W9-BIA-602

Strategic Debate

Strategic Debate

FOURTH EDITION

LTX
9-06-305

Roy V. Wood
Provost and Dean of Faculties
University of Denver

Lynn Goodnight
National High School Institute
Northwestern University

LAMAR UNIVERSITY LIBRARY

National Textbook Company
NTC a division of *NTC Publishing Group* • Lincolnwood, Illinois USA

Photo Credits

Alexandra Hoecherl, Appleton High School, Appleton, Wisconsin: page 250

Harold Keller, Davenport West High School, Davenport, Iowa: pages 190, 204, 227, 241

National High School Institute at Northwestern: pages 64, 98, 140, 260, 273

Odis Richardson, Du Sable High School, Chicago, Illinois: pages 2, 6, 72, 268

Art Shay, Photographer: pages 22, 40, 104, 181

1990 Printing

Published by National Textbook Company, a division of NTC Publishing Group.
© 1989, 1983, 1977 by NTC Publishing Group, 4255 West Touhy Avenue,
Lincolnwood (Chicago), Illinois 60646-1975 U.S.A.
All rights reserved. No part of this book may be reproduced, stored
in a retrieval system, or transmitted in any form or by any means,
electronic, mechanical, photocopying, recording or otherwise, without
the prior permission of NTC Publishing Group.
Manufactured in the United States of America.
Library of Congress Catalog Number: 87-63585

9 0 BC 9 8 7 6 5 4

TO
ALAN G. PRICE,
WHO WAS A TESTIMONY TO THE
BEST IN OUR PROFESSION

Contents

Introduction

Academic debate is surely one of the most exciting and valuable experiences for the high school or college student. The student who learns to debate well learns how to research a significant social-political question in depth. He or she learns how to organize research into a meaningful and persuasive presentation. The debater learns to defend his or her presentation against the attack of a well-trained opponent through critical listening and thinking. Finally, the good debater becomes a serious student of oral communication through a process of communicating his or her ideas to a third party under the most rigorous conditions.

And, of course, the competitive excitement that goes with debating cannot be discounted. Unlike many other interschool activities, good debating does not depend on the size, wealth, or prestige of the schools involved. It all depends on the individual student and a willingness to do the hard work required to excel in this activity. There's no doubt that the competitive element is one of the prime incentives for debaters, though later they generally cherish most the lessons debate taught them that have helped in other facets of their lives.

This, then, is a book about how to do well in academic debate. It is a text that discusses the strategies and tactics of the championship debater. The reader will soon see what these strategies and tactics are. They do not constitute "ten easy steps" to easy, win-at-any-cost debating. Instead, they represent the factors the student must consider and the things that must be done to become a good debater. The reader will discover that the debater's task is not an easy one because there are no ten easy steps, and unethical, win-at-any-cost debating is the surest way to lose debates and the best way to guarantee that the student does not learn what he or she should from the activity.

To fulfill their purposes, the authors have simply described what the best debaters actually do. Starting with debate fundamentals, they have followed the debater through the various stages of debating: research, building the constructive argument, the presentation of debate, refutation and rebuttal, and communicative persuasion in debate. This approach has led, naturally, to several necessary and intentional limitations of the text. Some of the more obvious limitations include the following:

1) Since this book is designed specifically for the academic debater, it necessarily focuses on those things that apply to competitive debate. In doing so, the authors have chosen not to deal extensively with the many applications of debate to other aspects of life. Certainly, the serious student of debate should consider its applications to the political and social arena. The debater should also study the many uses of debate research skills in any area of scholarly work.

2) Again, as a book for the practicing debater, this text does not attempt to deal with the scholarly theory of logic and argumentation as they apply to advocacy in general. As writers such as Glen E. Mills have shown, this is, itself, material for an entire book.

3) This book is primarily a reflection of what the authors have actually observed championship debaters doing as they prepare for and participate in debate. It does not, therefore, lean heavily on the literature of debate. The reader should not feel, though, that the lack of references to the literature means that the writers in the field have not had a profound influence on the practicing debater. Debaters, and certainly these writers, have been greatly influenced by such writers as James H. McBurney, Austin J. Freeley, Charles Willard, David Zarefsky, Tom Goodnight, Bill Balthrop, Tim Hynes, and Donn Parson.

The authors sincerely hope that these limitations have been overcome by the discussion of the practical aspects of academic debating. The book was written with only one audience in mind: the student. The final test of this book will be whether or not it helps the student become a better debater.

Finally, the authors would like to express their gratitude to the many people who helped formulate the material presented in this text. The members of the Northwestern University Debate Team and the high school students enrolled in the Northwestern Forensics Institute helped generate insights into debating and served as convenient "guinea pigs" for the authors' ideas. Doni Reiter and Scott Maeberry of the Northwestern University Debate Team provided their time and insights in tracking new material and examples for this edition. Special thanks go to Tom Goodnight for his time and patience in reading and critiquing each chapter.

RVW and LG

Strategic
Debate

Chapter 1

Fundamentals of Strategic Debate

Objectives and Key Terms

After studying Chapter 1, you should be able

1. To discuss the educational as well as competitive values of debate.

2. To explain the differences between propositions of fact, value, and policy.

3. To formulate a properly worded proposition that meets the characteristics of a proposition.

4. To explain the requirements of a prima facie case.

After reading this chapter, you should understand the following debate terms:

critical listening

critical thinking

proposition

proposition of fact

proposition of value

proposition of policy

burden of proof

presumption

prima facie case

burden of rejoinder

E very year tens of thousands of high school and college students participate in interscholastic and intercollegiate debate. Because so many students are involved, the range of approaches to the activity and the depth of experience in debating vary greatly. Some students, who engage in debating only briefly, gain slight but valuable exposure to the skills required in academic debate. Others, who compete for six or seven years during their high school and college careers, become expert on a variety of debate topics and authoritative on debate theory.

The majority of participants, no doubt, fall somewhere between the two extremes. Their experience is not so short that they gain only a brief exposure, but neither do they make a career of interscholastic and intercollegiate competition. Most school debaters regard debate as an extracurricular activity that is to be learned for its educational value and enjoyed for its competitive thrills. This text is written to meet the needs of that large group. It is designed, first, as an introduction to the concepts and skills that form the basis for the educational benefits of debating and, second, as an exposition of the basic and advanced aspects of debate as a competitive, strategic activity.

Debate as a Competitive-Educational Activity

The authors' bias is that debate is neither solely an educational activity nor a competitive activity. Debate is a competitive-educational endeavor. The skills and values that can be learned from it are as vital to the educated, democratic person in the twentieth century as they were to the Greeks who developed debate as an aid to training orators. Debate teaches much, and the context for learning is the competitive situation.

One of the most valuable skills that debaters acquire is the ability to communicate orally with another person in a situation that involves both spontaneity and pressure for excellence. Few students, except debaters, get the opportunity to speak to trained, adult listeners whose assignment is to give speakers feedback on the quality and effectiveness of their presentations.

Debaters also learn to design concise, cogent arguments that can stand up under almost immediate attack from a skilled opponent. Again, there are not many other situations in which speakers can find such highly motivated critics of their own thinking. The debater can be sure that if the judge does not comment on arguments that are logically weak, the opposition will.

One of the most valuable skills learned through debate is critical listening. In general most people tune out the majority of what is said around them or directly to them. Often politicians, businesspeople, teachers, parents, and even students argue endlessly over issues because they are absorbed with what they will say next instead of listening to what their opponents are saying. In debate you must listen to what your opponent is saying, or your reply is likely to be ineffective or irrelevant. Consequently, debaters take notes of what is being said and tailor their responses to the point—many times using their opponents' words—and turn their opponents' arguments to their own advantage. The ability to listen critically is widely recognized as an important skill.

Debate also teaches students to verbalize thoughts extemporaneously. It is not enough to think of a brilliant rejoinder hours after the argument, as so often happens in most other kinds of encounters. The debater must think of it immediately and express it fluently to the audience.

Finally, the debater learns the skills of organization that will enable him or her to lodge arguments in a framework that makes the ideas easy to follow but difficult to forget. In debate the critic and the opposition take nothing for granted. If the organization of arguments or case construction is even slightly confusing, the debater's opponents will push for clarity. This kind of pressure in debate forces the debater to become highly skilled in presentation.

In addition to the specific skills that can be developed, the student who debates well learns various values that surely are basic to the democratic man or woman. The debater not only learns to recognize a valid argument when it is presented but also develops an appreciation for the case that is well developed, no matter which side it represents. Conversely, the student of competitive debate learns to identify the fallacious or sophistic argument and to abhor it and what it represents.

But competition should not be separated from the educational element. Although "winning at any cost" can never be condoned, the primary values and skills to be found in debating can best be gained by students who are willing to commit themselves to the intellectual rigor required to learn debate on the competitive level. Too often the cry that debate is an educational, not a competitive, activity is a rationalization for not winning. It's often an excuse for not caring enough about debate to learn the persuasive, research, analytical, and refuting skills that are so necessary to winning. The techniques needed to win a debate embody the very skills and attitudes that are identical to the educational benefits of debating.

In short, long hours in the library, serious practice in critical thinking, and careful study of the strategies of the competition are not sophistic tricks of win-at-any-cost debate. They are the essence of oral argumentation, which, by its very nature, is a competitive endeavor.

Competitive success, then, should not be a means of gratifying the ego of the coach or the debater or for building the reputation of a school; it should be one of the measures of how much the student is learning about debate. These things, in turn, become very useful tools to the educated person who lives in a republic. They are the reasons for debating.

Debate is a highly competitive activity, offering recognition to those who succeed.

Debate as a Thinking Activity

Another bias of the authors is that if debate is a competitive-educational activity, one of the essential features of the competition is critical thinking. A theme of this text is that one of the worst, but most frequent, approaches to debate is the nonthinking approach. It is quite possible for a debater to participate in debate for an entire year—or for several years—without ever straining a brain cell.

The coach teaches the students the standard organizational and procedural processes. The debate manuals and other debaters provide the content. Simple imitation of other debaters can yield the speaking style. Nonthinking debaters, therefore, need never understand the debate topic, the strategies of organization and refutation, or the persuasive tactics of debate as communication. They never need to *think* about what they are doing.

Thinking, however, is a prerequisite for successful competitive-educational debating. Debaters need to know *why* a particular organization and procedure are used. They must seek the best evidence—from the library, correspondence, debate manuals, or many of the other resources discussed later in this text. They must think about the evidence being used and know exactly what it does for their arguments. Style and language must be continually examined so that they do not become imitations of other successful debaters but an expression of the individual as a communicative speaker.

Debate as a Strategic Activity

Military cadets, early in their courses in military science, learn that there are two elements to winning a war. First, a commander must have a general plan of attack. Should the enemy be taken by land or by sea? Will the enemy be demolished or starved into surrender? After arriving at a general plan, the commander must then discover methods that will make the goal attainable. Will aircraft carriers or submarines be used? Will nuclear weapons or the infantry be employed? When the battle plan has been completed, having answered such questions, the commander will have arrived at the strategy and tactics to be used in the campaign. Strategy is the *overall* plan of attack; tactics are the *specific* techniques to be used to fulfill the plan.

A symphony conductor must also develop a strategy and tactics. What is the general plan? Will the performance provide a demonstration of perfect technique and mathematical skill in interpreting the work? Perhaps a less mechanical performance to bring out the subtleties of the emotions of the piece is preferred. Whichever direction is taken, the conductor must employ specific techniques for getting the desired effects in the polished performance.

The debater is no different. When a student is preparing to enter a competitive setting, he or she is also approaching a strategic activity. Thinking debate requires an overall plan of attack and specific methods for carrying out that plan. To arrive at its strategy for a debate, the debate team must weigh many important considerations. What are the demands of the topic for debate? What are the potential strengths and weaknesses of the research materials that have been gathered? Which approach to analysis, based on the evidence, seems most potent for the debate? What might the opponents be expected to do? How might the critics be expected to react to various plans of attack?

After the strategy has been developed, the team must decide on tactics. When and how will the arguments be presented? What will each speaker do? What evidence would be the best to use during the debate? What mode of presentation would be the best to use under the circumstances?

Debate, then, is a strategic activity. In its best form, debate involves careful consideration of the best strategic approach that should be taken in light of the topic, team, opponents, and audience. That is why this text is titled *Strategic Debate*. This book evolves out of a consideration of the strategic implication—the strategies and tactics—of competitive debate.

The authors will never discuss unethical strategies for winning debates, although some debaters look for them. Indeed, there are no tricks, deceits, or gimmicks that really help in debate. Even if trickery were ethical and even if its use would not lead to the ruin of debate, all shortcuts to winning have serious disadvantages. The debater will never be successful in the long run if he or she uses unethical tactics. Moreover, many real benefits will be sacrificed. The authors have learned, from watching debaters at all levels of competition and at all levels of competence, that there is only one path to successful competitive-educational debate— the path of *most* resistance.

Purposes and Scope of the Text

Although there are many reasons for debating, most students get involved in debate for about the same reasons that they join other school clubs or organizations. The activity looks interesting, and other students seem to be enthusiastic about what they are doing. The new debater soon discovers that, although debate is very difficult to learn, it is a great deal of fun. There's a real joy in matching one's research and verbal skills against those of another person.

As the new debater struggles through the process of learning to debate, he or she discovers that good debating involves being able to perform well on many levels: in the library, intellectually, analytically, and verbally. He or she quickly discovers that learning to do all this well takes a year or more of hard work and practice. But somehow it is worth it.

As students who are learning debate begin to master the skills (usually, let's face it, in order to win more debates), they discover that how to win is not the only thing being learned. Classwork improves because a language is being developed and mastered. Suddenly, the debaters are able to listen to persuaders on television in a critical manner. They are becoming increasingly well informed about current events and contemporary issues.

This book is designed to help the debater in all phases of development. It is written as an aid to the new debater and to the advanced debater who has participated for a number of years.

The beginning debater is first confronted with the vocabulary of debate. Coaches talk about preparing a prima facie case to meet the affirmative "burden of proof." Speeches are called "constructives" and "rebuttals" (each with a different purpose and set of rules). Debaters are sent out to get as many "quotes" as possible to support the "contentions." This text defines these basic terms and attempts to explain why such concepts are essential to strategic debate. Until new debaters understand the rationale behind the concepts, they will never be thinking debaters.

New debaters also must develop a thorough understanding of the strategic and tactical obligations and possibilities of both the affirmative and the negative. The ability to refine their use of the basic tools of debate to the greatest competitive advantages must be developed. This text deals with the practical aspects of strategic debate for the beginner.

Finally, new debaters must understand the strategic implications of debate as a communication activity. The thinking debater realizes that, no matter how well the fundamentals of debate are mastered, arguments and analysis must be communicated to the judge. Experienced coaches know that their beginning debaters (and in some cases experienced debaters) "have arrived" when they stop explaining losses by blaming the critic and begin to study their failure to communicate with that critic as a listener.

This text is also designed to aid the advanced debater. Analyzing the "path of most resistance" to championship debating, it includes insights into the legitimate strategic approaches that are used by championship debaters. Debaters at the advanced level often are surprised at the refinements that really good competitive debate involves. The fundamental concepts and techniques take on new subtleties, and an understanding of the subtleties takes on a new fascination, even for the advanced debater.

The Fundamentals of Strategic Debate

Certainly it is possible for debaters to get by on their natural abilities, just as an unpracticed athlete might get by on natural talent; but the really good debater knows that to get the most out of debate one must continually refresh one's fundamental understandings of the activity.

For this reason, the rest of this chapter has been designed to fill two needs: to serve as an introduction to the fundamentals and to provide a review, and even new insights, for the experienced debater. It does not belabor the sophisticated arguments of debate theory; instead, it deals with the fundamentals of strategic debating in the context of what the debater must fully understand to be an accomplished advocate in the competitive situation.

The first question debaters ask at the beginning of a new season is "What's the topic this year?" There are various things debaters can be sure of as they wait for the answer to their question: (1) The debate topic always involves a particular type of proposition; (2) The debate topic is always worded in a particular way; (3) All the other debaters in the country will be working on the same high school or college debate proposition.

Types of Propositions

By definition, a **proposition** is no more than a judgment expressed in words. If one person says to another "I think it's going to rain today," that person has offered a proposition to the other for his or her acceptance or rejection. To say, "I think physics is a much more useful subject than English," is also to offer a proposition. To suggest, "We should all go to the party together," is again to express one's feelings in the form of a proposition. Each of these examples, however, involves a different type of proposition, a different type of judgment.

The first sentence, "I think it's going to rain today," is an example of a **proposition of fact**. The speaker expressed a judgment about an actual event—a belief that it's going to rain. The validity of this judgment can be checked rather easily. All the speaker and the listener have to do is to wait and see if it rains.

Types of Proposition

Proposition of Fact
"It's going to rain today."

Proposition of Value
"Physics is a much more useful subject than English."

Proposition of Policy
"We should all go to the party together."

"I think physics is a much more useful subject than English" is a different type of proposition. It is a **proposition of value**. The advocate has expressed a value judgment about a particular situation. The validity of this judgment is not as easy to verify as a proposition of fact. In fact, propositions of value often make the best topics for "rap" sessions because the participants can argue for hours and never arrive at a solution.

The last example, "We should all go to the party together," illustrates the third type of proposition. It is what most debaters call a **proposition of policy**. The speaker has suggested that a specific policy should be adopted by her or his friends: They should all go to the party together. The proposition of policy, unlike the propositions of fact and value, does not involve verification. It involves a decision as to whether the suggested policy should be adopted. Sometimes the decision is easy to reach, and sometimes it is not. In the example above, the other person might simply say, "Okay," and the question would be settled. In other cases, such as the proposition that capital punishment should be abolished, an argument might ensue that could last for many years.

It is possible to debate any one of the three types of propositions. Lawyers debate propositions of fact when they argue their cases about whether a person is guilty of a crime as charged. Legal procedure provides a carefully worked-out system for deciding whether a charge is true. The jury is allowed to hear only certain types of evidence, and the judge makes sure that the rules are not violated and that the jury fully understands the implications of the law.

Many people enjoy debating propositions of value. Anyone who listens to television talk shows is bound to hear debates about value judgments. Value questions create great audience interest because the listeners can get personally involved in questions dealing with "the new morality" or whether "God is dead." Even though it is difficult to arrive at answers to such questions, the purpose of such a debate generally is to create interest and to clarify points of view rather than to arrive at solutions.

Policy questions also frequently come up for debate. When a legislature debates a bill, it is almost always trying to decide whether a policy should be adopted. When a student council argues about how the student body treasury should be spent, it too is concerned with policy matters. The decision, then, about whether to accept a policy usually comes in the form of a vote that expresses the feeling of the majority. The majority simply decides whether a proposed change represents the best policy for the organization to adopt at that time.

Any one of the three types of propositions, therefore, could become the topic for an academic debate; however, the debater can be sure that a proposition of policy will be chosen for the national debate topic. Propositions of fact usually are too easy to settle—or almost impossible to settle (RESOLVED: *That the Communist regime in China has been successful*). Propositions of value tend to involve too much subjectivity for standard or cross-examination debate. Although it's enjoyable to argue value judgments, so much personal opinion would be involved that it would be impossible for a judge to reach a decision in standard or cross-examination debate. A proposition of policy, if worded correctly, can be just right. The exception is Lincoln-Douglas debate. In Lincoln-Douglas debate, the proposition used is generally a proposition of value (see Chapter 7).

The first demand placed on a potential national debate proposition is that it be debatable for an entire year; there should be enough evidence on both sides of the proposition to keep students interested throughout the season. Most policy questions can meet this criterion. Second, the proposition should deal with a subject area that interests and challenges serious students. Propositions that suggest a change in national or international policy often are interesting to students, and after a year of research they generally learn some worthwhile facts about the real world. Finally, the proposition for debate should deal with contemporary issues that will make debaters feel that they are engaging in more than just an academic exercise. There are almost always pressing policy problems, involving issues of national or international policy, that can be selected for the academic debate topic.

A further advantage of the proposition of policy is a very practical one. Over the years, debate coaches and critics have arrived at a set of criteria for judging policy debates. Debaters, then, can be fairly sure—no matter which part of the country they might debate in—that the critics will expect about the same sorts of things from the affirmative and negative teams. More important, debaters from Vermont, for example, who meet a team from California, can be comfortable in the knowledge that their opponents will interpret the proposition within the relatively limited framework of the proposition of policy.

Wording of the Proposition

Competitive debate is standardized not only by the type of topic used but also by the wording of the proposition. A debater can always be certain that the topic will be phrased in such a way that the obligations of the two teams will be implied in the proposition. A look at these sample propositions will clarify this point.

Resolved: That the federal government should initiate and enforce safety guarantees on consumer goods.

Resolved: That the United States should significantly change its foreign trade policies.

Resolved: That the federal government should establish a comprehensive program to significantly increase the energy independence of the United States.

Resolved: That the federal government should guarantee comprehensive medical care for all citizens in the United States.

Resolved: That a comprehensive program of penal reform should be adopted throughout the United States.

Resolved: That the federal government should provide employment for all employable United States citizens living in poverty.

Resolved: That the federal government should establish a comprehensive national policy to protect the quality of air and/or water in the United States.

Resolved: That the federal government should implement a comprehensive, long-term agricultural policy in the United States.

Resolved: That the United States government should adopt a policy to increase political stability in Latin America.

It is apparent that these sample propositions, although some deal with national affairs and some with international problems, have several common characteristics. First, the propositions are worded so that the affirmative team (the side advocating the proposition) is on the side suggesting a change in the present system. The negative team, which would answer no to the proposition, is always placed in the position of defending the status quo. Debaters are never asked to debate a question that would put the affirmative in the position of defending the present policy. The topic RESOLVED: *That the United States should not significantly change its foreign trade policies* would have to be changed to read RESOLVED: *That the United States should significantly change its foreign trade policies.*

Also, national academic debate topics advocate only one change in the present system. The affirmative is asked to advocate only one suggested alteration of policy, and the negative is asked to defend only one element of the present situation. Although it might be interesting to debate RESOLVED: *That law enforcement agencies should be given greater power and Congress should have the right to overrule decisions of the Supreme Court,* such a topic would be subdivided into two separate propositions, and a decision would be made about which topic should be adopted for national use.

Resolved: That law enforcement agencies should be given greater power.

Resolved: That Congress should have the right to overrule decisions of the Supreme Court.

Whereas the resolution or topic itself will advocate only one change in the present system, the affirmative may advocate the solution of a number of harms within the resolution. For example, under the energy topic the affirmative might decide to present two problems—danger of strip mining and inadequate availability of nuclear power. The solutions to these problems would be separate—improving regulations for safety of strip mining and a program to increase the safe use of nuclear power—but each would fall under the energy topic.

Should is perhaps the most important word in the national debate topic, and a debater can be quite sure that it will always be included. *Should* implies the policy change, and it characterizes the nature of the affirmative's position. The affirmative does not suggest that the policy change will be enacted, nor that it can be adopted, but that the change *ought to* be made. The affirmative team, therefore, is usually relieved of the obligation of showing that the change would be accepted by the government. It also would be irrelevant for the negative to prove that Congress, for instance, would vote against the proposal. The affirmative need only demonstrate that legislators *should* vote for the change. However, the negative may find it profitable in some cases to argue that lobby groups or attitudes of the administration would prevent the implementation of the affirmative plan. Also, the negative could not profitably argue that the change would be unconstitutional and therefore could not be adopted. The affirmative would only have to suggest that the Constitution should be amended.

Should is generally defined by the affirmative as meaning "*ought to* but not necessarily *will.*" More fundamentally, the word means that the proposal of the affirmative would be *the most desirable policy at the present time.* The affirmative is bound to demonstrate that the proposition, as it develops and analyzes it, would be the best policy and that the status quo therefore should be changed.

Finally, the proposition is worded so that it does not reflect a bias and so that the terms will be relatively clear to both the audience and the debaters. The topic above, which deals with a program of comprehensive medical care, would have been improperly worded if its author had written "burdensome, incompetent comprehensive medical care." Also, the negative can be much more certain of the affirmative's interpretation of the topic if the wording contains a specific formulation, such as "comprehensive medical care."

Returning to the mythical debater who asked, "What's the topic this year?" it is easy to see that the answer will fall within certain limits: (1) The national debate topic will always be a resolution that is expressed in the form of a proposition of policy; (2) It will deal with a subject that is controversial and that will yield ample evidence for both sides of the question; (3) The affirmative team will always be placed in the position of advocating a change in the present situation, the status quo; (4) Only one change in the status quo need be suggested; and (5) The debate topic will always contain the word *should* so that the duties of the affirmative will be clearly spelled out and, at the same time, limited.

Obligations Inherent in the Proposition of Policy

Because a properly worded proposition of policy implies obligations for the two teams engaged in a debate, there are certain things a team must do before it can hope to win the debate. If the affirmative and the negative both confront their obligations, the decision may well depend on the critic's judgment of which team best met its obligations. These fundamental duties of debaters can best be seen by first turning to another situation.

Criminal action against a person, for example, involves a carefully developed set of rights and obligations that closely parallel those of the debate situation. The state, represented by the prosecution, brings charges against a citizen, who is represented by the defense attorney, and the trial begins with a basic presumption: The defendant is innocent until proven guilty. This premise, a characteristic of most Western law, defines several elements in the criminal trial. The defendant does not have to prove he or she is innocent; the prosecution must establish guilt. Lawyers say, then, that the **burden of proof** is on the prosecution. The **presumption** of innocence is with the defendant, and the only way the prosecution can overcome the presumption is by meeting its burden of proof.

The burden of proof is so important in the law court that the defendant does not have to go to trial until the prosecution has demonstrated to the court that it has at least the minimal case required for it to meet its burden of proof. Accordingly, the prosecution is usually asked to show its evidence to a grand jury or to a magistrate at the time of the arraignment so that the trial judge can be assured the state has a minimal case. Such a case, which represents the minimum required to meet the burden of proof, is called a **prima facie case**. If the prosecution does not have a prima facie case, it cannot meet the obligation implied in the fundamental presumption that the defendant is innocent until proven guilty.

If the prosecution has a prima facie case, the trial continues and new obligations come to the fore. The defense is then faced with a case that was judged prima facie without rebuttal, and it must establish that the case does not prove, beyond a reasonable doubt, that the defendant is guilty. The defense's obligation to answer is called the **burden of rejoinder**. Only by meeting the burden of rejoinder can the presumption of innocence be regained.

A final obligation that falls on both the prosecution and the defense is that they must prove what they assert. Much of the training of a lawyer involves learning the criteria for proof and the legal precedents for proof.

The order of presentation in a trial also is standardized. The prosecution always begins and ends the trial. The district attorney initiates the action against the defendant in a carefully developed case that is composed of arguments and evidence that are designed to satisfy the burden of proof of the charge. As the prosecution proceeds, the defense is allowed to cross-examine the witnesses and to question exhibits of evidence in an attempt to refute the basic case being constructed by the district attorney. After the prosecution has rested its constructive case, the defense presents its side, provided the state's case was prima facie. After the defense has developed its arguments and the prosecution has cross-examined, both sides are given the opportunity to present a summation of their stands for the jury. The defense begins the summation period, and the prosecution ends it.

As the reader may have guessed, the obligations of debaters are very similar to the obligations of lawyers. At the outset, the affirmative team is in the position of advocating a change in the present situation, as summarized in the proposition. As in the case of the defendant, the status quo is held to be "innocent until proven guilty." It is the job of the affirmative to present an indictment of the status quo (some district attorneys measure their success by the number of indictments they can get) that will overcome the presumption held by the negative team. In debate this obligation is called the burden of proof of the proposition.

Although some debaters get confused about this point, the burden of proof is always with the affirmative team. Although the negative must prove what it asserts, it is never in the position of trying to prove that the proposition should be adopted. Even if the negative agreed that the present system should be changed, it would never argue in support of the specific change suggested in the debate proposition—if it did, there would be no debate. Similarly, the defendant might admit to being guilty, but a trial could nevertheless ensue over the specific charge that the prosecution brings against the defendant (for example, first-degree murder). The prosecution would still have the burden of proving that the defendant is guilty as charged. The affirmative still has the burden of proving that the status quo must be changed to the policy suggested in the debate resolution.

Debate also operates under the assumption that the affirmative can overcome presumption and thus meet the burden of proof only by presenting a prima facie case. In debate, a prima facie case is the minimal argument required to support the resolution, without refutation. As a trial judge can begin by assuming that the prosecution has at least a minimal case, the debate critic can assume that the affirmative would not advocate a change unless it had a case that would support the proposition without refutation. The specific approaches that the affirmative can take to develop a prima facie case are considered in a later chapter.

After the affirmative has met its burden of proof, overcoming negative presumption, the negative team is faced with the burden of rejoinder. Obviously, it cannot win its argument that the proposition should not be adopted unless it presents a well developed argument that contradicts the affirmative position. Negative approaches are also discussed in detail in a later chapter.

Questions for Discussion

1. In a court of law, lawyers debate what type of proposition? Why?

2. Outline the criteria necessary for a debatable proposition of policy.

3. The term *should* is described as perhaps the most important word in the national debate topic. Why is this so?

4. Why does the burden of proof always rest with the affirmative team?

5. What obligations must the affirmative fulfill in order to have a prima facie case?

6. Persons who debated in high school or college often say that the debate experience was one of the most valuable things they ever did. Why do you suppose they say this?

7. It is argued in this chapter that honesty and fairness in debate are even more important than in other activities because the responsibilities of the skilled persuader are heavy. Comment on this.

8. Discuss debate as a thinking and as a strategic activity. What role do strategies and tactics play in everyday life?

9. Presumption is a jealously guarded feature in criminal law in the United States. Why? What are its implications in nonlegal areas, such as politics and debate?

Activities

1. Attend a meeting of the city council, school board, or student activity group. During the meeting take notes on the issues being discussed and proposals put forth. Write as a proposition each of the proposals discussed. Is it a debatable proposition as proposed in the meeting? Why or why not?

2. The following are examples of poorly worded propositions. Identify the problem with each and rewrite it correctly.

Resolved: That efforts should be made to curtail our rising unemployment.

Resolved: That this winter has been worse than any other.

Resolved: That harmful unemployment should be stopped.

Resolved: That English study develops skills in grammar and punctuation.

Resolved: That the United States should adopt programs to fight inflation and guarantee a future supply of energy.

Resolved: That the jury system in the United States should not be significantly changed.

3. Formulate a proposition of fact, a proposition of value, and a proposition of policy on one of the following general topics: arms sales, education, "star wars" technology, the disposal of toxic wastes, the federal deficit, air safety, age and sex discrimination. Outline and be prepared to give a two- to three-minute speech on the basic areas you would explore in the analysis of the topic chosen.

4. Identify which of the following propositions are propositions of fact, propositions of value, and propositions of policy:

Resolved: That Americans drive more imported cars than American-made cars.

Resolved: That the United States should provide a guaranteed annual income for all citizens.

Resolved: That enlistments in the armed forces are decreasing.

Resolved: That the federal government should take measures to guarantee the United States' military superiority.

Resolved: That infant mortality is highest among the poor.

Resolved: That high medical costs create needless death and suffering.

Resolved: That reading skills in elementary and secondary schools are declining.

Resolved: That three years of physical education is not necessary for a well-rounded education.

Resolved: That the United States' balance of trade deficit is continuing to rise.

Resolved: That the United States should significantly change its foreign trade policies.

Resolved: That a judge is better qualified to render a verdict than a jury of one's peers.

Resolved: That the jury system should be abolished.

Chapter 2

Strategy and Tactics of Research

Objectives and Key Terms

After studying Chapter 2, you should be able

1. To explain what to do first, what to look for, and how to make the best use of research time.

2. To conduct a useful library survey on the current debate resolution. This should include a knowledge of indexes, books, periodicals, legal publications, and government documents.

3. To explain how to make a list of places and sources to write to for material on a particular debate resolution.

4. To explain and test the guidelines for ethics in research.

5. To process a primary source and properly record and file evidence cards from that source.

6. To explain the criteria for high-quality evidence.

7. To make a list of key terms to use when researching a debate resolution.

To research effectively, you will need to know the following terms:

competent	empirical evidence
form	opinion evidence
fact	validity
value judgment	reliability

To the casual observer, debate doesn't seem to be a very difficult activity. If a person is sufficiently glib and has a better-than-average knowledge of a subject, it might be assumed that he or she would be a fairly decent debater. Moreover, the typical debate takes only about an hour and a half to run its course, and each speaker spends only about fifteen minutes speaking. Our observer might think, then, that all a debater has to do is be prepared to give the equivalent of a fifteen-minute speech—hardly an overwhelming task.

Like many other things, however, the true nature of debate is hidden beneath the surface. For every minute that he or she spends before the audience or judge, the good debater spends several hours in preparation. The bulk of this time is devoted to research, to getting the evidence to support the arguments that will be used in debate. The championship debater is quite willing to work for many days to obtain the evidence necessary to develop a single argument in thirty seconds.

Why is research so important? The main reason is that debate, by its very nature, requires a tremendous amount of evidence. Debate is formalized argument, and argument is the process of reasoning from the known to the unknown—from *evidence* to a *conclusion*. Any argument, then, requires evidence if the audience or judge is going to accept it as valid.

But the debater must be prepared for more than just one argument. A typical debate might contain as many as a hundred different arguments, and the debater must be prepared for more than just one debate. It is necessary to be ready to deal with many different cases and analyses. Thus, the advocate knows that tremendous amounts of evidence will be needed just to deal intelligently with the arguments that will be advanced in the course of a debate season. In addition, the debater knows that specific bits of evidence are not enough. A thorough understanding of the issues and elements in the topic area is also necessary so that analyses will be as strong as the evidence.

Championship-level debating demands even more research because the really good debater wants the best and most recent material available on the topic. In fact, one national collegiate champion asserted that, although all the other elements of debate are important, the most successful debaters are those who have the most thorough knowledge of the topic and the best evidence to support what they assert.

This chapter, then, deals with the strategy and tactics of debate research. The first matter for concern is the overall strategy of research—what to do first, what to look for, and how to make the best use of research time. Then the tactics of research are considered—where to get evidence, how to file it, how to retrieve it, and how to maintain it.

Research Strategy

One theme of this text has been that debaters should have the highest standards for their own work. It is never profitable to look for the easy way out. Instead, the path of *most* resistance should be sought. This attitude is essential if the participant is going to get the maximum educational advantage from debating, and it is also vital if the debater hopes to be successful as a competitor. The research strategy, therefore, should grow out of this philosophy.

The research strategy of debate can be stated in one sentence: *The debater should strive to obtain a thorough knowledge of the topic and the highest-quality evidence to support the arguments.* The debater who succeeds in carrying out this strategy will learn a great deal and will win more debates than other less-informed colleagues.

Knowledge of the Topic Area

Good research involves much more than merely gathering "quote cards." A debate topic involves much more than isolated statistics and assorted quotations that pertain to its major issues. A debater who operates on the superficial level makes a serious mistake.

Some debaters can spend hundreds of hours looking for quotations and statistics and can end up, when the season is completed, knowing very little about the topic and its issues as they actually exist. Such an approach only shortchanges the debater. Isolated research for quotations and statistics might yield opinions of a few "authorities" who have studied the topic, with little understanding of how or why the experts arrived at their conclusions and practically no knowledge of how their opinions relate to each other. A thorough understanding of the topic area, on the other hand, could produce a great deal of information about an important problem that might well affect one's life.

Superficial research has its disadvantages on the competitive level as well. The authors have seen several debates lost—even at the end of the season—simply because the debaters didn't understand the topic. They had plenty of evidence cards, but they didn't know or understand the important background facts that any informed person would know about the topic.

How does the debater succeed in getting thorough knowledge of the topic and the highest-quality evidence? The first step is to decide to carry out the research strategy. It does very little good to *want* to be a good debater; the student must be willing to do the hard work involved. Second, the debater should develop specific criteria for judging the quality of research. Again, it does very little good to want to have good evidence; the debater must *know* when supporting material is good. Finally, the debater should develop specific tactics for carrying out the research strategy.

Obtaining the Highest-Quality Evidence

Deciding upon the kind of evidence that is best is not easy. Because evidence is used to try to obtain agreement from an audience or judge, the basic question is: What does it take to get the listener to decide that the argument is valid? No doubt some people require very little in the way of evidence to support what they already feel to be true. Even the best evidence might not cause other people, whose opinions have already been formed, to change their minds. And some audiences require extremely sound evidence, while others seem to believe anything that has appeared in print.

Fortunately, although it is true that debate judges are people first and judges second, the debater can be more certain of what the debate judge will require in the way of evidence than can, say, a public speaker who addresses lay listeners. Debate judges have arrived at some fairly standard criteria for judging the quality of evidence. They are inclined to award the debate to the team that has done the best job of meeting the evidence criteria in supporting their arguments.

In examining the criteria for debate evidence, it is best to look first at the general standards. The critic who listens to a debate and the debater who searches for evidence start by considering two general questions: (1) What can be said about the *external* qualities of the evidence—how can the *source* of the evidence be evaluated? and (2) What can be said about the *internal* qualities of the evidence—how *truthful* is it?

External Criticism

Questions of external criticism (how good is the source?) can be divided into two areas: the excellence of the publication from which the material is drawn and the competence of the author of the material. Debaters use several criteria in judging the quality of the publication and the qualifications of the author.

How Good Is the Publication?

First, is the publication **competent** to testify for the validity of a given argument? Here the debater should seek sources that are known to be objective and responsible in reporting factual and opinion material. If a magazine, for instance, claims to report current events, does it report these events reliably and responsibly or does it slant and interpret events to fit a particular editorial bias? Many debaters have fallen into the trap of believing a publication that sounds good but really is biased. In most speaking situations an advocate can get by with biased material, but debaters can be very sure that their opponents will have done enough research to show that the evidence is faulty.

Second, what is the **form** of the evidence? This question is quite complex. For example, two debate teams may differ as to what was or was not said in a presidential address, only to find that one team has been quoting from a source that utilized an advance copy of the speech, while the other team has been quoting from a source that used the speech as it was actually given. Another team may find that an authority has said something in a television discussion that is different from what was written in that person's most scholarly book.

The general rule on the form of a source is that the more permanent the form, the more reliable the information. Authorities are likely to be more careful in a scholarly book that will be available for many years than in a television encounter that is only transitory. The president is likely to weigh every word carefully in the prepared text of a speech, simply because every word will be carefully read. A president may feel freer to exaggerate and dramatize in off-the-cuff remarks. The debater, therefore, will seek the most permanent forms of evidence because they typically represent the best material.

How Competent Is the Author?

The first question to ask here is: *Who is the author?* Most debaters demand that an author be considered an expert, not a layperson, in the area being discussed. The author should be professionally qualified and competent to state facts or opinions, should be respected by other authorities in the field, and should have a reputation for responsible reporting. An author should not be biased. An authority with a vested interest should be avoided. One would expect, for instance, that a physicist who is paid to test nuclear weapons would say that such testing is necessary. Teachers can be expected to support the value of an education, and heads of government agencies usually are eager to point out the effectiveness and the necessity of their agencies. At the same time, however, when researching a given authority, look out for evidence that supports opinions other than that authority's own biases. Take the example of the physicist. Evidence by the physicist stating that nuclear weapons did *not* need testing would be very valuable evidence.

A very common pitfall is that authorities in one field may state opinions about other fields in which they are not qualified. An expert in military strategy might be heard advancing opinions about foreign policy. A physicist might offer medical advice to a friend. However, being a layperson does not make one's opinion false, any more than being an expert necessarily makes it true. The good debater is careful to gauge accurately the qualifications of the author of the evidence.

Third, the debater should ask *when* the author got the information. Generally, the closer the author was to the event, the more likely it is that the information will be right. In current events this usually means that the most recent evidence is the best. On many issues or arguments, the date of the evidence could determine who wins the issue. For instance, a magazine article on a specific international proposal could become outdated with tomorrow's headlines. A poll of public opinion on a given subject might be out of date as soon as a new poll is published. In historical events it may well be that the oldest source is the most accurate. An ancient Greek's comments about life in ancient Greece may be more accurate than comments in a modern, idealized history of that country.

The debater should also be cautious about the copyright date on books. Books, generally, are not printed with the same speed as magazines or newspapers. A book with a copyright date of 1988 was probably written in 1986 or 1987 at the very best. A good way to judge the timeliness of a book is to check the footnotes. The dates on footnotes and in the bibliography will give the debater a good idea of when a book was actually written and how current the research materials are.

Internal Criticism

Internal criticism, the truth of the evidence, frequently is overlooked by inexperienced debaters. They feel that if the source is sound and the authority reputable, the evidence must be true. This is not always the case. The U2 incident is a good example of the kind of exception that can develop. One can easily find quotations from the president of the United States, and in the best sources, that the U2 was a lost weather plane that had strayed over Russia. Later the president was forced to admit that the plane was on a spying mission, deliberately flying over the Soviet Union. One should always read materials with a sense of cautiousness.

What Does It Say?

In evaluating the validity of evidence, the first and most obvious consideration is: *what does the evidence say?* What does it report, and does this report make sense?

Does the evidence report actual events—**facts**—or does it make inferences about what is probably true, based upon what is already known? Or perhaps the statement is a **value judgment** about the nature of events, based on inferences drawn from facts. Most logicians and debate judges feel that the farther the statement is from the fact level, the more likely it is to contain error. The following is an example of an irresponsible leap from fact to inference to conclusion:

Fact level: Some American tourists are obnoxious.

Inference level: All American tourists are obnoxious.

Value level: Yankee go home!

Many inexperienced debaters depend on opinion evidence in which bias and error are likely to exist. It is best to present evidence that is factual in nature and let the judge follow the debater's logic in arriving at her or his conclusions.

How Consistent Is the Evidence?

The debater can judge the truth of evidence by checking to see if it's *consistent within itself.* It is not unusual to discover inconsistencies in evidence, and a careful researcher often can disprove the opponent's arguments by showing that the opposing team didn't read enough of the quotation to indicate the true opinion of the authority. Or the debater can read further from the same article or from other articles by the same person or source to show that the so-called authority seems unable to make up his or her mind. Inconsistency, then, may be one of the first indications that a piece of supporting material is not valid.

Criteria for Selecting the Highest-Quality Evidence

A. External criticism (How good is the source?)
  1. How competent is the source of the evidence?
     a. Is it objective?
     b. Is it responsible?
     c. Is it relatively free from bias?
  2. What is the form of the evidence?
     a. How permanent is the form?
     b. Did the source intend permanence and strict interpretation?
  3. Who is the author of the evidence?
     a. Is the author an expert in the field?
     b. Is the author relatively free from bias?
     c. How was the information obtained?
        1) Firsthand observation (primary source)?
        2) Obtained from someone else (secondary source)?
     d. When did the author get the information?
  4. How recent is the evidence?
     a. Does it represent the latest available material?
     b. Have important events occurred since the evidence was written?
B. Internal criticism (How truthful is the evidence?)
  1. What does the evidence say?
  2. On what level of abstraction is it?
     a. Is it a factual report?
     b. Is it an inferential report?
     c. Is it a judgmental report?
  3. Is the evidence consistent within itself?
  4. Is the evidence consistent with other information?

Finally, the validity of evidence can be gauged by determining whether it is *consistent with other information*. Do other authorities or sources agree? Is the same fact consistently observed by others? The researcher should beware of arguments for which only one supporting source can be found. Debaters also should be careful of a quotation that runs counter to the bulk of other information.

The criteria for fulfilling this phase of the research strategy are rather complex, but the adjacent outline should help clarify the situation.

Research Tactics

A tactic in debate is nothing more than a procedure for implementing the strategy of the debater. The tactics of research are simply the procedures that debaters use to get the best knowledge of the topic and the highest-quality evidence to support their arguments. This section, devoted to these two general topics, concludes with a discussion of evidence-filing, retrieval, and maintenance.

Acquiring a Knowledge of the Topic

Although all research obviously contributes to the debater's knowledge of the topic, the debater usually has something more specific in mind when referring to "acquiring background knowledge." A reference to a fund of background information and to a pool of evidence—"quote cards"—are two different things. The evidence represents specific, relatively independent information that pertains to the arguments the debater expects to use or encounter. Knowledge of the topic— background information—refers to the debater's understanding of the issues, ideas, and relevant facts that pertain to the topic area as an important real-world issue. Good debaters put almost as much emphasis on understanding the topic as they do on gathering evidence.

The process of acquiring background information begins on the day the proposition for the debate year is announced. At this point, usually in the spring, the debater begins background reading. However, he or she does not proceed without first organizing time and energy.

Surveying Current Knowledge

The first step in organizing the background reading phase of research is to find out what is already known about the topic. One reason why students who are interested in current events and political issues do so well in debate is that they already know a great deal about most debate topics.

Many debaters, at this point, simply make a rough outline of what they know about the debate topic. Then, often working with their colleagues or other squad members, they can list the major areas that are likely to be important, along with sub-issues that will probably come into play.

Reading In Depth

The next phase of acquiring background knowledge involves the careful reading of three or four key books about the topic and its major issues. Because debate propositions are concerned with important, controversial issues, many books will have been written on the subject. The debater's reading, at this point, should attempt to cover one or two major books that reflect relatively objective approaches to the problem. Each debater should also read one book that represents the bias of those who tend to support the topic and one book that represents those who tend to oppose it.

In familiarizing oneself with the extreme biases, the debater will locate the standard and the emotional arguments that will be encountered during the forensic year. Also, the authors of the more biased works will refer to other, similarly biased "authorities," whose names the debater can keep in mind for later reference. A good way to locate the prejudiced sources is to write to the pressure groups that usually are active in any major policy question. They'll be happy to recommend "a good book" on the subject.

Although standard, objective sources usually are more difficult to find than biased ones, there are ways to locate them. The school librarian may offer suggestions, or a teacher may be available to recommend the text on which most experts depend. Objective texts should acquaint the debater with the major arguments and issues as well as provide other authorities who can be investigated later.

Since researching a topic is time-consuming, the researcher needs to be as efficient as possible. Efficiency begins by reading only relevant material. In selecting materials you should check the title, table of contents, index, and chapter heads to focus the search for evidence more precisely.

When researching, skim rapidly, skipping all material that is clearly irrelevant and reading slowly any materials of possible importance. One should not worry about missing something by skimming; it will be more than compensated for by the increased amount of material read.

At this point it should be remembered that there is a difference between gathering evidence and gathering background material. During this early phase in the research, the researcher should read for an understanding of the major issues. Although notes may be made for later evidence-gathering, the debater should not at this time read for the compilation of quote-card material.

The background reading phase of research should not be limited to reading books. The debater should also turn to magazines, newspaper reports, government documents, and pamphlets.

Terminating Background Reading

It is not easy to decide when and how to terminate the general knowledge part of research. Of course, this process must continue throughout the entire debate season, but there comes a time when the debater feels ready to move on to gathering specific evidence for actual debating. At this juncture many persons simply stop their background reading, letting their knowledge of this element in the topic lie fallow in their minds. Others feel it is important to synthesize their background reading formally.

To gain a formal synthesis, some debate squads divide into small groups to discuss the major issues or points of controversy. After the groups have reached some consensus as to what seems important, they frequently assign specific issues to various students. These issues are researched individually or in groups. An analysis can be done of the affirmative and negative aspects of the issues. While the analysis will not be extensive, since all the debaters are still learning about the topic, group discussion and analyses can speed up the process of gathering background material. It can also help a squad spot potential affirmative cases. It is generally a good idea to have each group or individual write up statements to be duplicated for distribution to the entire squad. Those statements should provide background material, highlights of areas that need additional research, sources for background reading, and any viable arguments that were discovered while researching.

Regardless of what is done, the debater now is ready to gather evidence—a development that most debaters eagerly await. Now is the time to compile quote cards.

Research for Specific Evidence

It was mentioned earlier that argument is the process of reasoning from evidence to a conclusion. Most debaters have little trouble arriving at conclusions, but they have to work hard to find evidence that will support those conclusions. That is the purpose, however, of this phase of research. The debater should approach each piece of evidence with four questions in mind: (1) What does the evidence say? (2) How good is the evidence? (3) How does the evidence say it? and (4) What will the evidence do?

What Does the Evidence Say?

This first question is rather obvious. As one reads quickly through masses of material, one becomes "tuned in" to the material that seems most applicable to the debate topic. The researcher is looking for factual, inferential, or judgmental material that will support affirmative or negative arguments.

How Good Is the Evidence?

"How good is it?" is a question that is conditioned by the many standards that are used to judge evidence. The general standards of external and internal criticism have already been discussed. In addition to these, many debaters like to place evidence in a hierarchy of value that can give them a practical standard for judging the quality of evidence.

Most people would agree that evidence can be divided into two general categories. **Empirical evidence** represents the results of controlled observation to obtain factual and inferential data. **Opinion evidence** usually is judgmental in nature. Each of these can be further divided into two subclasses and arranged in a hierarchy, or ordering, that ranges from the best to the most doubtful evidence.

Empirical Evidence

Experimental Data

The first class of empirical evidence is experimental data. Experimental data are simply the evidence reporting the results of a scientific experiment that has been conducted to explore some causal relationship. The experimenter begins with a hypothesis. A hypothesis may be defined as a prediction about the nature of things. It supposes a relationship between two or more things or concepts. For example, the experimenter might hypothesize that "A causes B to happen to C." To test the hypothesis, the experimenter would conduct a laboratory experiment in which B would be exposed to A in order to see if C results. If it is suspected, for example, that a particular virus causes polio, the virus would be injected into mice to see if polio follows. If it does, the experimenter can be more sure that the virus is the cause. Or a supposed cause might be removed. If, for instance, a police chief thinks the crime rate is high because there aren't enough police officers, the force might be doubled in an experimental area to see if the crime rate drops. If it does, the cause of the high crime rate may have been found.

Of course, there are many more types of experiments. The point is that such data often are considered the very best debate evidence because they represent the best way to establish causation. However, experimental evidence is superior only when correct research design and application provide a superior basis on which to draw conclusions. In any case, evidence that can be verified is always preferable to evidence that cannot.

The current trend in debate, in both high school and college, is to rely more heavily on statistics and quantitative studies. In recent years there has been increased experimentation in social, economic, and political areas, as well as more valid data. While this may improve the quality of available evidence, it can create problems for the debater if not approached with caution.

In evaluating experimental data, the debater should ask three questions: (1) How well were the variables controlled? (2) Has the experiment been replicated with the same results? and (3) Can the results of the experiment be generalized to more than just the cases that were used in the experiment?

Methodology should always be examined carefully. The debater should have some idea of how the data were collected. When studies are used to support an affirmative proposal or negative repair, the debater should check to see if the proposal contains the same conditions and mechanisms as the studies being cited for support. Most abuses of experimental data occur in this area.

Observational Data

Observational evidence is information that reflects controlled observation of events. Types of observational data include statistics and carefully developed examples. The main criteria for judging the quality of observational data are **validity** and **reliability**. The validity consideration asks whether the observer actually observed what he or she claimed to be measuring. Reliability asks if the same results would be obtained if the observations were repeated or if they had been gathered at the same time by a different observer.

Political polls are good examples of types of observations that have had to overcome major validity and reliability problems. Early pollsters picked Alfred Landon to defeat Franklin D. Roosevelt in 1936 because their measures weren't valid. They thought they were gathering data about the feelings of all the voters when they conducted telephone interviews, but they overlooked the fact that millions of Democratic voters couldn't afford telephones during the Depression.

Reliability, on the other hand, was the problem for the pollsters who picked Thomas Dewey to defeat Harry S Truman by a landslide. Polls that were taken two weeks before the election simply weren't accurate two weeks later. The 1980 presidential polls certainly did little to add either validity or reliability to political polls. An election that was "too close to call," according to the polls, turned out to be one of the biggest landslides in American history. Pollsters are still trying to rationalize their way out of this blunder.

Experienced debaters like to use observational data. If the data are reliable and valid, such evidence is difficult to overcome in a debate and is frequently very persuasive. An opinion quotation is just somebody else's opinion, based on the facts as seen by the individual. If, on the other hand, the judge can examine the facts to arrive at a conclusion, the argument may be accepted, even though the judge may have disagreed with the same conclusion from an expert. Every debater should learn early that every person's own logic is the best logic.

Opinion Evidence

Opinion evidence also is divisible into two categories: *expert testimony* and *testimony from a layperson*. A person who fulfills the standards mentioned earlier in this chapter is probably an expert. Otherwise that person should be considered a layperson, no matter how prestigious the qualifications.

Even though most debate coaches would like to see less use of opinion evidence, they know that debaters will always make great use of it. Opinion evidence usually is easier to find and easier to use than other evidence. It is easier to find because almost everybody is anxious to state an opinion or conclusion in print. Some students feel that it's easier to use because an authority does their thinking for them. The debater draws inferences from the evidence and conveniently supplies a value judgment about the nature of the situation.

The biggest danger in using opinion evidence is that it contributes to the nonthinking style of debating. The debater who can get enough opinion quotations doesn't have to think; the experts can do the thinking. Usually these debates are no more than a string of quotations, interlaced with something called contentions.

Despite the prejudices of a large number of coaches (including the authors), opinion evidence can be very useful to the debater. It can be useful, however, only if the debater takes the time to understand *why* the authority arrived at a particular conclusion. If he or she does this and can explain it to the critic, the opinion card can save a great deal of precious time in a debate. Expert testimony, however, is the only variety that can be used for proof. Testimony from laypeople should be reserved for the persuasive effect of illustration.

The hierarchy of evidence, then, is as follows:

Best: experimental data

Second best: observational data

Third best: expert opinion

Weakest: layperson opinion

How Does the Evidence Say It?

It is always sad when a researcher finally finds just the information he or she has been looking for, only to discover that the material is so poorly written or so lengthy that no judge would respond to it. There is little the debater can do in such a situation, because no one has the right to rewrite the evidence to make it more palatable. Some people would paraphrase the material, but it's best simply to keep looking for usable evidence.

The researcher, then, should look at more than just the logical aspects of evidence gathering. He or she should try to get evidence that is readable and clear. The focus, or point, of the material has to be very clear if the debater expects the critic to see the connection between the evidence and the conclusion that it is supposed to support. Occasionally the speaker must sacrifice the best evidence card for another, more persuasive source.

What Will the Evidence Do?

This criterion has many elements. The debater primarily wants to know what the evidence will do in a debate: (1) Will it support the argument in the mind of the judge? (2) How will the other team react to it? (3) How easy will it be for the opposition to cast doubt on it? and (4) How does it fit with or contradict the other evidence the speaker plans to use?

These questions can be at least tentatively answered before actual competition begins. However, the best way to find the answers is to use the material to see what it will do. Sometimes debaters are pleasantly surprised to find that a piece of evidence they thought was weak appears to have won a debate for them. At other times a student may find that a favorite quotation had disastrous effects or caused more trouble than it was worth.

The basic consideration is: *does the evidence have the power to convince?* If the researcher carefully examines the material from the standpoint of the four questions, there is every likelihood that the evidence will be convincing. Then it can be tried in debates, against good opposition, to see how it stands up. Having given careful thought to these matters, the debater can be well on the way to meeting the strategic objective: to have the best evidence possible.

How to Look for Evidence

Most debaters use a two-pronged attack in looking for evidence. Early in the season, they search for material that looks as though it will be useful for background reading. Later they look for evidence to support specific arguments and cases.

The most productive time begins when the team has tentatively arrived at the affirmative case that they will use. The team members can then sit down and work out the major topics and subtopics that fit under their particular analysis. Then they exhaustively research each element of the case to get the evidence they need and to see what the weaknesses of the case may be. Usually, the team members divide their efforts to avoid duplication. They not only research the arguments that support their case but explore the arguments they would use if they were on the negative team. In this way they can anticipate negative attacks, or they may even throw out a case because of the weakness of such arguments if the opposition should use them.

It is important to note that many good debaters double-check one another on the most important evidence. They know that debates have been lost by teams that copied quotations inaccurately. Therefore, by making sure the evidence is correctly cited and recorded, they avoid the embarrassment of having a judge think they cheated.

To prepare for the negative side of the question, most teams detail probable affirmative arguments for thorough research. Because many arguments often are involved, some debate squads divide the labor among all the members.

The values of thorough and exhaustive research have been extolled. Now it is time to suggest some tactics for doing such work. These tactics vary considerably from person to person, inasmuch as most researchers develop systems that work best for them.

Very few debaters begin their research by reading the first book or article they encounter; such a system is simply too inefficient and the researcher has no guarantee that the first find will be the best. In fact, a researcher is likely to become tired of reading or to run out of time before finding the best data. Instead, it is better to begin by building a bibliography of the material that is available; then, the researcher can get an overview of what lies ahead.

A bibliography can be built by first making a list of words that might relate to a topic. It does not hurt to use imagination when compiling the list. Once a list of key words has been completed, the next step is to go to the periodical indexes and the card catalog. Looking up each word will provide a tremendous supply of possible sources. The debater should start with the source that looks best and then work down through the list of sources. Do not hesitate to add to the list of possible sources while you read through material. Footnotes and bibliographies can prove invaluable in locating good source material.

At first the student should read quickly, skimming the material and marking the parts that look good enough to commit to evidence cards. By skimming, even the slowest reader can at least superficially exhaust the available evidence. Then he or she can return to the most valuable sources and authors for in-depth reading.

The main tactic, at this point, is to have a tactic. So much evidence is available on most topics that debaters rarely can cover all of it. By carefully following the best plan of attack, many debaters end the season with as many as 7,000 to 10,000 evidence cards. Their equally energetic, but disorganized, colleagues may end up with just a few hundred or, at best, a thousand cards. Quantity, however, should never be confused with quality in debate; and it is often possible—and necessary—to have both.

Where to Find the Best Material

This section attempts to detail ten major areas in which the best debate evidence can be found. The list includes only sources of evidence that generally have proved to be the most profitable to debaters over the years. The major categories include: (1) bibliographies and indexes, (2) computer indexes, (3) books, (4) periodicals, (5) legal publications, (6) government documents, (7) newspapers, (8) pamphlets, (9) debate handbooks, and (10) material that can be obtained through the mail.

Bibliographies and indexes are among the most useful debate resources.

Bibliographies and Indexes

Many debaters are surprised to discover that some reference books are entirely bibliographical; there are even bibliographies to bibliographies. And, of course, many indexes contain useful references to source material. Listed below is a sample of available bibliographies and indexes. This list is by no means exhaustive.

Bibliographical Index. A bibliography of bibliographies.

Readers' Guide to Periodical Literature. This is probably the most widely used source among debaters. It is the most comprehensive guide to popular materials.

Education Index

Resources in Education

Current Index to Journals in Education

Books in Print. An annual listing of published works by subject, author, and title.

Forthcoming Books. A bimonthly listing of all books scheduled for publication within the next five months.

International Index to Periodicals

Economic Index

New York Times Index

Official Index of the Times (London)

Catholic Periodicals Index

Social Sciences and Humanities Index

The Bulletin of the Public Affairs Information Service

Public Affairs Information Service

Book Review Digest. An excellent place to find critical reviews of major sources.

Book Review Index. An excellent source of references to critical reviews.

Cumulative Book Index

United States Government Printing Office: Monthly Publications Catalog. A reference catalog all debaters should know. It lists all government publications by subject headings.

United States Government Printing Office: Congressional Information Service Index. Contains annotated listings of all publications from the legislative branch since 1970.

United Nations Document Index. Very useful but frequently overlooked.

External Research. This State Department list is of scholarly interest.

Index to Legal Periodicals

Foreign Affairs Bibliography

Biography Index

Current Biography

Who's Who in America. A standard source for sustaining the qualification of authors. In addition, there are several specialized *Who's Who*-type journals.

The Congressional Quarterly of the Bulletin of the Public Affairs Information Service

Vertical File Index

Computer Indexes

One important change in libraries across the country is an increased use of computerized indexes. More and more libraries are installing computerized data systems as replacements for the traditional card catalogs and bound indexes. For the library user who can understand such a system, the advantages this system holds in facilitating research both qualitatively and quantitatively are great.

To be sure, some library users may view computerized indexes with some hesitation. Some will see the advent of computerized library indexes as another annexation of everyday life by computer technology. In addition, this group might automatically assume that a computerized index is useful only to the expert programmer who can speak the language of the computer. But this is not so. Computerized indexes are designed to be "user friendly." That is, they are designed so that anyone can use them, and it usually takes only a few minutes to master a particular system.

Although there is a wide variety of computer systems presently in operation in libraries, most can be placed in one of two categories. The first includes systems that index items ordinarily found in a card catalog (primarily books). Most of these systems, like card catalogs, are indexed by author, title, and subject. All a person needs to do to find a listing under a particular heading is to enter the heading into the system (usually by way of a terminal, which has a keyboard similar to that found on a standard typewriter). For example, let's say you wanted to find out which of Mark Twain's books were available in your local library. You would first indicate that you wanted to make an author search (perhaps by typing the letter *a* and entering it; this will vary from system to system). Then, depending on the particulars of the individual system, you might type in "Twain, Mark" and enter it. The computer would then give a variety of information about each listing. It would give all the information you would find in the card catalog, such as the call number of the book, its publication information, and perhaps a short summary of its contents. In addition, the computer might also list the present status of the book—whether it has been checked out, other libraries where the book might be found, and so forth. This latter kind of information can be very helpful. A researcher doesn't have to waste a trip to the shelf to discover that the book has been checked out. In addition, he or she can know immediately whether the book can be found at other libraries.

The computerized catalog can also help facilitate subject searches. Using a standard card catalog to find information on broad topics can be quite inefficient. One can only find listings under very narrow, precise headings, and looking under broad references can be time-consuming. If a student were researching West Germany, for example, a card catalog would only allow her or him to examine subheadings (such as economy, history, geography, or demographics) one at a time. With a computerized system, though, the student could enter the broad topic of West Germany into the terminal, and it would display all the subheadings at once. A user would then know immediately how all the material on West Germany has been subdivided and would be able to get all the listings under a particular subheading quickly. This technique of entering broad topics to examine subheadings can also improve the breadth of research because the subheadings themselves can spark ideas for new cross-references to check out.

The second category of computerized indexes are those with periodical listings. These systems index periodical articles that might be found in bound indexes such as the *Reader's Guide to Periodical Literature* and the *Social Sciences Index*. The operation of these systems is similar to that of the computerized catalog: You enter a particular heading, and the listings for it are then displayed on the screen. Most of these systems, like the bound indexes, are limited to subject searches.

There are two advantages to computerized periodical indexes. The first is that a computerized system permits the search of many years at one time. With bound indexes, if a user wants to find all articles written on the MX missile in the past five years, he or she must go through five or more bound editions of a particular index. A computerized system allows the search of five years at one time. This can be particularly useful in newspaper searches. There is one computerized index that has compiled listings from the five biggest newspapers in the United States (the New York *Times*, the Washington *Post*, the *Christian Science Monitor*, *The Wall Street Journal*, and the Los Angeles *Times*) over a number of years. The second advantage, peculiar only to a few systems, is that the system may be attached to a printer. This means that after you call up the headings you are looking for, the listings can be printed out as hard copy. Needless to say, there is a great deal of time saved in not having to copy out by hand all the listings one finds. Of course, one may find a system of the first category (listing card catalog items) connected to a printer also.

The trend to computerized data systems should not be feared as diminishing the usability of the nation's libraries. Such systems are relatively easy to use, even for someone with virtually no computer experience. The advantages of such systems are great, however, in facilitating both the efficiency and breadth of research.

Books

Reference books are a good starting point for any researcher. In many cases they are an excellent place to find specific pieces of information. Most of these books are also useful for gathering background material.

Statistical Abstract of the United States. An exhaustive summary of current statistics.

Economics. By Paul Samuelson. It should be difficult to find an experienced debater who did not carry this book to most tournaments. It is an excellent and very readable text in beginning economics.

The United States in World Affairs. Published by the Council on Foreign Relations, it provides a good history and analysis of world affairs for each year.

Editorial Research Reports. Outstanding reference series. Available only to newspapers and libraries, it presents in-depth analyses of currently important topics.

Political Handbook of the World. A good reference for specific information about foreign countries.

Yearbook of the United Nations

Yearbook of World Affairs

Britannica Book of the Year

New International Yearbook

New York Times Economic Review and Forecast. Very good review of economic development in world areas.

Relations of Nations by Frederick H. Hartmann. A good examination of foreign policy and foreign relations.

Documents of International Affairs

Treaties in Force. Department of State's annual list of all the treaties to which the United States is bound.

Legislation on Foreign Relations. By the Committee on Foreign Relations, U.S. Senate.

Annual Report of the Council of Economic Advisors. Outstanding source for an analysis of the economic problems facing the United States and how these problems can best be met.

Brookings Institute Publications. A series of in-depth analyses of important issues.

Documents of American History

Black's Law Dictionary. The unquestioned standard work for legal terms and court precedents for concepts of law.

Constitutional Criminal Procedure. American Casebook Series.

American Constitution. By Lockhart, Kamisar, and Choper.

Constitutional Law. Gilbert Law Summaries.

Encyclopaedia Britannica. A thorough discussion of various topics at an adult level; thought by many to be the best encyclopedia.

World Almanac

Information Please Almanac

Reader's Digest Almanac

Book of the States

On any topic, the debater will be concerned with more than just reference books and textbooks. Listings can be found in the card catalog, using the list of key words discussed earlier. As the debater uses the card catalog, new key words will continue to crop up and should be added to the list.

In reading books, the researcher should pay special attention to footnotes, bibliographies, and the index. These specific sections of a book will often direct to other materials worth reading. In addition, they may save the debater time in finding subjects that may prove to be of special interest. In most cases, a quick look at the title page, table of contents, author's qualifications, and the date of publication will produce a reliable indicator of a book's merits.

There are, to be sure, different types of books. The debater needs to be able to distinguish between the survey of a subject intended for the general audience and the intensive, scholarly study of a subject. The latter is more likely to contain useful evidence. When reading anthologies of individual articles, the debater should keep in mind that the credibility of the evidence will depend on the qualifications of the authors and the dates of publication of the individual articles, not the dates of the edited collection.

To keep abreast of newly published books, you should consult *Books in Print*, which is an annual listing of published books by subject, author, and title. It is supplemented by *Forthcoming Books*, a bimonthly listing of all books scheduled for publication within the next five months.

Periodicals

Periodicals are a good source for recent evidence. Evidence from periodical literature should be carefully judged, however, against the criteria of evidence; they frequently represent one political bias or another. The best periodicals clearly separate editorial comment from reporting. The list below contains some of the more obvious publications. On many topics the most productive reading will come from the limited-circulation periodicals, which are intended for a more specialized reading audience. Indexes to some of these are listed in the section on bibliographies and indexes.

> *The London Economist.* A fine source.
> *Time*
> *Newsweek*
> *U.S. News and World Report*
> *Fortune*
> *Business Week*
> *Nation's Business*
> *The Nation*
> *The Reporter*
> *The New Republic*
> *Atlantic Monthly*
> *Saturday Review*
> *Harper's*
> *Foreign Affairs Monthly.* An excellent source of foreign affairs material by the best authors.
> *Annals of the American Academy of Political and Social Sciences*
> *Great Decisions.* Published annually by the Foreign Policy Association; very objective.

Vital Speeches
U.N. Review

Because some of the journals listed in the more specialized indexes have a very limited circulation, not all high school and college libraries carry them. If the debater does not have access to such periodicals, many of them can be procured in either of two ways. Some can be obtained through an interlibrary loan, a procedure by which the librarian makes arrangements to borrow materials from another library that does subscribe to the specific journals requested. Or single copies of most publications can be purchased from the publisher.

Legal Publications

With a few exceptions legal periodicals are not available in general libraries, but only in law and bar association libraries. Within the law library, the debater will find three especially valuable types of publications.

First, law libraries usually keep a large collection of books and pamphlets that are referred to as treatises. These are indexed in a card catalog similar to the catalog in a general library. Second, texts of court decisions in cases you may wish to investigate are also found in the law library. The need to investigate these materials on a topic involving international law may not be great, but they may be quite important in the case of domestic issues.

The decisions of our federal and state courts are printed in volumes referred to as court reports. Some of these reports, especially those of the Supreme Court, also may be available in general libraries that are classified as government depositories. If you are familiar with the system of citation employed in these reports, you will be able to find the cases you want without difficulty. A Supreme Court decision will be cited as 391 U.S. 1015 (1968). Translated, this citation means that the case in question was printed in Volume 391 of *United States Reports*, at page 1015, and that the case was decided in 1968. Similarly, a state citation such as 5 Cal, 3d 584 (1971) would mean that the case may be found in Volume 5 of the third *Series of California Reports*, at page 584, and that the case was decided in 1971. Citations for cases tried in courts of other nations or tried before international tribunals will be difficult to trace in American libraries although the process would be roughly analogous to this procedure.

Even after reading the actual decision, however, the debater may still be uncertain about the implications of the ruling or about the current state of the law. Clarification of these matters for American law would require consulting *Corpus Juris Secundum*, a reference work that is available not only at law libraries but also at major courthouses and in many general libraries. The Lawyer's Annotated Edition of *United States Reports* also includes annotations and commentary that may be helpful.

The third type of legal publication is the legal periodical. There are two principal kinds of legal journals. First, professional societies or groups publish journals containing material pertinent to their special interests. Examples of such journals are the *Journal of World Trade Law* and the *Journal of International Law and Economics*. Second, most of the nation's law schools publish law reviews. Law reviews usually are divided into two parts. The front section contains articles by judges, law professors, and practicing attorneys. These articles provide broad treatment of legal problems and should be read with great care. The back section, often titled "Notes" or "Comments," should be approached with some caution. These sections are written by student editors of the journal. They focus on new court rulings and discuss current problems in the law. Frequently, several law reviews will include comments pertinent to the case. These reviews may be sufficiently repetitive that it is unnecessary to read them all. Finally the debater should recognize that unsigned citations to law reviews usually refer to the student-written "Notes" section.

Government Documents

The debater will probably find that government documents can provide valuable information. On most topics they can be a direct source of information as well as a major summary source for materials that are difficult to obtain directly. Special reports, for example, typically contain the results of commissioned studies, which may not be available elsewhere.

Another type of government document is the annual report of many of the executive agencies of the federal government. For previous high school topics, such sources as the *Economic Report of the President, Federal Bureau of Investigation Uniform Crime Reports*, and the *Task Force on Medicaid and Related Programs* were found to be particularly useful.

Congressional hearings and reports are especially valuable sources of evidence. Hearings of the greatest value will vary from topic to topic. On a topic such as consumer product safety, debaters would want to focus their attention on the House Agriculture Committee, the Senate Finance Committee, the House Appropriations Committee, and the House Commerce Committee. On the other hand, with a topic such as U.S. foreign policy a debater would want to look at the hearings of the

Senate Armed Services Committee, Senate Foreign Relations Committee, and the House International Relations Committee.

To remain knowledgeable about current developments in congressional committees, a debater should frequently consult the *Congressional Quarterly*—a weekly résumé of activities in Congress. The calendars of these committees, which list the most recent committee publications and scheduled hearings, may be obtained free of charge, along with single copies of the transcripts of hearings, by writing either the chairperson of the committee or the individual debater's senator or representative.

A few hints may be helpful in reading the transcripts of congressional hearings. The debater will quickly discover that the transcripts of hearings are voluminous, so it is necessary to select with care those sections that are especially worthy of attention. The debater should concentrate primarily on the statements of professors and professionals from such fields as sociology, pathology, toxicology, medicine, political science, economics, chemistry, and the law; representatives of academic research bureaus or technical organizations and pertinent government agencies; and directors of reputable foundations or groups.

A tremendous amount of time can be saved if the researcher realizes that hearings contain repetition. The same witnesses may give almost identical statements at different hearings concerning the same problem. There may even be repetition within the same hearing. Frequently, a witness will read a prepared statement orally and then will have the written version of the same statement also included in the record.

The dialogue between witnesses and committee members following the witnesses' formal statements should not be overlooked. This interchange often is a source of excellent information, particularly of qualifications or limitations that witnesses may have forgotten to place on their overly generalized preliminary remarks.

Finally, the reports of the committees, printed after the conclusion of the hearings, are also worthy of attention. Although frequently there is duplication between the hearings and the report, it also is true that the reports contain many ideas and opinions not presented in the original hearings.

Individual publications of executive agencies represent still another type of government document. While some agencies, such as the Department of Agriculture, publish valuable pamphlets and reports, the student should be wary of propagandistic publicity pieces that are used by some agencies primarily as promotional items—leaflets, brochures, or handouts. Single copies of specific government agency publications generally can be obtained by writing directly to the issuing agency. It is a good idea to request, at the same time, a bibliography of related materials published by the same agency. The bibliography may contain publications not listed elsewhere.

It is always possible that unexpected evidence may turn up in the *Congressional Record*, the final type of government document. Unless you have virtually unlimited research time, however, reading the *Record* should be given a low priority. Many of the reprints in the *Record* are letters or editorials from obscure local newspapers. Should someone cite evidence from such a newspaper or periodical, however, your best chance of locating it is to peruse the *Record* for ten or fifteen days following the date cited. It usually can be found.

Federal government publications, of all the types that have been discussed, are indexed in the *Monthly Catalog of United States Government Publications*. Numbers in the subject index in the back of the volume refer to listings in the front section. These listings contain the complete citations to the pertinent publications. The February issue of each year consists of references to periodicals issued by government agencies. The *Monthly Catalog* is cumulated each year. Normally, however, its listings run about three months behind actual publication dates. Therefore, the *Congressional Quarterly of the Bulletin of the Public Affairs Information Service* should be consulted for notices of very recent releases. The *Monthly Catalog*, by the way, is not complete in its listings—some publications are not listed there.

In addition to the *Monthly Catalog*, the *Congressional Information Service Index* contains annotated listings of all publications from the legislative branch since 1970. The best bet for locating government publications, however, is to consult directly with the government documents supervisor or librarian at the nearest depository library. Designating a public or university library as a government depository means that the library regularly receives copies of most government publications. Also, most federal publications may be ordered at minimal cost from the Superintendent of Documents, U.S. Government Printing Office, Washington, D.C. 20402.

Newspapers

It is wise to stay abreast of current developments by reading a daily newspaper regularly. We recommend the New York *Times*. The *Times* contains reports of congressional committee hearings as well as reprints of important testimony. Finally, the Sunday edition of the *Times* includes a special section, "The Week in Review," which summarizes and analyzes developments of the past week.

Carried by most major libraries, the New York *Times* publishes its own semi-monthly index, which is cumulated annually. Each entry in the index includes a reference to the date, page, and column of an article (Nov 8, 16:6). For Sunday editions, section numbers are also included (Dec 16, IV, 9:1). The index is valuable not only for finding articles in the *Times*, but also for locating accounts of similar events contained in other newspapers of the same day. In addition to the New York *Times*, the debater will want to consult other newspapers, such as the *Christian Science Monitor*, *The Wall Street Journal*, the Washington *Post*, the *National Observer*, and the Los Angeles *Times*, just to mention a few.

Pamphlets

Another, although less recognized, source of evidence is the large number of pamphlets published each year. Pressure groups, foundations, and academic departments are among the many issuers of pamphlets. A sampling of pamphlets from all issuers is listed in the *Vertical File Index*, carried by most libraries. Most libraries maintain a vertical file of pamphlets and will order materials for it upon request. The *Vertical File Index* also indicates places from which the debater may order pamphlets directly and the cost, if any.

Debate Handbooks

Despite the protestations of many debate coaches, nearly all debaters make some use of a debate handbook during the early stages of their research. These special references are compiled to aid the debater in identifying the major issues, basic evidence, and important authorities. The vast majority of debaters find such help very useful at the beginning of the debating season. Others, especially those who debate at the championship level, will admit to ordering handbooks, if only to see what they can expect from their weaker opponents. Despite some of their weaknesses, we would recommend their early use, as long as the debater keeps their function in proper perspective.

Handbooks are designed merely to introduce students to a topic. They are not to be considered definitive sources. Because they must be prepared quickly and then condensed into a few hundred pages, it should be obvious that even the best handbook is likely to have its shortcomings. As long as the researcher knows that such shortcomings exist, there is no reason why he or she should not use a handbook as a beginning source. It is, of course, not appropriate to quote directly from a handbook during a debate round. Evidence should be quoted from the original source and then only after it has been checked for accuracy and context. Checking handbook evidence is important; an error might have been made in the production of the handbook. As was mentioned earlier, it is always wise to double-check evidence that was not personally researched. This simple precaution will always insure that the evidence is accurate.

Because handbooks are limited to a certain number of pages, there will always be evidence that was not included in the handbook. This usually does not mean the evidence was of no value. It means that there was not enough room because the researchers wanted to provide information from as many sources as possible in the limited space available. The debater should always go back to these sources to look for additional evidence. The sources cited in the handbooks may also produce valuable leads to additional primary sources.

Many coaches protest the use of handbooks because some lazy debaters feel that they need go no further in their research for evidence. (Such students would be more properly called "oral interpreters.") One of the principal values and strategies of debate is learning the technique of independent research. The debater who begins the season by buying as many debate handbooks as possible and spends the season "cutting and pasting" will find little long-term success in competition. As new ideas are developed by opponents, handbook researchers will find themselves lacking evidence unless they take the initiative to begin some original research.

Care should be taken in deciding which handbooks to buy. Each year new handbooks enter the market, while others drop out. Choose only those with complete citations and a reputation for being thorough and accurate. Below is a partial list of some handbooks currently on the market. Because the value of a handbook is a personal decision, no effort has been made to evaluate those listed.

> NTC Annual Debate Handbook. This handbook is sometimes
> referred to as the Northwestern Handbook.
> The Jayhawk Handbook. Prepared by the University of Kansas.
> The Baylor Briefs. As the title indicates, most of the evidence in
> this handbook is put together in brief format.
> Mid-America Research

The Loyola Handbook
The Golden West. Previously called *The Redlands Handbook.*
The UCLA Handbook
Cross Currents. Published by the Alan Company.
The Wake Forest Handbook
Texas Briefs
Ithaca Handbook. Prepared by Bates College.

Each year the National Federation of State High School Associations publishes a journal covering the current high school debate topic. This publication, *The Forensic Quarterly*, is not a handbook of evidence cards, but rather four issues analyzing the debate topic for the upcoming year. These issues can provide an excellent starting point for background information as well as an extensive bibliography for beginning a library. *The Forensic Quarterly* can be ordered from the National Federation of State High School Associations, 11724 Plaza Circle, P.O. Box 20626, Kansas City, MO 64195.

Materials Obtained Through the Mail

Many debaters overlook private sources in their frantic search through books and periodicals. This avenue can be the *most* useful of all sources of information.

Private agencies with causes frequently offer large amounts of free materials that explain their points of view. Some of the materials are so biased that they are unusable, but a great many of them contain relatively objective data that can be obtained just by writing to the agencies.

As soon as the topic for debate is known, the student should search out all of the potentially helpful private agencies and send them brief, polite requests for any materials they might have. There are two excellent sources available in most libraries for identifying the agencies that would have material on a debate topic:

Encyclopaedia of Associations. A comprehensive list of
    American associations.
The International Encyclopaedia of Associations

High School Debate Institutes

Each summer dozens of universities around the country offer institutes for high school debaters. The structure varies from one institute to another, but to some degree each offers instruction in debate theory, topic lectures, access to a university library, practice rounds on the new topic, and an opportunity to work with debaters from other high schools. Institutes vary in length, as well, with the shortest being two weeks and the longest five weeks. Costs vary as greatly as content, but many institutes offer scholarships.

An institute is like a handbook; it can be very beneficial when chosen with care, but it is not a guarantee of a successful season. Work cannot stop with the institute; it must continue throughout the entire season. When choosing an institute, compare and shop around. Look at staff, university facilities, reputation, and program offerings. Below is a partial list of current institutes run by a number of universities. Again, no attempt has been made to evaluate the programs.

Northwestern High School Debate Institute
Baylor Debate Workshop
University of Kansas Midwestern Speech and Debate Institute
Louisville High School Debate Institute
Northern Iowa Debate Institute
Wake Forest Debate Institute
Lewis & Clark Debate Institute
Northern Arizona University Debate Institute
Emporia State University Debate Institute
Golden West Forensic Institute, University of Redlands
National Forensic Institute
Emory University Debate Institute
Bradley University (Lincoln-Douglas debate)
Dartmouth University Debate Institute
University of Iowa Debate Institute

Each year the Speech Communication Association (SCA) publishes a *Directory of Collegiate Summer Workshops.* You can request a copy by writing SCA, National Office, 5105 Backlick Road, #E, Annandale, VA 22003. The SCA makes no attempt to evaluate the programs listed.

Recording Debate Evidence

The question that faces the debater after finding evidence is what to do with it, which entails three considerations. First, the evidence should be reduced to a form that exactly represents the wording and intent of the author. Second, it should be recorded in a manner that will be most useful to the debater. Third, it should be recorded in such a way that the speaker can immediately answer any questions about the accuracy of the citation.

With these three considerations in mind, it should be obvious that some material is so important to the debate case or to a specific argument that it should be carried in its original form. Most skilled debaters carry with them the actual copies of important books, articles, or hearings. If the entire work is not needed, the researcher can have the important parts photocopied. Less vital material should be copied on cards, to be filed away in the debater's file case. The procedure for recording the material on cards is dealt with below, and the filing procedure is the next topic for discussion.

The first step in developing an evidence card is marking the material to be copied, after carefully rereading the passage to see what part is wanted. The appropriate material is marked for later copying (or is copied out by hand from library books). The information should then be placed on a file card in such a way that it will be easy for the debater to use. Most researchers prefer to type the evidence on a 4" by 6" card. Typing makes it easier for both colleagues to read, and the 4" by 6" card is easy to handle but large enough to accommodate all the material without crowding. However, with the increasing amount of evidence being carried by debaters, many squads are now using 3" by 5" cards.

The card should be clearly labeled with the citation of the source. The full bibliographical reference should be typed in block style on the card. For the judge's and opponents' benefits and for later reference, it is especially important that the source and page number be accurately noted. A good quotation can lose its impact if the opposition points out that it cannot find the quotation on the page that the debater reported. (Recall our earlier discussion of always checking out evidence researched by someone else before using it.) The author's qualifications should also be included on the card, and space should be left in one corner for a filing index code.

Only one piece of evidence should be placed on a card. The researcher won't save much money by including two quotations on the same card, but can avoid a great deal of confusion by limiting the cards to a single quotation each.

Although it is not recommended that the debater omit words from a piece of evidence, many debaters often find some authors to be quite wordy. It is felt that these words are not necessary to make the point.

If unnecessary words are omitted, the omission should be clearly indicated with ellipses (. . .). Adjectives, qualifiers, and such words as *not* are not considered unnecessary words. It is strongly suggested that ellipses be avoided wherever possible. What one debater considers unnecessary may be essential to another. Also, NFL rules require that internal ellipses not be used unless the team is carrying the original, or a copy of the original. Below is a sample of what a finished evidence card should look like.

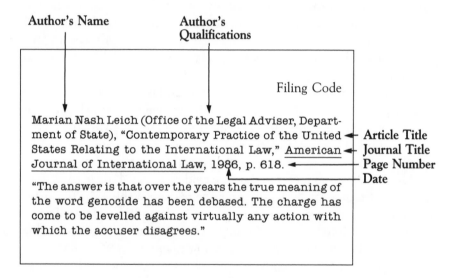

Filing Material

If the debater has done all the work thus far indicated by the strategy and tactics of research, he or she has invested a great deal of time and energy in accumulating a store of material. However, we have watched a number of students collect as many as 2,000 evidence cards, but use only ten or twenty on each side of the question. Frequently, the reason for this is that they simply don't know what evidence they have in their file boxes and probably couldn't find it in any event. Information retrieval, as any professional will affirm, is as important as any other phase of scholarship.

It is certainly true that each debate team will develop a filing system that is best for its own use. Any system is adequate if the students know at all times what they have and can quickly retrieve the evidence during a debate. The important thing, again, is not so much which system is used but that there is a system. There are, however, several commonly used filing systems that vary in complexity, depending on how much evidence the researcher has gathered.

The common feature of all the systems is that the student divides the evidence into categories. Then the material is stored in a file box behind index cards that indicate the category. No matter what system is used, it is important that the number of cards in each category be kept small. If there are more than ten cards under a single heading, the chances increase that the debater won't know what the file contains and will use the first card found. Even if the debater knows what evidence is in the file, a category that contains a great many cards will take too long to sort through in an actual debate round. A filing system should make it as easy as possible to find evidence during a round.

Simple Alphabetical System

The most elementary filing system involves dividing the cards into subject areas and filing them accordingly. If the researcher has several cards on the United Nations, they are filed behind an index card labeled "U.N.," with "U.N." written in the upper right-hand corner of each card to facilitate refiling. This system is used most often by new debaters, and it works fairly well as long as you have a small number of evidence cards. More evidence, however, requires a more elaborate system.

Elaborate Alphabetical System

As debaters get more and more evidence, many of them simply elaborate on the system they learned as novices. They get two file boxes, one for the affirmative and one for the negative evidence. Then the cards are filed behind the major affirmative and negative headings. To help in filing, two different colors of cards often are used to indicate the two sides of the question. (To use two colors of cards requires greater care on the part of the researcher in recording evidence. To avoid having to recopy a tremendous amount of evidence, the researcher must decide in the beginning if a card will be used for affirmative or for negative arguments. In many cases this may not be possible.)

Such a system, unfortunately, presents problems. To begin with, it takes a great deal of time during a debate to find the appropriate heading and then to find the best card. Also, a sizable amount of material cannot easily be classified as either affirmative or negative. For these reasons, the best debaters usually move to a notebook index system for their evidence filing.

Index Sheet System

A notebook index system means that the index file cards are lettered and numbered instead of labeled by subject. "U.N." might become "Category A." Cards that deal with the effectiveness of the veto might be numbered "A14." A master notebook is then kept for the entire filing system. All of the material in each file box is noted on a single index sheet to which the debater can quickly refer for the code numbers that apply to specific subjects. The number of cards in each category is kept small by expanding the number of categories and by eliminating the weakest evidence.

If a debate team has five file boxes, it would first assign a code number to each box. Then it would letter the major headings and number the subcategories. The index sheet provides the summary for the filed material. The following is part of an index sheet that was used by a student debater.

The index cards in the evidence file were tabbed with the appropriate letters and numbers. The evidence cards were labeled with the proper box numbers and subject letters and numbers. If, during a debate, the debater wants to prove that minimum competency testing improves the quality of education, the index sheet would show that such material is filed under "B3." After the debate, the cards that were used could be quickly refiled under the B3 heading, which would have been noted in the upper right-hand corner of the card.

Debaters who have used the index sheet system report that it is a very effective way to handle large amounts of evidence. They say that the cards can be easily filed, quickly found, and just as quickly refiled after a round. This is probably true because many index headings are possible under a code designation and because the entire subject subcategory does not have to be written on each index and evidence card. Also, it is considerably easier to read the code than to read a lengthy heading when you are searching through a file box. A word of warning: if the debater loses the notebook that has the evidence sheets, there is no way of knowing where the evidence is filed. It would be wise to carry a duplicate or two at all times.

Sample Index System

I. The Character of the Military Situation in Latin America
  A. Position of the Military in Latin America
    1. United States policy is driving Latin America to
      the Soviets
    2. Outcomes of revolutions are not predictable
    3. Military regimes are not necessarily repressive
    4. United States has economic interests in Latin America
    5.
    6.
    7.
    8.
    9.
    10. United States intervenes regularly in Latin America
    11.
    12.
    13.
    14.
    15. Latin America is a place for superpower confrontation
    16. Moscow is the cause of instability in Latin America
    17. U.S.–Latin American policy is inconsistent
    18. Soviets will be increasingly involved
    19.
    20.
  B. Terrorism, Violence, and Revolution in Latin America
    1. Violence is part of an ongoing cycle
    2. Human rights and violence
    3. Human rights issues include state violence
    4. Torture is supported by foreign aid
    5.
    6.
    7.
    8.
    9. Revolutions cannot be brought by aid
    10. Dictatorships always fail
    11. Authoritarian regimes invite revolution
    12.

Continued on next page

Continued from previous page

C. Central American Military Problems
  1. The military helps sustain democracy
  2. Terrorism is the norm of authoritarians
  3. Most terror is Marxist and not state
  4.
  5.
  6.
  7.
  8. Democracies are fragile
  9. Democracies need security protection
  10. Military aid helps to defeat guerillas and maintain democracies
  11.
  12.
  13.
  14. Democracies are growing
  15. Aid to Contras will result in military involvement
  16. Military aid is not the way to solve problems
  17.
  18.
II. The support for Contras in Latin America
  A. Contra Support: The General Policy
    1. Contra support deters Soviets
    2. Contra support develops allies
    3. Contra support deters Cuba
    4.
    5.
    6.
    7.
    8.
    9. Contra support unjustified legally
    10. Contra support creates backlash
    11.
    12.

NOTE: The debater should be sure to allow blank spaces in the index outline in order to add new categories as the number of evidence cards grows.

Maintaining the Evidence Files

The last matter of relevance to research in debate is the process of carefully maintaining the evidence file. Periodically, the team should go through all of its material to see what it has. Cards that are never used should be discarded if reexamination indicates they are not as useful as they once appeared. More often, however, debaters will find material they have been overlooking because it was not used at first. That material might suddenly become the best evidence in the file.

The important thing is to extend the thinking approach to debate to the evidence file. Because it has become a kind of status symbol among debaters to carry large amounts of evidence, useless material often hides valuable information—there are so many cards that going through them to see what is good and what is bad becomes an overwhelming task. The debater may neglect checking the files and, thus, may overlook new and valuable material. Also, the size of the evidence file can lull the researcher into thinking the research job is done. Such nonthinking debaters can typically be identified by the large number of late-season losses they accrue. Debaters should always remember that a large file is useful only if they know what is in it and can retrieve the information quickly. If that is not the case, the debater will develop only a good set of muscles by carrying around so much evidence.

Summary

This chapter has outlined some of the major strategies and tactics of debate research and is, in many ways, the keystone of this text. Because argument in debate depends so much on evidence, the debater often is only as good as the evidence. Research should be approached with a planned strategy, and a sound procedure should be followed. The strategy has to be to collect better evidence than any of your opponents will have. The tactic or procedure should involve the careful gathering of background material and specific evidence. Finally, all the work will be lost if the evidence is not recorded, filed, and maintained in a logical, practical way.

The thinking approach to debate applies as much to this area as to any other. If a student researches in a particular way because "that's the way everybody else does it" or merely collects quote cards instead of convincing evidence, that student will become one of the many victims of nonthinking debating. The student won't learn much from the debate experience and won't win many debates.

Questions for Discussion

1. Outline the criteria for judging a source both externally and internally. Provide an example that does not meet the criteria and explain why it does not.

2. Evidence can be divided into two categories: empirical evidence and opinion evidence. Explain the difference between the two. Which would be the preferred form of evidence? Why?

3. What applications can you make of your knowledge of research techniques? Would they help in other classes on other subjects? How?

4. Discuss the differences between research based on the nonthinking approach and research based on the thinking approach to debate.

5. The authors outline a procedure for recording evidence. Why is it important to include all the information outlined?

6. Once a significant amount of evidence has been collected it becomes necessary to store it in some fashion. Describe the filing systems suggested in this chapter. Which system would work best for you? Why? If you have another system that you believe would be efficient describe it and what you feel its advantages are.

Activities

1. Listen to the nightly news for one week. During this time choose an issue of importance and also follow it in the weekly newspaper. Evaluate the evidence being used to support various claims. Provide an example of evidence that meets the criteria outlined in the chapter. Also provide example(s) of evidence that fall short of the criteria.

2. Using the current debate resolution or one provided by the teacher, make a list of key terms that could be used for beginning your research.

3. Compile a list of organizations that might have useful information on the resolution used in Activity 2. Compose and mail letters requesting information concerning this resolution. When the information arrives, be prepared to explain why it is or is not useful for research.

4. Using the resolution from Activity 2, make a list of congressional committees that might have information about the topic. Write to each of these committees for information. Be sure to ask for any bibliographical information.

5. Using the resolution from Activity 2, collect five articles. Research the articles, cutting evidence and listing categories for filing. Once this activity has been completed, it should become an ongoing activity to prepare for future debates.

Chapter 3

Building the Affirmative Constructive Argument

Objectives and Key Terms

After studying Chapter 3, you should be able

1. To explain how the affirmative decides what case area to offer in a debate.

2. To discuss what makes a harm inherent and significant.

3. To explain the essential characteristics of each type of affirmative case construction.

4. To explain the process of constructing an affirmative plan.

5. To produce an affirmative case and plan complete with evidence.

To effectively debate the affirmative, you will need to know the following terms:

defining terms	comparative advantages case
definition by authority	criteria case
operational definition	net benefits case
traditional need case	systems analysis
structural inherency	affirmative plan
attitudinal inherency	

T he affirmative case constitutes the position to be developed by the affirmative throughout the debate. It includes a justification(s) for change, a plan, and the advantages of the plan. Most debate resolutions are open to a number of interpretations. Since any of these may be a topic for debate, the affirmative decides which area of the resolution it wishes to discuss. Many novice debaters are eager to begin work on the affirmative, but shy away from the negative. Novices seem to find a sense of security in knowing ahead of time what case will be debated and having one speech already prepared.

Confidence in the easy road soon vanishes as the debater learns the responsibilities and obligations of the affirmative. In this chapter you will learn these obligations by examining three areas of the affirmative position. First, you will look at the definition of terms. Here you will explore where to look, as well as how to use the definitions found. Second, you will take a look at four specific types of affirmative cases and the obligations and responsibilities they must meet. The case areas to be discussed include the traditional need case, the comparative advantages case, the criteria case, and the net benefits case. Although these are not the only types of affirmative cases used, they are the ones used most often. Finally, you will explore the development of the affirmative plan.

Definition of Terms

In preparing for either side of the question, a basic fact must be remembered: The affirmative's definition and analysis of the topic determines the direction of the debate. The affirmative has the right to make any interpretation of the topic, as long as it clearly maintains the spirit of the proposition. But how does the affirmative decide what case to offer?

Each affirmative team starts by **defining the terms** in the resolution. The debater begins by identifying each important term and discerning its various meanings from a number of sources. Sources used to define terms of past resolutions are listed below.

Dictionary of Economics and Business
Dictionary of Political Science
Dictionary of Development Banking
Systematic Glossary of Selected Economic and Social Terms
Webster's Third New International Dictionary

Funk & Wagnall's College Dictionary
The Oxford English Dictionary
Penguin Dictionary of Economics
A Dictionary of Politics
The American Heritage Dictionary of the English Language
Black's Law Dictionary
Chambers Twentieth Century Dictionary
Random House College Dictionary
The Scribner Bantam English Dictionary
The Living Webster Encyclopedic Dictionary of the English Language

This list of resources is not exhaustive. Depending on the topic, there will be various specialized dictionaries and resource materials that can be used. The debater should always consult more than one source for each term. Not only does this give the debater a better idea of possible affirmative cases, it will also help the negative to anticipate what cases might be used by its opposition. In past years coaches and debaters alike have seen resolutions made almost meaningless by the unexpected definitions of what previously seemed to be a harmless term. A couple of past resolutions can illustrate this:

Resolved: That the federal government should establish minimum educational standards *for* elementary and secondary schools in the United States.

for: for the benefit of

This definition would open up the topic to include cases that *helped out* elementary and secondary schools. The affirmative then could advance a case setting standards either for preschools or for education departments at the university level. Both would have an *effect on* elementary and secondary schools. Setting standards for preschools would affect the ability of the child upon entering kindergarten, thereby benefiting the elementary school system. To set standards for university education departments would upgrade the quality of teachers and thus benefit both elementary and secondary schools.

Resolved: That the United States should significantly change its *foreign trade* policies.

foreign trade: all transportation by merchant ships between countries other than under whose flag a vessel is registered

Such a definition opened the door for an affirmative case that sought to change waterborne commerce between two ports. That is, the affirmative sought to alter the regulation of goods and services between the United States and another foreign government. Many negative teams described these cases as "the regulation of aid" as opposed to the "regulation of trade."

Using such definitions tends to broaden the topic to the extreme. Most resolutions are written to allow significant leeway in case development without stretching the definitions. Most judges would consider the examples given here to be off the topic. The debater should examine the definitions with the intent of the resolution in mind.

Generally, terms are defined in one of two ways. There is no set rule of thumb for which method to follow. The choice is usually left up to the debater's instinct.

Definition by Authority

When using **definition by authority**, the affirmative defines its terms at the beginning of the first affirmative speech. It is not necessary to define all the terms of the resolution. The first affirmative need only concentrate on those crucial to his or her particular case. The sources used are generally those listed earlier. They may also include authorities in the field being debated. For example, on a topic involving economics the affirmative might choose to cite Professor Milton Friedman, of the University of Chicago.

Debaters tend to define terms more frequently at the beginning of each debate season. As the season progresses, the definitions often drop out of the debate. This occurs because the definitions of terms tend to be agreed on and are no longer needed. However, if the affirmative is running a case that does not use the commonly accepted definition, it is strongly suggested that terms be defined to avoid any misunderstanding.

Operational Definitions

The terms of the resolution can also be operationally defined in the affirmative plan. This means that the plan serves as an example of the resolution. When using an **operational definition**, the affirmative merely states this fact after stating the resolution.

The affirmative defends the position that the future will help human-kind, as long as people help themselves. To bring meaning to these words, _____ and I support the resolution RESOLVED: *That the U.S. should significantly change its foreign trade policies.* All terms will be operationally defined in the plan.

Let's look at an example on the topic RESOLVED: *That the federal government should establish a comprehensive program to significantly increase the energy independence of the United States.*

Plank 1. Establish oil reserves.

A. A one-year supply of oil based on total domestic consumption in the previous year will be stored. Initially 5 billion barrels, to be received and adjusted annually.

B. Crude and refined products will be stored. Refined products will be located especially in areas lacking capacity. Incentives for refining development as necessary.

C. Salt-dome and steel-tank storage located throughout the country will be utilized.

Plank 2. Oil for the reserve shall be acquired from Naval Petroleum Reserves and North Slope oil and secondary and tertiary recovery of nonproducing, onshore domestic supplies. Government with private companies to deliver the oil to the reserves, using existing pipelines where possible. The government will be a producer as a last resort.

Plank 3. Use of the reserve may be authorized by the president, Congress, or the agency responsible for administration. Authorization will include responses to artificial or natural supply interruptions. When used, sale will be at prevailing domestic market prices.

Plank 4. Administration. A federal agency will be created to oversee the establishment and maintenance of the reserve. The agency will ensure completion of the reserve by 1992.

Plank 5. Finance. Reduction of money from duplicative programs. Sale of oil from Naval Petroleum Reserves. Value Engineering on Federal Contracts, general federal revenue.

Plank 6. Enforcement. Will be through judicial review, citizen standing. Violators will be subject to civil and criminal sanctions.

Unusual Definitions

Debaters have always been known for their creativity. No matter how carefully the topic committee words a resolution, there will be loopholes through which the affirmative might crawl. The authors would like to draw a distinction between the "unusual" case and the "squirrel" case.

The unusual case centers around an area of the topic few have thought of. On the energy topic, the MHD (magnetohydrodynamics) case would be considered unusual. The affirmative presented an alternative that was unusual but that could solve a significant portion of our electric energy need. The MHD case also adhered to the intent of the resolution. That is, it provided a form of energy that would help to alleviate our dependence on other countries.

The squirrel case involves a case idea that the affirmative tries to work into the topic. It usually involves searching endlessly until the debater finds a definition that will incorporate the case idea. The energy topic provides a good example. The affirmative defines energy as a source of power. This definition seems innocent enough until the affirmative also defines fire as a source of power. From these two definitions, the affirmative offers a case on fire prevention. Of course, the case does not remedy the energy crisis, which was the intent of the resolution.

Another test for the squirrel case is a test of its definitions. The definitions provided by the affirmative are placed back into the resolution. Most of the time, when this is done the resolution will make no sense. The success of the squirrel case is usually short-lived. If it is successful at all, it is because the negative team panics and allows the affirmative to run the show.

In recent years debate resolutions have tended to be very broad. Without stretching their imagination, debaters have been able to think of dozens of possible cases. Usually, there are one or two key terms in the resolution that can have many definitions. In the resolutions that follow, the key terms have been underscored.

Resolved: That the federal government should establish minimum educational standards for elementary and secondary schools in the United States.

Resolved: That the federal government should establish <u>uniform standards for</u> testing and marketing all products with <u>potentially</u> carcinogenic effects on humans.

Resolved: That the United States should significantly <u>change</u> its <u>foreign trade policies</u>.

Resolved: That the federal government should establish a <u>comprehensive</u> program to significantly increase the <u>energy independence</u> of the United States.

Resolved: That the federal government should <u>guarantee comprehensive medical</u> care for all citizens in the United States.

Resolved: That a <u>comprehensive</u> program of <u>penal</u> reform should be adopted throughout the United States.

Resolved: That the <u>development</u> and <u>allocation</u> of scarce world <u>resources</u> should be controlled by an international organization.

Resolved: That governmental <u>financial support</u> for all elementary and secondary education should be provided <u>exclusively</u> by the federal government.

Resolved: That the federal government should implement a <u>comprehensive long-term</u> agricultural policy in the United States.

Resolved: That the United States should adopt a policy to increase <u>political stability</u> in Latin America.

In an effort to limit the range of interpretations of the topic, the collegiate topic committee has begun to provide "parameters of the resolution." This means that the committee provides a statement of what the committee had in mind when framing the resolution. Although this statement is not binding on the debater, it does help the negative to build a framework for a topicality argument against any affirmative off-the-wall definitions.

Should vs. Would

All academic debate resolutions contain the word *should*. When the affirmative proposal is shown to be workable and desirable, it is argued that it *should* be adopted. The affirmative is not compelled to show that it will be adopted. While the affirmative must provide enough detail to show that the plan will work, there is not enough time in a debate to provide the kind of detail found in a piece of legislation. For example, in a debate on the energy topic, the affirmative would be expected to show which energy source would be used, but it would not be expected to outline the details of how the energy source would be developed or the finite details of how it worked. Or, when debating the resolution RESOLVED: *That the United States should adopt a policy to increase political stability in Latin America*, the affirmative would not be expected to show how private organizations would actually implement aid programs with the end result being increasing political stability. In most cases it would be pointless for the negative to try to show that public opinion would keep the affirmative plan from being adopted.

The exception to the foregoing occurs when the affirmative utilizes attitudinal inherency. In such a case, the affirmative will argue that present attitudes preclude the status quo from adopting the affirmative plan. When arguing that attitudes are the barrier to status quo adoption, the affirmative must also show that its proposal can overcome those attitudes. If it does not, then the negative can present a strong argument that the status quo would not adopt the affirmative proposal either. Attitudinal inherency will be discussed further in the next section of this chapter.

Preparing the affirmative case includes practicing speeches and cross-examination strategies.

Traditional Need Case

The **traditional need case** is built on the conservative philosophy that there is no reason to change the status quo until it has been demonstrated that serious evils exist in the present system. It is not enough, however, to demonstrate problems in the status quo; the new proposal must be shown to have the capacity for correcting the evils without generating new problems that would be worse than those in the present system. An example will clarify this traditional position concerning the adoption of new policies.

A debater supporting the affirmative side of the proposition RESOLVED: *That automobiles should be prohibited in Gotham City* might argue that automobiles are unattractive and that they destroy the esthetic

---

Traditional Need-Plan Case

I. The United States is vulnerable to nuclear attack.

   A. The Soviet Union has thousands of nuclear weapons.

   B. The United States has no defensive shield.

II. Vulnerability inheres in status quo policy.

   A. The ABM treaty prevents deployment of defensive weapons on a broad scale.

   B. Disarmament negotiations are unlikely to succeed.

   Plan: Develop a space-based defensive shield for the United States; deployment negotiated with the Soviets to maximize deterrence values.

III. The plan will meet the need.

   A. Defense technology is promising.

   B. Long-term development by science can work.

   C. The technology will be good enough to at least stop accidents and function as an insurance policy against major wars.

beauty of the city. It might be suggested that automobiles cause large traffic jams that jangle the nerves of the citizens and create great difficulties for the police. The negative, however, could respond to such arguments by saying that they do not meet the requirements of the traditional prima facie need case. If the beauty of the city is marred by the presence of cars, so what? Where is the serious problem? The advantages of having cars far outweigh the disadvantages. If traffic problems are caused, so what? Automobiles are so beneficial to Gotham City residents that everyone wants to drive, and some difficulties naturally follow.

It would be possible, however, to build a traditional need case on such a topic. The affirmative could argue that some change is necessary because there is a significant air pollution problem. The toxic content of the city's air is so high that the health of a large part of the citizenry is in danger. Children may die because of smog. In addition, people are leaving the city and new businesses are not moving into Gotham City but are looking for new, clean locations. The affirmative could go on to demonstrate that the heavy automobile traffic of the city is the prime cause of the pollution problem. It could also show that, until cars are banned, the problem cannot be solved.

Having proved a need for a change, the affirmative would suggest that automobiles should be prohibited in Gotham City. It would show that banning cars would solve the problem and that many advantages would result. The health of the citizenry would no longer be in danger. People would no longer feel a need to move from the area, and new businesses could again be attracted. Finally, the affirmative might demonstrate that the disadvantages of not allowing automobiles in the city could easily be overcome by expanding the public transportation system—an added feature that would bring in more revenue, cut the accident rate, and settle the nerves of the citizens.

In the traditional need case, the affirmative begins the process of building a prima facie case by demonstrating that there is a need for a change—not, thus far, a need for the proposition but *a need for a change in the present system*. After it has demonstrated the need for change, the affirmative will say that it also has a *proposal* for change—the affirmative plan—that corrects the problem and that also has several *advantages*. If the affirmative meets these basic arguments, it has met its burden of proof by presenting a prima facie case.

A prima facie case is one that any reasonable person would accept at face value. That is, it must include a plan to implement the resolution and a justification for the plan. The justification can be an inherent need in the present system, a comparative advantage, or some other accepted grounds. Finally, all parts of the case must be presented in the first affirmative constructive speech. The affirmative team that holds back part of the case until the second constructive speech would run the risk of losing the debate on grounds that they did not present a prima facie case.

Most debaters feel that the most difficult phase in the traditional need case is establishing the need-for-a-change argument. What constitutes a need for a change? Generally, there are three elements to a sound need-for-a-change argument. The affirmative must demonstrate that: (1) A problem exists; (2) The problem is inherent in the status quo; and (3) It is sufficiently widespread to cause concern.

The Problem Exists

In advancing this kind of argument, the affirmative does not yet advocate the need to adopt the proposition; it argues first that a change is needed in the present system. Naturally, it designs the need argument carefully, so that the only proposal that could meet the requirements of a change is the affirmative's plan, implied in the resolution.

The first step in constructing the need-for-a-change argument is identifying a problem that clearly exists in the present system. This identification is not very difficult because debate topics are framed in response to situations of policy controversy that many people feel pose serious problems. The problems that the affirmative looks at are those that currently exist but that, at the same time, could be remedied by the proposal implied in the proposition.

During the 1986–87 debate season, high school debaters dealt with the proposition RESOLVED: *That the federal government should implement a comprehensive long-term agricultural policy in the United States.* The problem identified by a number of teams was the devastation of the small farmer in times of high interest rates and falling agricultural prices. The 1987–88 topic, RESOLVED: *That the United States should adopt a policy to increase political stability in Latin America,* concentrated on a variety of foreign policy issues (drug smuggling, sale of arms, and illegal immigration, to name a few).

In each of these examples, the affirmative debaters researched the topic and combined their background knowledge and specific evidence to focus on a problem in the status quo. Identification of the problem as a fact became the first step in justifying the first affirmative contention that a change was necessary in the present way of doing things.

As indicated, however, identification of the problem is not the end of the need-for-a-change argument. The affirmative still must establish three things about the problem in order to persuade the judge that it has presented a prima facie case. It must demonstrate that the problem is inherent in the present system, that it is harmful, and that its effects are sufficiently widespread to justify a change.

The Problem Is Inherent in the Status Quo

Most debate coaches feel that *inherency* is the key to the need argument. For this concept the affirmative must show that the problem is inherently a part of the present system. This flaw can be one of two types, commonly labeled structural inherency and attitudinal inherency. When using **structural inherency**, the affirmative argues that the problem cannot be corrected until basic changes have been made in the structure of the present system. The problem cannot be solved simply by doing more of what is presently being done, nor can it be corrected simply by spending more money on present methods. Generally, the affirmative will identify some law(s) or set of regulations that stands in the way of the affirmative solution.

Attitudinal inherency deals with the attitudes of the bureaucracy, not with laws or regulations. Here it is argued that the attitudes of the government or those of industry stand in the way of the status quo's solving the affirmative problem. An example of attitudinal inherency can be found under the foreign policy topic. The affirmative would argue that the attitude of the government has been to sell arms to foreign countries. Although there are no laws (short of specific treaties) that indicate that arms must be sold, nonetheless the policy has been to do so. Thus, the attitude of government would preclude solving the evils of arms sales that the affirmative has outlined.

Chart 1 indicates the inherency argument that a team might have given on each of the propositions. In each case the argument is causal. The defect is claimed to be the cause of the problem that was established by factual argument. The good affirmative team identifies a problem and shows that it is inherent in the present system because of a structural or attitudinal defect in the system. This, however, is not enough to overcome a "so what?" question from the negative.

Chart 1 Need-for-a-Change Argument		
Topic	*Problem*	*Inherent Defect*
foreign trade policies	export of products banned in the United States	no safety regulation for the export of products banned in the U.S.
comprehensive long-term agricultural policy	small farmers financially ruined	lack of government subsidies

The Harm Is Sufficient to Cause Concern

At the next point in the development of the need-for-a-change argument, the affirmative uses a value argument to establish the problem as an evil in the present system. The conservative philosophy of this case requires that the change be made in response to evils, not merely for the sake of change itself.

Remembering the steps for providing a value argument, the advocate tries to show that the relevant parties' interests are presently being hurt by the problem. The failure to provide small farmers with economic support causes hardships and suffering. Or current import policies regarding steel and textiles cause unemployment, hurting both the people who are unemployed and the nation's growth potential. Chart 2 includes an added category: harm.

Chart 2 Need-for-a-Change Argument			
Topic	*Problem*	*Inherency*	*Harm*
foreign trade policy	export of products banned in the U.S.	no safety regulation for products banned in the U.S.	injury and death to children from non-fire resistant pajamas
comprehensive long-term agricultural policy	small farmers financially ruined	lack of government subsidies	suffering and financial ruin

It is worth observing that some harm arguments of value are easier to establish than others. Few people, for example, would argue against the claim that malnutrition results from poor use of infant formula, but many might question other harms that might be cited. Perhaps unemployment is only temporary and mild and therefore not really bad.

The next affirmative contention is not so much an argument as an explanation. The affirmative must develop a carefully thought-out plan for change. This plan must represent a basic change in the present system. Somehow the structure for the present procedures must be changed, or the affirmative is advocating only an increase or decrease in the present system, which it has already shown is in need of change. Only one proposal can solve the problem, and the affirmative has it. It should, moreover, be *inherently* capable of correcting the faults, just as the present system is inherently incapable of remedying the situation. Over the years the role of the affirmative plan has changed significantly. Affirmatives started out by "standing on the resolution." They then progressed to offering skeleton plans that set up only the bare essentials for solving the affirmative problem. Now affirmative teams propose lengthy, greatly detailed plans with great elaboration involving executive boards, oversight boards, enforcement boards, and financing. In recent years affirmative plans have been delivered with such detail as to take 2½ to 3½ minutes to read in the debate. This is not to suggest that such painstaking detail is always necessary or appropriate. The length and detail of the plan should be determined by the specifics of the affirmative problem. A plan to solve both safety and reclamation problems in strip mining would probably necessitate significantly more detail than a plan to solve the problems of cumbersome regulations that slow the construction of new nuclear power plants.

Some planks of the plan have become standardized; that is, they appear in almost any plan, no matter what the affirmative problem area. These planks are designed to anticipate possible negative disadvantages. Chart 3 is an example of an affirmative plan. Standardized planks have been labeled for easy identification.

Chart 3

Plan

1. An independent, self-perpetuating, affirmatively appointed, munificently salaried, limited-term seabed Nodule Ocean Resources Enterprise will be established. Reasonable retirement ages. All necessary power, staff, funding, and resources provided to fulfill plan mandates. Removal for mis-, mal-, or nonfeasance. *Standard.*

2. Mandates

   A. All new investment in South Africa by U.S. affiliated firms is prohibited. Future investment allowed only if investment decision was made prior to today. Trade incentives to other countries for reductions in South African investment.

   B. An independent sub-agency created, with membership open to all recognized countries. Voting power determined by relative share of GNP. The sub-agency is authorized to lease blocks of international waters for the purpose of deep seabed mining. Leases issued based on competitive bidding, concentration of market, and optimal rate of production. Revocation of leases for nonmarketing of assurance of investment integrity. No other areas of ocean resource management are to be affected by the operation of this plan. Domestic processing assured.

   C. Compensation to all affected parties as a result of potential mineral price reductions and/or decreases in output. Profit compensation to affected industries must be used for diversification. No compensation to South African-based or -operated companies, nor to the government itself. Employee compensation based on need. Cost control monitoring, auditing, and spot checks.

   D. Research and development into all environmental consequences of deep seabed mining and related activities. Technology transfer with subsidization provided. Standards developed and enforced to assure safe operations. Environmental impact statements published and disseminated periodically.

   E. Assurance of scientific research outside of territorial waters. Exceptions granted after review.

   F. Research, development and encouragement of mineral exploration alternatives. Those initially examined include recycling, substitution lunar and asteroid mining. Conservation encouraged where feasible and desirable.

   G. Research into all aspects of the affirmative plan, including all reasonable alternatives.

3. Enforcement. Independent special prosecutors and the Supreme Court will review all plan actions. Enforcement will include assumption of assets, fines, imprisonment, economic sanctions, withholding of plan benefits. *Standard.*

4. Financing. An off-budget, unbreakable trust fund created with revenues from countercyclical funding, enforcement provisions, international graduated GNP tax of member nations, and general revenues. *Standard.*

Advantages of the Affirmative Plan

The advantages that would accrue if the affirmative's proposal were adopted form the last part of the traditional need case. The advantages contention gives focus to the entire affirmative argument, and it adds extra persuasive effects when the affirmative calls for the adoption of the debate proposal.

The basic affirmative advantage usually is presented as the first advantage that would occur if the plan were enacted. This advantage, of course, is that the proposal would eliminate the problem in the present system. At this point in the case, the affirmative should carefully explain why and how the proposal will eliminate the harmful effects of the structural or attitudinal defect in the present system. Then the speaker should specify how the nation or the individuals involved would be helped after the problem has been corrected. This explanation brings the full affirmative case into focus for the critic. It provides the connecting material that ties the three contentions into an appeal for the proposition.

In addition to the plan-meets-the-need advantage, affirmative teams typically stress two or three additional or additive advantages of their proposal. The affirmative can point to the economy of the proposal, its greater efficiency, and specific side advantages. When this phase of the case is reached, the affirmative team obviously has completed a prima facie case that, in its three parts, meets the affirmative's burden of proof.

Comparative Advantages Case

Up until the early 1960s, debaters used the traditional need case structure when developing affirmative cases. Prior to the sixties, there was no alternative to the traditional need case. As the federal government developed more and more programs to handle needs inherent in the present system, affirmatives found greater difficulty in presenting an inherent case. Negatives argued quite successfully that the affirmative harms could be solved with existing federal programs. Or the negatives argued that current federal programs just needed more money, manpower, or enforcement (forms of minor repairs are discussed in greater detail in Chapter 4). Debaters almost always chose the negative in elimination rounds. If they could be negative, they probably had a better chance of winning the debate. However, the sixties saw the birth of a new form of affirmative case—the **comparative advantages case**. This new case format turned from attempts to solve the insoluble problems of the present system to comparing a new policy against that of the present system.

The comparative advantages case was greeted with resistance and hesitation. Many judges believed that this case format did not fulfill the burdens of the prima facie case. Others argued that only the weak teams would advance comparative advantages cases and that to do so was an attempt to take advantage of the negative. Debaters and some critics responded that the comparative advantages case was more like the real world than the traditional need case. New government programs do not solve *all* of a problem, but legislators argue that the attempt at resolution is better than what existed before. This situation is analogous to that in which a car salesperson is trying to get a customer to purchase a new model car. The salesperson could follow the traditional pattern by pointing out all of the flaws in the customer's old car: strange noises in the engine that surely indicate a major overhaul is just around the corner, worn tires, flaking paint, and the generally poor condition of the auto. All these flaws would be used to establish "inherent evils" in the present situation. On the other hand, the salesperson could stress the comparative advantages of the new model: the old car might be nice, even perfectly good, but wouldn't a new Cadillac be preferable to the customer's old Chevrolet? The salesperson then need only convince the customer that the advantages are worth the extra cost.

When developing a comparative advantages case, the affirmative begins by identifying a goal or goals that exist in the present system. The goal might be a restatement of the resolution. On the topic RESOLVED: *That the United States should adopt a policy to increase political stability in Latin America*, many affirmatives argued the goal of political stability. The debate then centered around who could best achieve political stability in Latin America—the affirmative or the present system. Or the goal may be more specific, as with the topic RESOLVED: *That the federal government should significantly change its foreign trade policies*. In this instance the goal could be to decrease our balance of trade deficit. The affirmative would argue that its proposed changes in our foreign trade policies would yield greater results than do the current policies.

Next the affirmative outlines the proposed change (the plan) before presenting any advantages. This change in structure from the traditional need case is a logical one. In order to compare the two systems, one must first know what the change is.

The plan is followed by the affirmative advantage(s). To use the comparative advantages format does not mean that the affirmative has fewer responsibilities. The affirmative must still show that the advantage(s) is significant and that it is unique to the affirmative plan. Under the traditional need case, the affirmative had to show that there was a *compelling* need or reason for change. The advantage must also be compelling or significant. The affirmative must show that the number of lives saved, money saved, or efficiency provided is significantly more than that provided by the present system.

What Constitutes a Significant Advantage?

The significance of an advantage (or harm, in the traditional need case) is generally determined by the evidence provided. Support for significance can be of two types: quantitative and qualitative. Most of the time, the debater will provide quantitative proof to support an advantage. This type of proof involves presenting facts or data to support a claim. On the topic RESOLVED: *That the federal government should establish uniform standards for testing and marketing all products with potentially carcinogenic effects on humans*, teams arguing for the banning of cigarettes found it easy to provide data supporting the harms of smoking. It was also easy to provide quantitative support for an advantage of saving lives or saving money.

Not all cases lend themselves to the use of quantitative evidence. The topic RESOLVED: *That the federal government should establish minimum educational standards for elementary and secondary schools in the United States* serves as a good example. Most cases dealing with educational standards are going to involve talking about beliefs and values. It would be difficult to provide quantitative evidence to support educational programs for the gifted. But there is qualitative evidence that indicates that there are advantages to be gained from such a program. The affirmative should not fear such questions from the negative as "How many people die?" and "How much money will be lost to the economy?" The right of the individual to an education should be considered a significant advantage. In this case it is the value that is important, not a statistical entity.

After the evidence has been provided, it is still necessary to ascertain whether the advantage is significant. Significance is a term of comparison. The advantage must be shown to be significant as compared with something else. It must be shown to be significant when compared with what is offered by the present system (including minor repairs) and then shown to be significant as compared with the disadvantages presented by the second negative. An advantage that saves 1,000 lives but runs the risk of nuclear war would not be significant. While 1,000 people might be saved with the adoption of the affirmative plan, far more would be lost in a nuclear war.

The comparison to be made will not always be one of numbers against numbers or values against values. In many cases the debater will be comparing the advantage of saving lives as opposed to the disadvantage of a loss of a value. The affirmative case that banned cigarette smoking serves as a good example. When the affirmative saves lives by eliminating cigarettes, it is also taking away a liberty of the individual— the right of free choice. In such a case, the affirmative must demonstrate why the advantage of saving lives *outweighs* the disadvantage of the loss of freedom of choice. The advantage is supported by quantitative evidence, while the disadvantage is supported by qualitative evidence. The comparison is a difficult one, but one that will have to be made in many rounds.

In the end the affirmative must be able to show that the advantage(s) outweighs both what the present system can do and whatever disadvantages may result from the adoption of the affirmative proposal.

What does it mean to say that the advantage(s) is unique to the affirmative plan? Remember, the discussion of the traditional need case pointed out that there had to be some structural or attitudinal barrier preventing the present system from solving the affirmative problem. This concept is known as inherency. In the comparative advantages case, the affirmative must also demonstrate a reason why the present system cannot do what the affirmative proposes. Most often the barrier to the attainment of the affirmative advantage(s) will be an attitude. The affirmative will be required to show that the present system, even with minor repairs, is incapable of attaining the affirmative advantage(s).

Take, for example, the topic RESOLVED: *That the federal government should establish minimum educational standards for elementary and secondary schools in the United States.* The affirmative could run a comparative advantages case on sex education. The advantage would be fewer teenage pregnancies. The negative might offer a minor repair with community-sponsored sex-education programs or information campaigns for parents. In order to win inherency (to show that the advantage is unique to the plan) in such a case, the affirmative would have to be able to show that, because of prevailing attitudes about sexual material, many teenagers would shy away from community programs and parents would continue to put off talking with their children about sex. The affirmative would argue that a program in the schools would better insure the dissemination of information and a resulting decrease in teenage pregnancy.

Comparative Advantages Case

I. The goal of the present system is to achieve peace in Nicaragua.

II. Plan is to endorse negotiations on a regional peace plan.

III. Advantage of peace.
   A. Military confrontation is destructive.
      1. Diverts economic resources from domestic help.
      2. Causes further instability.
   B. The status quo policy is not adequate.
      1. Bilateral negotiations are not effective.
      2. Foreign intervention increases nationalism and prolongs confrontation.
   C. Regional peace plans are better than unilateral efforts.
      1. The OAS charter has appropriate procedures for conducting peace.
      2. Nations in Central America are willing to negotiate.
      3. The threat of U.S. military intervention if such plans fail can always be held in reserve.

IV. Plan: The United States should endorse regional peace proposals made by the Organization of American States and abide by the arrangements.

One last word about the advantage(s). It is quite possible (if not probable) that the affirmative will claim more than one advantage. A case arguing for energy independence might claim advantages of cheaper energy, more jobs, and a decrease in the balance of payments. The affirmative most likely will argue that each of the advantages is independent; that is, each advantage is a separate unit. When offering independent advantages, the affirmative need win only one advantage to win the debate. In our energy example, the affirmative could lose the advantages on balance of payments and cheaper energy but win the debate if the affirmative provides more jobs than the present system while becoming energy independent.

In the end the affirmative advantage(s) is compared to what the present system can do and then is compared to the disadvantages presented by the negative (discussed in Chapter 4), those harms that result from adopting the affirmative proposal. If there is still a significant advantage after these two comparisons, the affirmative will most likely win the debate. The following is an example of the structure of the comparative advantages case, both in theory and in practice.

Criteria Case

A common case format is the **criteria case**. This kind of case form focuses on the values or goals toward which a policy should be directed. The affirmative then demonstrates how its proposal best meets the criteria. The criteria case consists of two contentions. The first outlines the criteria—standards of evaluation—by which a proposal should be judged. It is important to present goals or criteria that are significant. They should also be a set of standards that can be readily agreed upon.

The second contention demonstrates how the affirmative proposal best meets the outlined criteria. Consider the example of a case advocating methanol (a substitute for gasoline) on the topic Resolved: *That the federal government should establish a comprehensive program to significantly increase the energy independence of the United States.* In this case the affirmative developed a set of criteria for a good energy policy. It was argued that any energy policy should meet four criteria: An energy source should be nonpolluting, inexpensive, renewable, and technologically proven. Once these criteria were outlined and agreed upon, the affirmative could show how methanol met *all* four criteria simultaneously. It proved very difficult for the negative to show that any present-system policy or future energy alternative could do so.

Criteria Case

I. The goal of present agricultural price supports is to help farmers remain solvent.
   A. The goal is expressed in laws.
   B. The goal reflects the value of supporting rural ways of life.

II. The best means of meeting this goal is for subsidies to be directed at small or medium farmers.
   A. Large-scale farming is without economic benefits.
   B. Large-scale farming does not need price supports.
   C. Medium-small–scale farming is ecologically wise.
   D. Medium-small–scale farming does need subsidies.

III. The present system offers a barrier to the goal.
   A. Subsidies go primarily to large farms.
   B. Debt collection on medium-small farms is still without relief.
   C. Farmers continue to be thrown off the land.

IV. Plan: Redirect farm subsidy payments to those who can demonstrate the need to stay in business.

The strategic value of the criteria case is found in the ability to refute negative counterproposals, minor repairs, or inherency arguments. Once it is proven that the affirmative case meets the criteria for a good energy policy, the negative must show that its counterproposals or status quo alternatives can meet all of those criteria equally well. Notice the problem this creates for the negative. Nuclear power may be technically proven and renewable, but is it cheap or safe? Oil and gas may also be technically proven and safe, but are they renewable or inexpensive? Exotic alternatives such as solar energy might be renewable, nonpolluting, or inexpensive, but have they been proven technologically? The strength of the criteria case is that once the affirmative has a proposal that meets all of the criteria outlined, the affirmative can use the criteria to defeat any policy that the negative presents. The affirmative will want to argue that the negative position fulfills some, but not all, of the criteria; therefore, the affirmative proposal alone is the superior alternative.

The criteria case can be constructed in two ways—as a traditional need case or as a comparative advantages case. That is, the affirmative can demonstrate that the present system cannot meet the stated criteria and set forth its plan, or the affirmative can present the plan (after outlining the criteria) and then demonstrate how it better fulfills the criteria. Both structures are outlined in the accompanying box.

Traditional Need Structure

I. Stated goal

II. Criteria to be used to meet the goal

III. Why the present system cannot achieve the goal while meeting the criteria

IV. Plan

V. How the plan meets the goal while meeting the criteria

Comparative Advantages Structure

I. Stated goal

II. Plan

III. Criteria
    A. How the present system fails to achieve the goal
    B. Advantage of the affirmative policy

In some instances, resolutions will not point to clear-cut criteria for evaluating policy. Criteria cases worked well on the energy topic because the value standards for energy resources were fairly well agreed upon. In debating some topics, however, there may be a number of different criteria that contribute to a good policy. In such cases it may be difficult, if not impossible, to choose one set of criteria. When this happens, the debate will most likely center around the criteria. In such a situation, the affirmative would lose any advantage the criteria case structure might give them. This format is best used only when the criteria are clear-cut.

Net Benefits Case

A final affirmative case idea is the **net benefits case**. The net benefits case does not evolve directly from existing debate theory. The net benefits case is based on systems analysis rather than stock issues.

Systems analysis assumes that legislation of policy takes place in an environment that is constantly changing because of growths in population, economic fluctuations, and demographic trends. Also, it assumes that policies already exist in all the problem areas considered by the current policy makers. It is argued that there is no need to debate over whether a policy should be adopted because policy has already been adopted. What is at issue, however, is how existing policies can be adjusted to accommodate the continual changes occurring all around. It is not assumed that policies should remain unchanged until a need is demonstrated to change them, but rather that what is being debated is the degree and direction of changes that should be implemented by law on an ongoing basis of revision and adjustment.

The net benefits case incorporates four steps: (1) Apply systems analysis to the problem area; (2) Determine the components that make up the system and the rules governing how the components are interrelated; (3) Analyze and project what differences could be predicted following a change in policy governing these interrelationships; and (4) Determine the most favorable ratio between the costs and the benefits of the proposed change in the system. In other words, the affirmative must not only show the advantages accruing from the plan, but also must demonstrate that the plan would result in the greatest net benefit possible considering both the predicted advantages and the predicted disadvantages. When defending the affirmative proposal, you would demand that the negative not only refute the affirmative case, but also present a counter-policy system on which the judge could base a comparison of the methods of controlling and guiding inevitable change.

Net Benefits Case

I. Open trade policy has mixed results.
   A. Open trade policy is good if nations reciprocate.
   B. Open trade policy is harmful if nations maintain trade barriers for U.S. imports while flooding the U.S. market.
   C. On balance, open trade has resulted in an unfair trade balance.

II. The United States trade deficit is harmful.
   A. Trade deficits lead to the devaluation of the dollar and interest rate instability.
   B. Trade deficits leave the United States a debtor nation and drive up interest rates.

Plan: The United States should consider trade legislation on a case-by-case basis and only have open trade with partners who do not practice restrictive trade policy.

III. The net benefits of such a policy would outweigh harms.
   A. If a country is not being protectionist, open trade remains.
   B. If a country is being protectionist, the plan provides an incentive for fairer arrangements.
   C. Unless the United States implements this plan, it will eventually be pressured into unlimited protectionism with disastrous results.

Proponents of this approach make the point that it is a closer approximation of how decisions are made in policy deliberations in government. Congressional committees and administrative agencies do not debate as often over whether the federal government should adopt a new policy (whether based on traditional need or comparative advantage) as they engage in a continuing process of amending, adjusting, and fine-tuning the laws already on the books. The basis for real-world decision making appears to be based on the relative net benefits of making the proposed change in the overall system as compared with other proposals.

Systems analysis has many implications for debate. First, the affirmative team is able to admit that the proposed resolution has disadvantages as well as advantages. The basis for systematic decision making is the net benefits after taking into account the advantages *and* the disadvantages.

Second, the basis for decision (in debate) cannot be simply the significance of the net benefits of the affirmative plan. Instead, there must be a comparison between the benefits of the affirmative plan and the benefits of an alternative system that might be proposed by the negative. If the negative team is not prepared to defend an alternative system, the affirmative system is then accepted because the known risk of a system is preferable to the incalculable risk of having no system at all. This does not mean that the negative is not obligated to present a counterplan. The defense of the present system is always an option. The important point is that the negative must be prepared to show that the benefits of continuing the present system—or any other system, for that matter—are greater than the net benefits of the affirmative plan.

Again, unlike the other cases discussed in this chapter, the net benefits is not an evolutionary outgrowth of traditional debate theories and practices. It is an approach derived from systems analysis as employed in contemporary governmental decision making. A primary distinction of the net benefits case is that it calls for the negative team to uphold a system of its own for purposes of deciding which competing policy system would produce the greatest benefits, using a comparison of the cost-benefit ratios of the two systems as the basis of choosing one over the other. In this case neither the affirmative system nor the negative system carries presumption. The net benefits case argues that the net benefits of a proposal, after considering both the advantages and disadvantages, is a better measure of the acceptability of a system than a consideration of the advantages alone.

The Affirmative Plan

Every affirmative team must specify the method it will use to implement the resolution. For example, once the affirmative has shown the need to

control drug smuggling in Latin America in order to achieve political stability, it must provide a way of setting a program to do just that. This
method is called the **affirmative plan**. Over the years the affirmative
plan has gone through a great deal of refinement. Originally, teams relied
on the resolution to solve the problem outlined. Then the affirmative
began to provide a skeleton outline of a solution. When the traditional
need case was the only structure in use, the plan was presented in the second affirmative speech. When the comparative advantages case came
along, affirmatives began to introduce the plan in the first constructive.
With the comparative advantages case, this was necessary in order to
compare the affirmative solution against the present system. Now judges
and debaters alike have come to expect the affirmative to present the
plan in the first speech, no matter what case format is used.

With the advances in negative strategies (discussed in Chapter 4),
judges feel that presenting the plan in the first speech promotes clash. If
the affirmative waited until the second affirmative speech to present the
plan, the first negative would not be in a position to choose the most appropriate strategy of attack against the entire affirmative case. The practice of presenting the plan in the first affirmative constructive speech has
become so widespread that the debater who has no plan (and merely
stands on the resolution) or waits until the second affirmative constructive speech risks losing the round.

All affirmative plans are constructed around plan planks. Plan
planks are statements that authorize specific kinds of action in order to
implement the resolution. Occasionally, a plan may need to have only
one plank. If a resolution called for the abolition of the Interstate Commerce Commission, a plan might be written that says simply that the
Congress of the United States is directed to follow appropriate procedure in the decommissioning of this agency.

In general, resolutions that call for a reduction of government power
have compact plans, because the affirmative can call upon the normal
processes of government to implement the reduction of power. Most resolutions, however, do not invite such a simple plan of action. Typically,
resolutions call for the creation of some kind of government action—a
new agency or increasing the scope of responsibility of an old agency.

In this section you will examine some strategic considerations for the
construction of affirmative plan planks. Basically the affirmative plan
can be divided into five parts: agent of change, means of change, enforcement of change, funding of change, and plan spikes.

The Agent of Change

The affirmative will want to indicate the persons responsible for carrying out the work of the plan. Sometimes this kind of plan plank need only indicate what agency, bureau, or level of government will be responsible for seeing to it that the plan mandates are carried out. Where there is an agency with a good record of cleaning up problems, similar to the one identified by the affirmative, this agency could be a useful institution for implementing the plan. At other times, however, part of the problem isolated by the case may be the failure of existing agencies to redress present problems. In such an instance, the affirmative may want to create a new board or agency. The new board should be constructed in such a way as to avoid the problems of the current institutions. Some of the following considerations need to be made.

First, the board must be competent. Perhaps the problem with the present system is that appointments are politically oriented. If so, the affirmative must discover a fairer selection process.

Second, the board must be independent of specious political influence. A typical problem with existing regulatory agencies is that the regulators are beholden to the industries they are supposed to be overseeing. The affirmative may need to take measures that assure independence— for example, limiting lobby influence, changing the composition of the board on a regular basis, restricting the working possibilities for a retired board member and the industry that member regulates.

Third, the board must be equipped with necessary information-gathering powers and research facilities. The problem with the present system may not be related to the competence of the people carrying out present laws or their political inclinations. Instead, present agencies may simply lack needed information to carry out their tasks. Congress itself, for example, before reorganization acted on information provided only by a very limited staff. In such a case, the agency would be empowered with the provisions necessary to gather the information.

Finally, a new board must be provided with the necessary personnel to operate, as well as funding, facilities, and retirement provisions.

The Means of Change

The affirmative may specify an exact means of enacting the resolution, or it can create a number of choices from which the board might choose. When the affirmative wants to defend specific alternatives, those alternatives should be listed in the plan. For example, on the medical care topic, screening cases were very popular. However, most affirmatives did not want (or could not defend) all forms of screening. The plan would identify which specific screening tests would be mandated. By being extremely specific, the affirmative can narrow the territory that is subject to attack by the negative.

On the other hand, there will be instances when the affirmative will not know which specific mechanisms the plan ought to choose. The future may be uncertain, the mechanisms may be in a state of development, and the alternatives may appear to be of equal merit. In such cases, the affirmative may wish to specify a range of mechanisms from which the board will choose the most appropriate combination.

Harvard University let the board choose when the colleges debated the topic of energy independence. Harvard wished to develop nuclear power at the expense of other energy alternatives. Because they were not sure exactly which type of reactor or fuel processing was best, they left it up to the board to decide which to use. The strategic value of this approach is that the affirmative subtly shifts the burden of proof to the negative. As long as the affirmative has general information saying that the development of nuclear power can be accomplished, the negative must show that all alternatives available to the board have no hope of success. Obviously, this is a difficult thing to do.

A word of caution is necessary here. The strategy just discussed can backfire if the affirmative becomes too general in listing its range of options. The energy topic serves as an excellent example. Many affirmatives tried to argue that the board would choose from all available energy alternatives to replace the energy that we were importing. Many affirmatives even listed a few of the alternatives but would not limit themselves to those mentioned. This made it very difficult for the negative to run disadvantages against an energy alternative because the affirmative would drop whichever alternative was challenged and shift to another. The time constraints of the debate did not allow the negative sufficient time to challenge all alternatives, thus leading a large number of negatives to cry foul. Many judges were sympathetic to the negative position and began to require the affirmative to be more specific or risk losing to a process disadvantage (discussed in Chapter 4).

Enforcing the Proposed Change

All proposals must be enforced in some way. The affirmative may use existing enforcement mechanisms, arguing that there is nothing wrong with the present system's ability to enforce laws. Or it can institute new procedures. These new procedures may be more or less severe than those employed by the present system. Many affirmatives set up independent prosecutors and outline specific levels of punishment. The amount of detail needed in this plank of the plan will depend on the form of inherency being argued.

Funding the Proposed Change

Almost all proposals will require money to operate. Even though the affirmative may claim an advantage of saving money, it will still need money initially to get the proposal into operation. The affirmative will usually specify where the money will come from. As with the means for change, the affirmative can be specific, or it can list several alternatives from which the board can choose. When financing a plan by cutting other government programs, the affirmative should be careful to investigate the possible ramifications of cutting a program. If avenues of financing are listed haphazardly, the affirmative may find itself with a significant disadvantage to counterbalance its advantage.

Plan Spikes

Plan spikes are provisions in the plan designed to eliminate a potential disadvantage or plan-meet-need argument. In preparing the affirmative case, the affirmative should make a list of possible disadvantages and plan-meet-need arguments. Once the list has been made, the affirmative works to develop answers to the arguments or modifies the plan to eliminate the argument. For example, if the plan is likely to cause unemployment, the affirmative may want to put in a plan spike that provides for alternative employment or compensates the unemployed, thus eliminating the disadvantage.

Summary

The affirmative position involves a great deal of work and a number of critical choices. The affirmative team must explore the definitions of the terms of the resolution. From these definitions the affirmative begins to narrow the resolution down to a specific case area. Once the area has been chosen, the debaters must decide what format to use when developing their case—traditional need case, comparative advantages case, criteria case, or alternative justifications case. To make this decision, the debaters must explore the options to see which will best fit the needs of their problem areas. After the case area has been developed, a plan is devised. The plan, like a model plane, must come with all its parts in order to work. If a provision is overlooked, the plan either won't solve the need or it will create a potentially serious disadvantage.

Most debaters enjoy being affirmative, for it is their chance to offer solutions to serious problems. Novices prefer the affirmative side of the proposition because they feel more secure on the affirmative. For many this is a false sense of security; only careful planning and continual research can help assure an affirmative victory.

Questions for Discussion

1. Discuss the essential differences between the four types of affirmative cases. Describe the advantages and disadvantages of each.

2. Why is inherency the key to the need-for-a-change argument? What is the difference between structural and attitudinal inherency?

3. Why is it important to define the terms of the proposition before choosing a case idea and case structure?

4. In the comparative advantage case, what constitutes a significant advantage?

5. What does it mean to say that the advantage is unique to the affirmative plan?

6. When looking at case types, what would be the advantage to the affirmative in using the net benefits format?

7. What are the five parts to the affirmative plan?

Activities

1. Using the current debate resolution (or one identified by your teacher), isolate the key terms of the resolution and define each. Use at least three sources to define your terms.

2. Using the resolution from Activity 1, outline what would be some unusual definitions of the key terms. Explain why.

3. Using the resolution from Activity 1, select an affirmative case idea. Attempt to outline the idea in each of the case forms outlined in the chapter. Explain which format best suits the specific affirmative case idea.

4. With the case outline from Activity 3, draft a first affirmative constructive speech in which there is a single contention or advantage. This speech will most likely be two to three minutes in length.

5. After reviewing the speech from Activity 4, expand the case to a full six minutes. The remaining two minutes will be used later for the affirmative plan.

6. Using the affirmative case outline from Activity 3, draft a plan. Be prepared to defend your enforcing and financing mechanisms. When you add this to your speech from Activity 5, you should have a complete first affirmative speech.

Chapter 4

Building the Negative Constructive Argument

Objectives and Key Terms

After studying Chapter 4, you should be able

1. To explain and present the three case arguments a negative can use against each type of affirmative case.

2. To produce negative arguments to an affirmative case, complete with evidence.

3. To explain topicality as an issue.

4. To explain and demonstrate how to construct plan-meets-need arguments against an affirmative case.

5. To explain and demonstrate how to construct case-related disadvantages, policy disadvantages, and process disadvantages.

6. To explain the characteristics of a counterplan and the guidelines for presenting and defending one.

To effectively debate the negative, you will need to understand the following terms:

straight refutation	minor repair
defense of the present system	plan-meets-need arguments

workability	turnaround arguments
circumvention	plan spike
disadvantage	policy disadvantage
case-related disadvantage	process disadvantage
uniqueness	counterplan

D ebating on the negative side of a proposition may seem a little frightening. After all, the members of the affirmative team get to choose the case area to be debated. As a result they are able to prepare their arguments well in advance. The affirmative argues its case every round and is experienced in defending it. The members of the negative team, in contrast, are usually not so well prepared on the specific issues. They don't have as much experience with the specific ideas being presented by the affirmative. Even though the negative team may have prepared general arguments against the resolution, it must still think quickly, improvise, and apply its best arguments to the specific affirmative case. This chapter is directed toward analyzing the best methods of planning and attack that the negative can use to overcome the seemingly overwhelming advantages of the affirmative.

The premise on which this analysis of negative strategy is based is quite simple. The authors believe that it is much better for the negative team to select important issues rather than to attack whatever affirmative statements appear in the round. The process of selecting the most damaging arguments against the affirmative is called the construction of the negative position. An example of this process is provided by arguments in a court of law.

In a courtroom the prosecuting attorney affirms the guilt of the accused and asks for appropriate punishment. The prosecutor maintains that the defendant was seen committing theft, that the theft was a crime, and that the court has the duty to punish the criminal. The defense could negate each argument presented by the prosecutor, maintaining that the defendant did not commit the act; that if the accused did commit the act, it could not be defined as theft; that even if it could be defined as theft, the quality of the action was such that it served some greater cause and is not deserving of punishment; and that, even if all of the above were incorrect, the court does not have the jurisdiction to punish the defendant. It is important to note here that the defense could make all of these arguments or only one. For example, even if evidence could be brought forward proving that the defendant took an apple, if that action was not covered by the code of criminal conduct, it would not be punishable as a crime. The process of selecting which arguments to use (one argument, all arguments, or a combination) is the process of selecting a negative position.

Although there are some similarities between a counsel for the defense and the negative, which is charged with arguing against an affirmative that indicts the present system, the options available to arguers and the tactics of selecting these arguments are quite different. The outcome of a trial is directed toward deciding the question of guilt or innocence. The reader will recall that this was defined in an earlier chapter as a proposition of fact. The outcome of a policy debate is the decision to do something or not. Consequently, the student should look at the options available to the negative in denying that the resolutional action should be undertaken.

Basic Negative Strategies

The easiest way to begin to understand position debating is to think about what all affirmative teams must do, no matter what case they are defending or what resolution they are arguing. All affirmatives must advance two basic ideas. First, that the future without adoption of the resolution is not as good as it could be. Second, that the future with adoption of the resolution is more promising than the future without the resolution. This may seem to be two ways of saying the same thing, but there is a difference. The first statement places the burden of proving inherency on the affirmative, for if the action proposed in the resolution would come about through the natural progression of the present system, there would be no need for the judge to vote affirmative. The future imagined by the affirmative would be identical to that brought about under the present system.

The affirmative must always call for a change, the adoption of new policies or ideas. There would be no necessity to vote for a resolution if the present system would naturally move toward the change supported by the affirmative. For example, suppose several members of Congress were supporting new antipoverty programs. Suppose, further, that the opponents were able to prove that the economy would soon expand to the point that poverty would be eliminated. There would be no reason to pass the resolution because the naturally evolving present system would be just as good in the future as would the results of all the effort undertaken to produce new programs.

The second basic affirmative idea requires proving that the adoption of the resolution would make our world better rather than worse. This idea follows the same logic that prevents doctors from administering drugs that might cure the disease but that have harmful side effects that could kill the patient. The affirmative must prove not only that the resolution resolves the problem it is designed to change, but also that the action does not bring about more harms than benefits.

Thus, at the outset, the negative debater should remember that the affirmative has two duties: (1) proving, in light of what has already been accomplished and soon shall be accomplished by the present system, that there is some reason to exert effort in behalf of the resolution; and (2) proving that the benefits of the proposal outweigh the costs.

Given these responsibilities, the negative has four strategies that can be used against any affirmative case. First, the negative may choose to deny that the affirmative's picture of the future without adoption of the resolution is correct, showing instead that probably little or no harm will exist. For instance, the negative can argue that the affirmative's measurements of harm are inaccurate or misleading; that the problem the affirmative isolates is not a problem at all because people desire risks; or that no one really knows at present what the future will look like. This position focuses on minimizing the affirmative's rationale for adopting the resolution: resolving a harm. This is generally referred to as the affirmative harm.

Second, the negative may choose to deny that voting for the resolution is necessary to bring about the good world the affirmative says will result if the resolution is implemented. Here the negative argues that self-limiting factors within the present system will solve the problem; that the present system has adopted programs which, if given a chance to work, will solve the problem; or that recent changes in conditions external to the harm will solve it in the future. This position focuses on negating the affirmative's claim that there are unique reasons for adopting the resolution, also known as affirmative inherency.

Third, the negative may choose to make the counterclaim that the future envisioned by the affirmative will not come about because the reso-lution is not very effective. The negative may argue that other factors that cause the problem will persist; that the plan cannot work because of some internal flaw (like limited manpower or technology); or that the plan will be circumvented. This position focuses on negating the affirmative's claims that any benefits at all will flow from the affirmative plan. The negative is demonstrating that the plan will not meet (or solve) the needs outlined by the affirmative.

Negative Strategies

1. Deny affirmative picture of the future. (Resolving the harm)

2. Deny that resolution is necessary to bring about the advan-tages the affirmative outlines. (Denying affirmative inherency)

3. Counterclaim that the future outlined by the affirmative will not come about because the resolution is very ineffec-tive. (Plan will not meet the needs)

4. Argue that the plan will result in great harms. (Disadvan-tages)

5. Offer a counterplan as a better way to resolve the problem.

Fourth, the negative may argue that, contrary to the affirmative's al-legations, the plan will result in great harms. Here, the negative usually maintains that the unintended consequences of the affirmative plan are more harmful than the benefits of adopting the resolution. This position focuses on constructing disadvantages to the affirmative plan. It is im-portant to remember these four basic options. The negative need win only *one* argument—*harm, inherency, plan meets need,* or *disadvan-tage*—to carry the debate. This always holds true.

But there is one other option you should be aware of. Suppose you are researching a case that a successful opponent is likely to offer and you find that the harmful effects of the present system have existed for a long time and seem to be spreading. The programs of the present system aimed at resolving the harms have made little progress and are likely to be continually ineffective. The affirmative programs, while not perfect, are likely to be much better than the shabbily constructed efforts of the present system. Finally, there are really no overwhelming disadvantages to giving the proposal a try. What can be done?

A poor strategy is to follow the tactics of the squid, who, confronted with a strong opponent, squirts out a cloud of ink, hoping to confuse the enemy. Certainly, negatives can cloud the issues by barraging the affirmative with questions, challenges, and weak evidence—covering the judge's flow sheet in inky red. But, even though this strategy might be successful against less well-prepared teams, it will not work in the long run.

In selecting a strategy, debaters should find one that enables them to overcome more experienced, even more talented teams, by virtue of its intellectual soundness. Such strategic thinking is not only intellectually sound, it is most likely to win—because debate tournaments are constructed to insure that teams rise to equal levels of competence. Confronted with the problem of a by-and-large "true case," the challenge to the negative becomes one of thinking of an even better way to resolve a problem other than the resolution. Thus, the counterplan must be placed in the repertoire of every negative team.

The counterplan focuses on a future world that is better than the one envisioned by the affirmative *and* that cannot exist if the affirmative plan is adopted. Here the negative suggests that the adoption of the resolution forecloses a future that would be much better if the alternative policy advocated by the negative were adopted.

Basic Negative Tactics

In standard debate formats, the negative has two constructive speeches and two rebuttals. By convention, the first negative constructive speech is used to deny most or all arguments of the affirmative case. The second negative constructive speech is used to construct arguments against the affirmative plan, either by questioning the advisability of each plan plank or by reading prepared arguments against the plan. These duties are rather clear and easily definable when affirmative teams argue traditional need plan cases.

The first negative almost always argues that there is no harm; that even if there were, it is certainly not significant; and that even if it were significant, the present system either can or will probably take care of it. The second negative almost always argues that the affirmative plan cannot resolve the harm or that, even if it can, the net result will be disadvantageous. This strategy is designed to avoid duplication of arguments.

If the second negative extends all first negative arguments, then the first negative rebuttal becomes useless, except perhaps for its entertainment value. So efficient is this organization of duty, that it still characterizes many—if not most—contemporary rounds of debate. This division of duties is probably wise for beginning debaters, because it simplifies the presentation of arguments and is probably useful in a large number of debates. But remember, there is no law of argument that the negative must argue all stock issues, nor is there any law of argument that demands that the negative present arguments in a certain sequence for constructive speaking. Indeed, the experienced negative debater should experiment with different combinations of stock issues and selective refutation.

Group discussions elicit new information and case approaches.

Before examining such complicated issues of strategy in detail, it would be wise to see how each negative argument is constructed. You must look closely at the pieces of a puzzle before you can put it together. Toward that end you will explore the possibilities of straight refutation, defense of the present system, plan meets need, and disadvantages. Each of these stock issues could be the framework of a complete position in and of itself. However, it is knowing how to use these arguments in combination that leads to the optimal construction of a negative position.

Straight Refutation Strategy

Straight refutation depends on methodically eliminating each of the affirmative's arguments. Imagine yourself listening to a round of debate. The first affirmative speaker presents a reasonably complete case, structured around several contentions and many subpoints. The first negative speaker stands up and makes the same three responses to every affirmative statement: (1) There is not enough proof to know that the affirmative statement is true; (2) There is some evidence to indicate that the affirmative contention is probably false; and (3) Even if the statement were true, it has no bearing on the question of whether or not the resolution ought to be adopted.

Imagine further that the second affirmative speaker is quite inept and cannot answer any of the negative charges. The debate continues like this throughout all the speeches. How would you vote? Negative, of course. But why?

The reason most argumentation theorists give for rejecting unsubstantiated policy resolutions is that it is better to know why action should be taken than to act upon whim or fantasy or caprice—even if we were so inclined. In other words, presumption rests with the negative unless or until the affirmative can demonstrate a reason to change.

Under presumption, the negative argues that we should not make a change just for the sake of change. There must be a net benefit. Thus, the judge is ultimately asked to vote against the resolution because the affirmative cannot present enough good, sound reasons for convincing a rational person to act. Consider how each of the proof challenges listed above can be employed.

There Is Not Enough Proof

In some debates key arguments are not supported by evidence. There may be no empirical studies that measure a harm. There may be no pilot programs that show the efficacy of a particular approach to solving a problem. There may be no authoritative sources that concur in the opponents' assessment of the gravity of a harm. In straight refutation, the negative speaker must look for such assertions, identify them as unsupported or weakly supported, and demonstrate why it is important that the affirmative prove the statement. For example, if the affirmative only asserts that its plan meets the affirmative need, then there is no proof that the resolution will bring about the claimed benefits on the basis of which adoption is justified. Suppose the affirmative were debating the resolution RESOLVED: *That the federal government should establish a program to provide for aging American citizens.* Unless the affirmative can demonstrate some pilot program that has provided the same protection for older Americans, the affirmative probably will not be able to prove with evidence how the affirmative plan will bring about the advantage claimed.

Of course, there are more subtle analytical problems. Continuing the example, the affirmative may have general evidence claiming that the problem can be solved but may only assert that the solution is similar to the one used in the plan. Consequently, the negative must look for implied premises that are assumed to be true but actually need to be proven before a warrant for the resolution can be said to have been established. For example, suppose that in the previous example the affirmative referred to a program in England or Canada that provided for its aging citizens. The affirmative would most likely outline the advantages that had been gained under such programs and claim that the same will come about in the United States under the affirmative plan. The negative would have to look for differences between the English and Canadian systems (or ways of life) and the system in the United States. The argument would be that unless all underlying assumptions are the same there is no reason to assume that the affirmative plan would gain the same advantages.

The Affirmative Statement Is Probably False

Tests of evidence are discussed in greater detail in Chapter 2, but remember that the adequacy of the proof is always a comparative question. Suppose one side in a debate quotes Senator Blooper as saying, "If we don't develop the Super-Back Fire Bomber, the Russians will attack." The other side responds with a piece of evidence from Senator Lackluster that reads, "The development of the Super-Back Fire Bomber has no bearing upon Russian defense policy, unless the United States builds it, in which case the Russians will attack." Unless the advocates explain why their evidence is superior, a judge is left in a quandary. Merely entering evidence to the contrary does not negate a point. The key tactic is to explain the comparative merits of the proof.

The process of explaining tests of evidence can become quite complicated. If both teams continue to argue the likelihood of Russian attack, then arguments such as these emerge: One side asserts that Senator Blooper is more expert than Lackluster and that more experts agree with him; the other side maintains that Senator Lackluster's statement is more recent and that Senator Blooper gets his information from self-interested military sources. This creates the need for an additional level of argument, source credibility.

It is not enough to state qualifications of the source. One must indicate *why* those qualifications are superior to those of the source used by the opposition. If the argument were to be left as it stood, how would a judge evaluate greater expertise against bias, consensus against timely information? The debater must demonstrate why greater expertise should be accepted over another source's bias or why having more experts agree with one's source is more valuable than recency of evidence. To win the evidence challenge, the advocates must be prepared to make the ultimate extension, proving why their criteria for credibility are superior to the criteria of the opponents. If this is not done, the judge has no way to evaluate the argument.

Even If the Statement Were True, It Has No Bearing

In addition to ferreting out unsubstantiated but crucial assertions and attempting to reverse the weight of evidence, straight refutation also involves testing the coherence and relevance of the affirmative contentions. It is possible that the affirmative has a lot of meaningless verbiage in the first constructive speech. *Meaningless* is used in a special sense: the truth of the contention has no relevance to whether the resolution should be supported. Consider an instance in which the resolution RE-SOLVED: *That the United States should adopt a minimal guaranteed annual cash income for all citizens* is debated. The affirmative case is a single, long oration on the horrors of poverty. Poverty, it is claimed, stunts social development, spreads disease, results in violence, and foments immorality. Need the negative necessarily refute *all* of these points? Need the negative *even* refute *any* of these points? No. Why? If the resolution does not solve or at least minimize the problem of poverty, then these contentions are irrelevant to the consideration of whether it ought to be adopted.

Before going on to the next section, you should examine another crucial consideration for a strategy of straight refutation. Many affirmative teams "hedge their bets" by claiming that several subpoints of a contention are "independent." For example, in showing that the present system can't solve poverty, the affirmative might claim that the failure of current efforts is caused by lack of coordination, by lack of manpower, and by conflicting jurisdictions. The net effect of this structure is to make it possible for the affirmative to lose two out of three of the subpoints and still be left with a reason why the present system programs fail. Thus, in the last rebuttal, the latitude of strategic choice is greater. Whichever subpoint the negative attacks with the least strength is featured as the determinant inherency argument.

The negative should be alert to the strategy just described. Wherever the affirmative claims reasons to be independent or wherever the case is structured in such a way that later in the debate the affirmative may bring up claims to independence, the negative should collapse the independent subpoints into a single argument. In the example given, the negative could argue that it is really the problem of jurisdiction that causes manpower shortages and coordination problems and, further, that the jurisdiction question can be or will be resolved without the affirmative plan. By collapsing the independent subpoints to a single issue, the negative reduces the likelihood that the affirmative can merely pick and choose according to its own desires.

Straight refutation is an important element in the preparation of almost any negative position. Forcing the affirmative to prove important, but unapparent, premises increases its obligations. Presenting contrary evidence robs the affirmative of sweeping claims. Questioning the relevance of claims focuses the debate on negative ground. But every debater should seriously consider whether straight refutation is enough. There are limits to this tactic.

One limit is imposed by a sense of fair play. While it is true in the abstract that we probably should test all actions before they are undertaken, sometimes severe testing is a facade, a mere tactic for delay. We are reminded of the opponents to the SALT treaty who claimed to be for arms control but against the particular treaty. Of course, some of these opponents had no concern for arms control whatsoever, believing on the contrary that America should be armed to the teeth to deter the advance of the Red tide. The barrage of questions, challenges, and counterassertions could not really be answered because no amount of evidence to the contrary would ever suffice.

It is perhaps for this reason that an increasing number of judges are demanding that the negative not merely question the affirmative, but also present an alternative policy, a defense of the present system, or some other approach as an alternative to the present system and resolution.

Although the negative is usually wise to present an alternative analysis and defend it, there is no logical obligation for the negative to do anything beyond denying the truth of the affirmative contentions. It may be the case that there is not enough knowledge to act; therefore, no policy is available at this time.

The negative should use straight refutation selectively and in combination with other constructive arguments. Although it may be true that some affirmative teams will be overwhelmed by questions, challenges, and demands made of every contention, this strategy is not likely to be successful in the long run—as teams continue to research their own cases and gather evidence. Moreover, it is difficult to sustain the credibility of a style of debate that seems to give the negative the right to question everything and prove nothing. If every affirmative argument is questioned with equal intensity, how much weight should be given to simply one more challenge? Abusing the strategy results in giving equal weight to the important and unimportant issues alike.

Defense of the Present System

A **defense of the present system** position always involves two arguments. Refutation of the affirmative claims, first, that life under the present system will be worse in the future; and, second, that the future looks promising in respect to the harm area isolated by the affirmative. There are three ways to defend the present system. Any or all of them may be chosen, according to the available evidence.

Affirmative Does Not Prove a Harm

This defense argues that the features that the affirmative claims to be undesirable in the present system are either necessary evils or do not exist. The debate turns on the question of values. For instance, a case may claim that the CIA violates individual privacy by wiretapping and eavesdropping. It may even prove that such intrusion upon important civil rights is likely to continue into the future. A negative position would defend the present system insofar as it consists of arguments to justify such violations for the greater good, namely collective security. To the extent that the negative could prove that in this instance the needs of a greater security were paramount, the present system would be defended. This may be a difficult position because the negative assumes the burden of proving that such vital information could be gathered in no other manner. But the "necessary evil" is always a possible option.

Another method of redefining a harm is to prove that the value structure of the affirmative is not acceptable. It is virtually undeniable that some lives could be saved if mandatory seatbelt laws were enforced. Moreover, it is probably difficult to prove that not wearing seatbelts is a necessary evil, serving some greater good. But it could be argued that even though saving lives is an important duty of government, in instances where individuals choose knowingly and willingly to take risks at their own expense, the government has no right to intervene; that such action would be the very essence of tyranny. The defense of the present system in this example is centered on arguing that the value of liberty outweighs the value of saving a number of lives. Thus, it can be admitted that people who could be saved by seatbelts die as a result of accidents, but it can also be maintained that this harm, though tragic, is not within the appropriate sphere of governmental action.

Most affirmatives identify a harmful area that is usually agreed on as being unnecessary and susceptible to some social or government action. Therefore, a negative position arguing that the harm is not really a harm—all things considered—is typically quite rare. However, in some topic areas, especially those touching on civil liberties—such as control of mass media by the federal government—the argument may become more common.

The Harm No Longer Exists and Is Not Likely to Recur

This position may appear silly with regard to some cases. It would be news indeed if war were eliminated or air pollution had migrated to another planet or the poor were no longer with us. However, in other instances the position becomes much more defensible.

Some social problems, it may be argued, are the product of a unique confluence of circumstances or climate of opinion. If the circumstances change or if the opinions are reshaped, the problem may be unlikely to recur. In arguing that the power of the president should be restricted, for example, advocates might point to Vietnam as an example of an unwarranted, disastrous intervention brought about by abuse of executive discretion. Of course, the negative would be hard pressed to refute this point. But the implication of the argument—that future interventions will be equally disastrous—may successfully be refuted by referring to the disastrous nature of the Vietnam war itself. It could be maintained that since Vietnam was so bad, no president would risk the political consequences of escalation, that the mood of the country is against intervention, and that, consequently, there is no reason to further limit the president's power. Where cases depend on historical example to prove the potential significance of a recurrent harm, the negative can defend the present system by arguing that measures have been taken to assure that past mistakes will not be repeated.

The defense of the present system in this manner must always be selected carefully. Proving that circumstances have changed may magnify the possibility of a harm recurring. For example, the anti-Vietnam sentiment might lead to more warlike actions on behalf of belligerents who calculate that the United States will not respond. Moreover, the affirmative may appeal to prudence. The harm occurred once. Even if it is unlikely to reappear, prudence demands that all precautions should be taken.

The Harms Isolated Will Soon Abate

This position is the most common defense of the present system, although it is becoming less useful. Combined with straight refutation, the defense of the present system is maintained by arguing that the harm is not growing. The defense continues by pointing out that new programs or measures have been designed to combat the problem to the extent possible and that additional efforts would be premature—perhaps even making the situation worse. The logic behind this position is that the multifaceted present system is better than the single approach suggested by the affirmative.

For example, let's consider a case for a national health insurance program based on the contention that existing programs leave gaps in coverage that result in many citizens' not obtaining medical care and therefore dying much sooner than expected. The negative defense of the present system centers on pointing to the expanding coverage of private health insurance, Medicare, Medicaid, and free care. Thus, it is implied that the present system may once have been delinquent but no longer is. The affirmative plan is unnecessary to the solution of the problem.

The utility of this approach is limited by the notion of comparative advantages. This idea allows the affirmative to admit that the present system may eventually solve a problem but, at the same time, also to contend that there is a better way of reaching a solution. Many affirmatives on the national health insurance question modified their cases merely to maintain that the national health insurance plan should pertain to catastrophic illnesses. Because at this time there were no programs for these kinds of illnesses, and because it was unlikely that insurance programs would respond with the comprehensiveness or largesse of the federal government, a unique advantage area justified adoption of the resolution. Finally, it was argued that *even if* private health insurance tried to cover catastrophic illnesses, thereby rendering the affirmative rationale for change irrelevant, the net effect of such an action would be to collapse private insurance, resulting in untold human suffering. Thus, affirmatives prepared for "trends of the present system" arguments by arguing that each trend that proved hopeful in resolving the problem either made the problem worse or resulted in some other effect that was less desirable than what the affirmative plan would achieve.

Another limitation of the trend argument should be noted. Although it is not logically inconsistent to argue that the present system is moving to solve a problem in a way similar to the affirmative proposal and that this movement is disadvantageous, such a position hardly constitutes a defense of the present system. What is the point of arguing disadvantages to a policy if the present system will adopt the policy in any case? Many judges expect the negative to defend the present system and show that it is doing something good. That is, the negative is expected to show that the problems outlined by the affirmative are not inherent in the system. To argue, then, that the present system is enacting or can enact a policy identical to the affirmative solution and that such a policy is bad is an inadequate and contradictory negative position. The negative must be prepared to show the differences between the movement of the present system and the resolution. And, most important, the negative must be prepared to show that the method of movement by resolutional means is what constitutes the harms.

To summarize, defense of the present system can often be a complicated task. The negative debater should select the defense that seems to be most feasible to support. There are three basic options: (1) Deny that what the affirmative says is a harm really constitutes something that ought to be eliminated; (2) Deny that the harm is likely to recur; and (3) Show that trends indicate that the harm is likely to be minimized with all possible dispatch. Because the status quo is imperfect, the debater should not expect that a defense of the present system can be conducted with unwavering success. In many debates a defense of the present system is combined with an attack on the affirmative plan. Nevertheless, the negative debater should pay careful attention to how such a defense can enhance a comparison of the status quo with the affirmative plan.

Minor Repairs in the Present System

One variation on the trend argument is the minor repair. A **minor repair** is a change advocated in the present system that falls short of the resolution. It gains the advantages that the affirmative claims as justification for voting for the resolution. A minor repair is often used in conjunction with a trend argument, because no matter how promising the trends of the present system, they will always fall short of an ideal affirmative plan.

Continuing the catastrophic illness case previously discussed, an affirmative might claim that while it is true that private insurance could cover the problem of large bills, the affirmative case is still warranted because of a special provision in the case. That provision sets up a special court system to adjudicate claims quickly, fairly, and inexpensively. Unless the negative can counter this claim, the affirmative wins because its system is still superior to the present system.

The negative might counter with a minor repair; namely, setting up its own court system for adjudicating health care claims. This is certainly *not* the same thing as a national health insurance plan, and it mitigates the only reason for adopting the affirmative case. Typically, a minor repair consists of isolating "small" problem areas in the present system, stipulating the desired change, pointing out how this action is not tantamount to enacting the resolution, and establishing that the minor repair can solve the problem identified in the affirmative analysis.

Minor repairs should be used sparingly. To advocate a repair does restrict the scope of negative argument. It would be logically inconsistent, for example, to maintain that a problem could be solved by a simple change in the present system and at the same time to argue plan meets need, which maintains that no efforts can solve a problem. Finally, some believe that if the net effect of the minor repair is to bring about the resolution, then the minor repair is really just a variation of the affirmative case. (See the discussion of the counterplan on whether the support of a "topical" change in the present system by the negative demands an affirmative ballot.)

Plan Does Not Meet the Need

Plan meets need is a stock issue that rarely appears as a complete position. If the negative were only to argue plan meets need, the reason presented for rejecting the resolution would be that any action undertaken under its aegis would be completely futile. Although it is possible to discover "absolute solvency arguments"—as the phrase goes—such are rare. **Plan-meets-need arguments** are more often combined with defense of the present system. The net effect of this combination is to minimize the weight of the affirmative advantage. If the harm is not as significant as claimed and if the degree of resulting advantage is not as great as claimed, then the disadvantages do not have to be very large to offset the rationale for the case. The following are methods of implementing this argument.

Alternative Causality

Alternative causality means that there are causes for the problem other than those dealt with by the affirmative. Many affirmative cases claim advantages from mitigating certain evils that are eliminated by the affirmative plan. Against such cases the negative could argue that the affirmative would not accrue an advantage because there are other causes for the harm than those isolated by the affirmative.

On the consumer product safety topic, affirmative teams argued that children living in older homes ate flaking paint chips. It seems the chips taste sweet but produce dangerous lead poisoning. The plan proposed repainting the houses and thus eliminating the deaths. Negatives were able to reduce the effectiveness of the plan by pointing out that the homes in question were within the inner city and that the lead levels from automobile exhausts were high enough to produce the same results. Thus, even if all chips were removed, there would be no guarantee that lead poisoning would not continue.

If the negative team can quantify the significance of the alternate causality, the argument is much stronger than if no quantification can be established. In the lead paint example, no study had differentiated the degree of responsibility for lead poisoning between car exhausts and paint. Thus, the affirmative could argue that since there were direct, known links between the paint and the children's illness—at least in some cases—some degree of effectiveness could be shown. Unless the judge is quite strict and demands that the plan completely meet the need, the negative does not make so great an inroad on the argument as it might.

A variation of the alternative causality argument involves some affirmative cases that claim to treat the symptoms of a problem, alleviating its effects rather than bringing about a solution. Just as a doctor may prescribe medicine to treat the side effects of a disease without eradicating the disease itself, an affirmative policy may treat the harmful effects of a problem, even though the problem itself persists.

In cases that purported to respond to United States energy needs, the affirmative commissioned many alternative technologies to respond to energy shortfalls, while at the same time instituting conservation. Thus, while it may have been true that conservation by itself could not cure America's rapid consumption of energy, the alternative technology could help to mitigate the problem.

This kind of affirmative position makes plan-meets-need arguments difficult for the negative to win. If the affirmative empowers a board to select from a dozen energy alternatives the one it finds to be useful, the negative has to defeat all proposals to prove that no benefit will come about. The affirmative need only defend the one that is not attacked by the negative. In this debate scenario, the negative would be fortunate indeed if plan-meets-need arguments became a voting issue.

Workability of the Plan

Sometimes even experienced advocates will have a flaw in the plan. A funding plank will be left out, no enforcement provided, or no topical action mandated. In such cases the plan will not work and ought to be rejected. Few judges will allow the affirmative the luxury of amending the plan. If such a procedure were allowed, the affirmative could simply add new provisions as the debate went along, and the negative would never catch up to debate the real affirmative case. Like a bill called to a final vote before Congress, the resolution is voted up or down as it is presented in the first affirmative constructive.

Most **workability** arguments do not come from obvious errors in the plan. Rather, workability emerges from matching the mandates of the plan to the external environmental factors that limit the objectives of the plan. A plan to make doctors work in a ghetto for five years, for example, would not work if such a mandate caused all doctors to go into research in order to avoid the injunction. A plan to control wages and prices would not work if all goods were sold illegally on the black market, despite government laws. To discover workability arguments, one must ask "Why has this plan not been tried before?" There are often many good reasons.

If a plan has a precedent, either at another time in the United States or presently in another country, the negative should pay careful attention to these analogous programs. If the plan was successful when tried elsewhere, then the negative should be prepared to argue that circumstances are not analogous in the present situation and that these dissimilarities are critical to extrapolating success rates. If the plan was not successful when tried elsewhere, the reverse becomes the negative position.

Circumvention

One form of plan-meets-need argument employed by negatives argues that countermeasures will arise that circumvent the objectives of the affirmative plan. This area of analysis becomes particularly fertile when the case depends on the attitudes of interest groups or social agencies (attitudinal inherency). The essence of this position is that unless the attitudes that perpetuate the problem are changed, the old problem will simply reappear in a new form. One can remove guns, it may be argued, but thrill-seekers will merely turn to knives. The plan-meets-need argument can be expanded into a disadvantage if the new manifestation of the attitude is more harmful than the old one. If knives are more lethal than guns, then the net effect of the plan is to worsen needless suffering and death—at least so the issue could be argued.

A **circumvention** argument always has two parts: the motive and the means. The motive for circumvention is generally isolatable from the inherency presented by the affirmative. Why do presumably good persons do evil? This core question identifies the reason that certain social groups or institutions perpetuate the problem: they benefit in some way from preventing the greater good. Unless the affirmative changes the structure of social incentives, imparting to these interests a motive for doing good, the ultimate reason for a problem continues to exist. If the affirmative does not buy off, break up, or ship out the wrongdoers, then the motive remains. The means for circumvention are as various as the negative speaker's imagination is fertile.

One debater from the University of Kansas always used to say, "Now, I am not one of these scoundrels causing this harm, so I don't know the area, and I have had only ten minutes to think about it, but here are the ways the affirmative plan can be circumvented." What would follow would be a series of imaginative scenarios that seemingly were not controlled by the affirmative board (the means of change).

In practice, the negative rarely reads evidence on circumvention; most of it is provided by the affirmative. The first negative might argue inherency and claim that the motives in the present system are not so adamantly evil as portrayed by the affirmative. This would not preclude the second negative from arguing plan circumvention, as long as the argument is prefaced by the phrase "To the extent you accept what the affirmative says is true, then . . . ." Otherwise, a circumvention argument might contradict inherency.

There are several means by which the affirmative can argue attitudinal inherency and not open itself up to such circumvention attacks. The most prevalent method is to argue that the motives of people under the present system are unknown or passive. People perpetuate the problem by bad habits, inertia, or poor coordination. Given no strong attitude one way or the other, they are not likely to circumvent the plan.

In such a circumstance, the negative must press for a motive, a way in which the plan contravenes interests that could become active if crossed. For example, under the topic RESOLVED: *That the federal government should establish a comprehensive program to significantly increase the energy independence of the United States,* some affirmatives argued that the present system was not taking action to solve the energy crisis because of the public inertia and bad habits.

The affirmative, which offered nuclear power or increased coal use as an alternative, was likely to hear circumvention arguments. The negative would agree that either of these alternative energy sources would create such harms that people would move to find ways to circumvent the plan. The affirmative might attempt to avoid circumvention by declaring all such attempts illegal. Sometimes this claim is sensible. Certainly, simple rules to circumvent the obvious objective of a law would be tolerated. At other times, the argument could become outlandish.

A disarmament case might isolate the cause of the current arms race to the attitudes of the military-industrial complex. The negative could argue that if the attitudes are really that powerful, the plan would result in the overthrow of the United States government by military fiat. The affirmative, extending the power of its plan to an absurd level, would point to the plank of the plan that would say, "Circumvention is outlawed." Of course, without reasonable expectations that the plan could possibly continue in such a hostile environment, such claims are meaningless—unless of course the affirmative had established a dictatorship. But that argument could be debated on its own questionable merits.

Plan meets need can be argued by pointing out alternate causality, impeaching the workability of the plan, or indicating that it would be circumvented. From the authors' point of view, these arguments are not generally so effective as they appear to be. In combination with minimization of harm and disadvantages, however, they may contribute to an effective position.

Disadvantages of the Affirmative Plan

A **disadvantage** is a harmful effect, or series of effects, brought about by the affirmative plan. Disadvantages, usually but not always argued exclusively by the second negative constructive speaker, must together outweigh the rationale for voting affirmative. Just as it would not be wise to reject a college that would otherwise provide you with a good education and enjoyable experience because you, say, didn't find the color scheme of the classroom buildings to your taste, it would not be wise to reject some overall beneficial policy merely because there are trivial harms that may come about. The reason the negative asks the judge to vote on disadvantages is that, overall, the affirmative program promises more net harms than gains.

Is it possible for the negative to argue only disadvantages? Of course, but in practice this is rarely done. Typically, disadvantages contribute to a balancing equation, an equation that involves many of the stock issues previously discussed. Think of the original affirmative claims as the gross benefit. In order to see what justification for the case is left at the end of the round, the judge must look at the net benefit.

The net benefit is determined by subtracting three things from the affirmative claim: (1) the degree of significance of harm area that has been overstated; (2) the degree of ineptitude that is falsely claimed about the present system with regard to the problem; and (3) the degree of solution that cannot be attained by the affirmative but nevertheless was initially claimed. What is left of the advantages is then compared to the disadvantages to determine if the case is still worth adopting.

If the net benefit is small and if the negative wins no disadvantage, then the judge may still vote negative on presumption. That is to say, since there is no really good reason for adopting the affirmative, it is re-jected on the grounds of unknown risk. There may be harmful unexam-ined side effects to the change. Since presumption is always an unknown quantity, many judges are equally as likely to vote affirmative, however, on the grounds of giving the policy a try in the absence of any proven dis-advantage. For this reason it is always important to try to extend through the rebuttals at least one winning disadvantage. The following are three different areas for finding disadvantages to affirmative cases.

Case-Related Disadvantages

Case-related disadvantages are the potentially bad consequences im-plied by the specific affirmative case. For example, a case that justifies so-cialized medicine may result in a doctors' strike, harming the quality of medical care. Socialized medicine might also result in discouraging stu-dents from pursuing a career in medicine, thus worsening the quality of the delivery system. What is being argued here is that to gain an advan-tage in one area of the topic will only make things worse overall. In the example, the affirmative would provide medical care for all but could de-crease the quality of that care by causing a doctor shortage. The disad-vantage has the effect of "turning the case"—making a problem worse rather than better. This is a powerful argument in most rounds. If it is won by the negative, the affirmative cannot win.

Any disadvantage is composed of two parts: the links and the impacts. The link can be defined as the "why" part of the disadvantage. It is the proof that explains *why* the affirmative plan will cause an undesirable effect and *why* it is unique to the affirmative plan. **Uniqueness** is an important element of the negative argument. If the disadvantage is not unique to the affirmative plan, the affirmative could argue that the disadvantage is not a reason to vote negative because it is possible for the disadvantage to occur under the present system.

A link may be either direct or indirect. In the disadvantage to socialized medicine, the strike argument would be a direct link to the affirmative plan. It would be the plan that brought about the condition of harm. A doctors' strike is not likely under the present system, but the negative would attempt to prove that it is certain to occur under the affirmative plan. The disadvantage of a future doctor shortage would be an example of an indirect link, because it must first be established that socialized medicine as proposed by the affirmative would reduce doctor profits, thereby reducing the incentive to pursue a medical career.

In either case, the negative must be certain that the disadvantage does not occur under the present system *and* that the affirmative plan is not effective in offsetting the harm. To continue the example, if the affirmative could prove that the number of doctors under the current conditions was declining and that the affirmative plan provided greater incentives that would offset the onus of socialized medicine, then the disadvantage would be "turned around"—it would be a net reason to vote for the affirmative.

Since **turnaround arguments** seem to enjoy growing popularity, the negative would be wise to take into account these possibilities and preempt the potential responses in structuring the initial disadvantage. The first step in discovering a potential turnaround is to answer the question "Why would this disadvantage not occur within the present system?" Or, alternatively, "Why is the disadvantage unique under the affirmative policy system?"

The second step is to look at the affirmative plan to see if there are special plan provisions that might arguably offset the harmful side effects of the policy system. These special planks are sometimes referred to as "plan spikes."

A **plan spike** is usually an ingenious means of implementing a resolution to avoid the ordinary objections made against the resolution. Certainly, in arguing socialized medicine, the affirmative should be able to predict that a recurrent negative objection will be the effect of the plan on doctors. In anticipation of these recurring objections, the affirmative would take measures in the plan to offset the potential harm. The affirmative would then be prepared to demonstrate that these measures are an improvement over the present system, thus turning the disadvantage around. For example, the affirmative could provide salaries that are competitive with private practice, or the affirmative might pay for a doctor's education. The net effect would be to restore the economic incentive to entering the medical profession while guaranteeing medical care for all citizens.

The negative should be prepared to defeat the viability of these plan spikes, arguing, for example, in the case of socialized medicine, that pay is not the primary factor in determining a medical career. Rather, it is entrepreneurial freedom—a core feature of socialized medicine that cannot be offset by any plan spike to increase salaries.

A negative, hedging its bets, typically argues several independent links to the harm. The affirmative has three possible responses. First, the affirmative may argue that any or all of the links are not unique to the affirmative plan. The link would be shown to exist in the present system, making it possible for the disadvantage to occur under the present system. Second, the affirmative could offset the link cause of a harm, the turnaround. The turnaround would add another advantage to the affirmative case and thereby add another reason to vote affirmative. Finally, the affirmative could argue that the "threshold," the significance of the causal relationship between the link and harm, is not established. The net result of this argument would be to diminish the likelihood or scope of the impact to the disadvantage. The negative should be prepared to rebut each argument.

What should the negative do if the affirmative argues all three positions against a single disadvantage? First, the negative must decide if it wants to extend the disadvantage or concede it and concentrate on another one. If the negative decides not to extend the disadvantage, it could concede the affirmative threshold argument. This could be done by admitting that the negative has not presented sufficient evidence to relate the link to the harm.

The result of the negative's conceding the affirmative threshold argument would be that the affirmative could not claim a turnaround; if the link is not sufficient to cause the impact, then there is no disadvantage for the affirmative to turn. In any case it should be remembered that if the negative claims a disadvantage to be significant and if the affirmative claims to turn the disadvantage around by virtue of its plan, the negative simply cannot ignore the disadvantage without impairing its own position. The "impact" or harm to a disadvantage may fall into one of two general areas. You will recall that the link in the disadvantage explains why the disadvantage will occur. The impact is the end result or outcome of the disadvantage. In the socialized medicine disadvantage, the doctors' strike argument tells why the quality of medical care will decline. The death and suffering that will result when people have inadequate medical care due to a shortage of doctors is the impact of the disadvantage.

The impact may be quantitative or qualitative. The quantitative disadvantage argues that adopting the affirmative proposal would result in a large number of deaths, a widespread increase in unemployment, or a substantial decrease in GNP. In this context, the debate focuses on the relatively simple question of which policy system will have the greater lifesaving benefits.

On the other hand, the negative could argue a disadvantage with a qualitative harm or impact. The negative might, for example, argue that the plan will significantly restrict liberty. This type of disadvantage can be very difficult to compare with the affirmative advantages, particularly if the affirmative is arguing quantitative advantages.

The difficulty lies in comparing two different values, quantity versus quality. When the impacts flow from different value areas, the negative should be prepared to argue the superiority of one value over another. Unless this is done, the judge is left to pick between apples and oranges. There is no way to decide the round on the merits of intrinsic argument, for there is no criterion of choice. Anytime the negative is arguing disadvantages with values different from the implied value of the affirmative, the negative must also argue that the judge should accept their values.

Common disadvantages are discovered by looking to subject matter related to the topic. If the area is foreign policy, for example, and the traditional areas for advantage are security, stability, prestige, peace, cooperation, and prosperity, then the negative should search for the unique ways in which the resolution will create a decrease in safety and increase international tensions, conventional or nuclear conflict, arms racing, and possible world collapse. Moreover, the negative should be able to select its own disadvantages, compare the possible impacts, and be prepared to argue for their importance as compared with the affirmative advantage. This selection process should take into account whether or not the present system will be subject to the same harm without the affirmative plan and whether the affirmative plan has unique measures that might offset the disadvantage.

Policy Disadvantages

Policy disadvantages, also known as generic disadvantages, look at the affirmative case and its impact on society as a whole. The disadvantage does not deal with a specific area of a topic but with the affirmative plan in the larger context. The policy disadvantage deals with policy in general and not with the specific action of the affirmative plan. A typical example, which will be discussed later, is the "social spending," or cost, disadvantage. As soon as the affirmative spends money to accrue an advantage or solve a harm, the negative can argue that money will not be available for other societal needs. It does not matter whether the affirmative case is energy conservation, socialized medicine, ocean mining, minimum educational standards for gifted students, agricultural subsidies, pollution control, control of illegal drug smuggling, or military intervention into countries fighting for "democracy." If the plan spends money, social spending can be argued.

In the previous discussion, it was assumed that the appropriate course of analysis was to investigate the impacts of a plan on areas specifically related to the affirmative case area. But why should that be the approach automatically turned to by the negative? There may be more important areas to consider before selecting a policy. If the United States were on the brink of nuclear war, economic collapse, or irrecoverable pollution, it would be important to see whether the affirmative policy would be the proverbial straw that breaks the camel's back and collapses the entire social order.

Policy disadvantages stem from the notion that there is no such thing as a discrete action or a delimited area; all policies are interrelated to some extent. Thus, in looking at possible disadvantage areas, first examine possible higher-order impacts—earth-ending threats.

Links are important to the extent that the policy effects are *directed* toward making the catastrophe more or less likely. Of course, it would be very difficult to prove that, say, increasing arms sales to Nicaragua would result in the final catastrophe of nuclear war. But given the disastrous consequences of such a war, it would be foolish to take the risk unless there were very significant advantages. Indeed, it might even be more foolish not to look at the impact of any of our policies in regard to nuclear war, to decide only on an incremental basis.

Social Spending Disadvantage

I. The affirmative will spend x to implement the plan.

II. Congressional budget restrictions will not allow increased spending, so existing programs will need to be cut to fund the affirmative plan.

III. Those programs with the weakest political constituencies will be cut first. These are often the programs that help the most people.
  A. Foreign aid will be cut.
    1. Money spent for foreign aid is more effective than money spent for the affirmative plan.
    2. Example of benefits of foreign aid (with evidence).
  B. Welfare programs would be cut.
    1. Traditionally, food stamps have been targets of budget cuts.
    2. Only a few dollars a year would save a life.
    3. Illustration of number of people currently receiving food stamps. Outline what is currently spent on food stamps vs. the money to be spent on the affirmative plan.

Perhaps an illustration of this kind of argument might clarify the concept. Consider the social spending disadvantage, an argument applicable to any plan that spends money. The development goes as follows. The affirmative claims that its plan will cost x dollars; of course, it will cost more because of inflation, cost overruns, corruption, and so forth. Congressional budget restrictions are such that any new spending will come about only at the expense of existing programs. The programs that will be cut are the ones with weak political constituencies.

Foreign aid has a weak political constituency. Dollars for foreign aid are much more effective than dollars spent for the affirmative plan. The greater the contrast between the cost-per-saving-a-life between the affirmative and the negative, the more effective the disadvantage. Or assume that the affirmative's plan is to implement air bags in automobiles on a nationwide scale. To do so would require an expenditure of hundreds of thousands of dollars to save a single life.

The negative might choose to demonstrate that the food support program would be cut and that food stamps save a life with an expenditure of only a few dollars a year. In such a case, even a small risk of actual cuts in food aid is not high. The decision-making calculus still favors the negative. One must remember to multiply the probability of result by the impact to determine the desirability of the policy system.

So far, the argument sounds simple, but it gets far more complicated. To begin, the policy disadvantage seems counterintuitive. Why would saving lives on the highways result in deaths in Angola? Why would Congress decide to cut foreign aid, as opposed to other low priority programs, especially given the logical desirability of foreign aid? Finally, how can claims to fiscal responsibility be taken seriously in light of federal largesse in previous years? The negative may never be able to approach the certainty that the affirmative claims in linking highway deaths and air bags, but given the significantly greater consequence of a foreign aid cut, the negative can give away a lot and still argue that the risk of harm mandates rejection of the policy system.

There are other policy disadvantages: trade wars, pollution, Malthusianism, nuclear war—to name just a few. Debate handbooks are filled with evidence related to these issues, largely because of their popularity and cross-applicability among topics. These rather common disadvantages should be explored by all teams. Members of affirmative teams are likely to encounter teams that do not wish to debate the content area of the case—it may be too good—and choose to debate on their own grounds. If one is on the negative, the reverse suggests itself. But it should be remembered that before embarking on an issue that almost all debaters will be thoroughly familiar with, careful preparation should be made.

Process Disadvantages

A **process disadvantage** focuses on flaws in the affirmative method of producing results. A process disadvantage relates neither to the particular content area of the topic nor to extrinsic considerations of policy effect. The judge is asked to reject the case because the plan is an inappropriate method of achieving any advantage.

The process argument is becoming popular for several reasons. First, as the variety of case areas and plans proliferate, it becomes more difficult to research each particular avenue of a topic. It is difficult to prepare hundreds of specific disadvantages. Given that the affirmative team is more likely to command expertise in its area of analysis, the success of such a strategy is questionable.

On the other hand, general policy disadvantages become difficult to prove. Most experienced teams know the consequences of their plan with regard to nuclear war, growth, or other recurrent disadvantages. A process disadvantage, on the other hand, may not be as obvious. It may result from a relatively unplanned element in the affirmative plan. The process disadvantage certainly has the important strategic edge of not being turnable. A bad process is simply that—a bad process.

Consider the example of a case that isolates harms to advertisements directed toward children. Millions of children ruin their teeth and become obese because of the beguiling pitches of their beloved cartoon characters on Saturday morning. The plan proposes to ban these advertisements.

A process argument may be launched against this plan, substantiating the importance of freedom of speech. The net effect of this position is to show that even if it is proven desirable and effective to ban ads for children with regard to health results, the result would be to interfere with the value of free speech, an antecedent and superior social value. Thus, even if there were some unique probability of helping children, after first negative trends, repairs, and significance arguments were counted, the process by which the affirmative plan achieves this goal is not worth the advantage.

Of course, there are answers to this position, but it should be noted that there is a low probability of a turnaround. The affirmative does nothing in the area to enhance free speech. The negative is not debating on affirmative ground—the lifesaving effects of media manipulation. Finally, the disadvantage can be applied to other cases that share in restricting media to gain their benefits.

Other process-related arguments stem not so much from a topic area, but from practices popular within the debate community. For years, teams appointed themselves and their coach to the regulatory board. The authors would argue that such practice hedges the educational value of debate.

Many teams also used cost-benefit decision making to select appropriate policy mixes. This strategy for writing a plan was designed to befuddle negative plan-meets-need arguments. The board would be empowered to choose, for example, from a variety of non-nuclear options (coal, oil, solar, wind, wave, fusion power) any alternative that would replace nuclear generation of electricity. The negative was thus left with the virtually impossible burden of proving that no alternative could be found. This strategy was successfully defeated by focusing directly on the process of selection. By proving that cost-benefit was a silly method of decision making, the affirmative no longer had the luxury of claiming that its board would necessarily do the right thing.

Finally, many affirmative teams found it useful to establish the inherency of a particular problem in terms of the attitudes of a group of people who acted to perpetuate social harms. Why are harmful consumer products produced? Because some businessmen and women can make money from such products. The negative found some success in arguing that these attitudes would manifest themselves in other ways. Barred from selling unsafe infant carriers at home, the socially unconscious villains would sell them abroad, modify the carrier a bit, or call it something else.

In order to get out of this trap, since the affirmative could not guarantee that it would think of and bar all the things that the negative might, the affirmative claimed that legislative intent would be determined by "the affirmative speeches in the round." Thus, when a negative would bring up a possible avenue of circumvention, the affirmative would declare that such an equivalent harmful action would be outlawed by the plan—that was their intent. This strategy, of course, makes it extremely difficult for the negative to lodge any plan-meets-advantage argument, for any flaw in the affirmative plan would be absolved by the intent of the affirmative to correct it. Such a maneuver steps beyond legislative authority.

Legislation called up for a vote is voted up or down on the basis of what is stipulated in the bill. A bill is never passed with the stipulation that the enacting body could outlaw future actions that would violate the intent of the bill. Therefore, the authors feel that the affirmative is beyond any realm of reason when it argues that affirmative speeches serve as affirmative intent.

In sum, the negative has the option of choosing from three different areas of disadvantage: case-related disadvantages, policy disadvantages, and process disadvantages. Each area has potential and limits. Finding a disadvantage that directly relates to the affirmative and is within the intuitive purview of the topic is closest to straight clash. And clash is what most judges still like to see.

However, preparing these disadvantages for every splinter case on a topic is not likely to be time-effective and, unless the affirmative is inept and unprepared, is not always likely to be successful. A policy disadvantage, because it relates to questions of more universal scope, such as nuclear war or economic growth, may be applicable to more cases. Moreover, because the impacts are quite large and not directly related to the affirmative case area, the argument takes place typically on negative ground. But it should be remembered that policy disadvantages are often counterintuitive, that not all judges multiply probability of harm times magnitude to determine comparative risks, and that many affirmative teams will be prepared to turn around the disadvantage.

Process disadvantages may be useful for defeating teams that take unusual measures to obtain rather trivial advantages. When a violation of process is intrinsic to action implied in the topic (banning commercials intrinsically relates to issues pertaining to freedom of speech), the argument becomes time-effective, even though affirmative teams will probably be well prepared on the issue. Process disadvantages that relate to particular means of implementing a plan (board appointments, decision criteria, legislative intent, and the like) may work against a particular team quite effectively *once,* but unless the team is quite inept, the plan will contain a different means of implementation the next time.

Counterplan

In the **counterplan** position, the negative admits that the affirmative's analysis of the problem in the present system is correct. However, the negative argues that the affirmative proposal is not the best method for correcting the problem. Instead, the negative's alternative counterplan is the best way to remedy the evils. The counterplan then is the negative's alternative to the affirmative plan. It will solve the affirmative problem without adopting the resolution. The negative counterplan is controversial in debate theory, but debate theory is always debatable.

Until recent years counterplanning was a little used strategy. Possibly, negative teams did not want to take on the burden of proof necessary to defend another, new policy system. Certainly, few negative teams have ever wanted to admit that the affirmative was right about anything, and perhaps to concede the harm and inherency area was just too much. Whatever the reasons, the negative counterplan is a relatively new, unsettled practice. It has raised many theoretical problems that remain unresolved. In this section, the discussion will focus on the method of constructing counterplans and some of the theoretical problems in defending such an approach.

Returning to the initial analysis, when the negative *advocates* a counterplan, the negative asks the judge to reject the affirmative plan because it forecloses a future that would be much better than that offered by the affirmative. This means that the negative has the duty to prove that: (1) The affirmative plan and the negative plan cannot exist side by side; and (2) The negative counterplan provides a better future world than does the affirmative plan. If the negative cannot prove the first premise, then both the plan and the counterplan could exist amicably side by side in the future. The counterplan would not be a true "counter" to the affirmative. If the negative cannot prove the second premise, then the counterplan is rejected on the grounds of comparative merit.

The primary requirement of a counterplan is that it must not be topical. If the counterplan turns out to be merely another way of implementing the resolution, then the negative has not done its job—denying the acceptability of the resolution. For this reason, the negative team must show how the counterplan differs from the resolution. Negative debaters thus should define the terms of the resolution and show how the counterplan does not meet those definitions. In addition to proving that the counterplan is not topical, the negative must also show that the counterplan is competitive with the affirmative plan.

The issue of competitiveness pertains to the question of whether the counterplan is truly counter to the resolution. Assuming that the affirmative plan is within the topic, then if the topic is to be rejected because it forecloses a competing alternative, the counterplan must be proven competitive. There are several ways to accomplish this end.

First, the negative might demonstrate that its course of action is antithetical to the plan. Disarmament is antithetical to armament; eliminating food aid conflicts with expanding food aid; expanding the use of wiretaps conflicts with eliminating wiretaps.

Second, the negative might demonstrate that the plans cannot exist at the same time. One way of doing this is for the negative to identify limited resources and to put these resources to work for a different purpose. If, for example, the number of genetic researchers have limited time, to use these people for certain kinds of research would necessarily restrict time spent in other activities. From the negative point of view, the other research might be more beneficial.

Where resources are not limited, the counterplan may not be competitive. To say, for instance, that the negative will take the money available for the affirmative plan concerning education research and spend it on space research does not render the counterplan automatically competitive. Congress could spend money on both. However, if the negative was able to show that Congress was limited in funding this area by political constituency, economic constraints, and the like, then the resource area would be proven finite, and the counterplan might be considered competitive. To make the artificial claim that both cannot exist at the same time merely because the negative stipulates that its plan will use the "affirmative's funding" only results in the conundrum that the affirmative would have to be voted into existence before the counterplan could work.

Another avenue for establishing competitiveness is to argue that both plans *should* not exist together. It may be the case that the direction of the counterplan is not antithetical to the affirmative and that resources for both abound. Nevertheless, because the existence of both would be less desirable than the benefits of both, the net system favors the negative. For example, an affirmative may appoint a federal board to deal with education for the handicapped; the negative counters with a number of state boards with the same responsibility. Both could exist, and the policy direction is similar. Yet, because the result would be a profusion of duplicative, perhaps contradictory regulations, the mutual existence of both would probably not be desirable. It should be noted that the negative has the duty to prove that this problem of confusing jurisdiction would be more significant than any advantage that might result from covering the problem from two different perspectives, showing that the net result is that the two systems should not be adopted simultaneously.

A final variation of the competitiveness argument is the claim of redundancy. Here the negative argues that since both systems solve the same problem, it is unnecessary to adopt both; rather, the more desirable should be chosen. This claim is effective only if all or a significant portion of the affirmative advantage is obtained.

Even after the negative has established that its policy is indeed counter, there may still be problems in the area of competitiveness. Depending on the answer to a single question, a debate may have quite different results: Must a counterplan be merely competitive as a whole, or must each part be an alternative?

Affirmatives usually claim that parts of the counterplan not in direct contradiction to the affirmative proposal must not be considered as reasons for voting negative. For example, suppose that the negative establishes that state-funded education programs are an alternative to federally funded education programs. Furthermore, the negative funds its proposal by raising alcohol and tobacco taxes. Could the negative claim, as a reason to vote for the counterplan, a decrease in alcoholism and tobacco deaths because of depressed buying? The affirmative will try to claim the negative could not.

The affirmative will argue that the question of taxation is not really intrinsic to the issue of education. Rather, it is only an "artificial by-product" of a plan. It may even claim that the present system or judge could adopt such taxes without necessarily rejecting the affirmative plan. The affirmative would be arguing that the advantage of decreasing alcoholism and tobacco deaths is not competitive with the affirmative education program advantage. The authors' own inclination on this issue, however, is to reject this line of argument.

Just as the negative cannot argue under inherency that the present system could adopt the affirmative plan if it wanted to, so too the affirmative cannot argue that the present system could adopt the not directly competitive aspects of the counterplan if it wanted to. Without establishing some level of probability, both arguments are made in fantasy land. Moreover, it seems unfair that good negative ideas be adopted at the judge's own arbitrary discretion. The judge is in a forced choice situation, voting either for the affirmative or the negative policy system and not parts of both—which could be done only in group discussion where a decision maker had the luxury of adopting whatever advice seemed to be good. The authors believe that the debate situation more closely approximates the final choice on alternative bills where the means of implementation, though perhaps not logically essential, constitute the only available choice, and even incidental benefits to both plans must be compared.

In summary, it is vital to remember that in any counterplan debate, the negative must prove that the counterplan is an alternative to the affirmative plan *and* does not support the resolution. A simple illustration should demonstrate the importance of this strategic rule.

Suppose an affirmative team, advocating a resolution that calls for increasing United States military weapons, chooses to build a new fleet of battleships. The justification for this plan is centered on the claim that the ships will enhance military security. A negative team could counterplan with increasing the land armies of this country, arguing that the counterplan is not topical because armies are not weapons. The negative may successfully defend the claim that increasing the army enhances military security, the very goal of the affirmative. But the negative, implementing this strategy, might still very well lose the debate, for increasing troops is not competitive with increasing ships. Both could be done. Both would enhance security. The counterplan furthers the goal of the affirmative, but it does not stand as a reason to reject the affirmative plan per se.

Now consider a somewhat different counterplan against the same affirmative case. In this instance, the negative bans all battleships and builds more guided missiles. The central claim is that the mix of battleships and guided missiles decreases security, whereas increasing the number of guided missiles enhances military security. In this instance the negative is competitive. Banning battleships is a direct alternative to increasing the number of ships. Furthermore, the counterplan results in a single system of missile defense that is superior to the mix of missiles and battleships, which is continued by the affirmative. But the negative still is in danger of losing the round. Why? Because missiles are weapons, and the topic calls for increased weapons development. All that the negative has accomplished with the missile counterplan is to advocate an alternative method for implementing the topic.

Even though in this scenario, the negative may have defeated the affirmative case for increasing one kind of weapon, the resolution itself is affirmed by the counterplan. Thus, from this illustration it should be apparent that the negative must always be wary of presenting a counterplan that, even though not topical, is not competitive or, alternatively, even though competitive, is topical. In both instances the negative position is unsound.

Besides competitiveness and topicality, the negative must also win the comparative merit of its policy. In comparing a plan and counterplan, there are really only two arguments. The first is comparative degree of efficacy. Developed in this manner, the negative argues that the plan is more likely to be circumvented than is the counterplan, the plan is less likely to work than is the counterplan, and the plan achieves fewer advantages than does the counterplan.

Comparisons must be made directly, lest the debate become inordinately complicated. For example, the affirmative might offer a case that would provide a guaranteed annual income for all citizens. The affirmative justification would be that many people go hungry, lack adequate housing, and so on because they do not have enough money. The affirmative would demonstrate that because the jobs these people are qualified for do not pay enough to sustain life, they go on welfare where they can get the same amount of money without working. The negative counterplan would propose to solve these problems by increasing aid to housing, education, food stamps, day care, and so on. The negative would maintain that its proposal is *comparatively* advantageous because the counterplan would guarantee that the specific needs of the affirmative would be solved, whereas under the affirmative proposal people could use the money for things other than housing or food.

The second comparison is comparative alternative advantages. After isolating the comparative degree of effectiveness achieved over and above the affirmative, the negative then may move to presenting other advantages. Note that solvency levels need not be an issue, nor need the negative necessarily win greater solvency. The negative simply needs to establish that the comparative degree of solvency, even if greater by the affirmative, is not worth the concomitant risks. However, in developing disadvantages to the affirmative proposal, the negative must be certain that such harms do not apply to the counterplan or to the present system (if the negative has a severability plank in the plan).

An example of comparative alternative advantages can be seen by looking at an affirmative case that claimed to save lives by mandating the use of seatbelts. The negative would counterplan by having air bags put in cars when they are manufactured. By using air bags instead of seatbelts, the negative could claim the comparative alternative advantage that no enforcement is needed to gain the same advantage of saving lives. Because the air bag would inflate automatically on impact, it would not be necessary to devise some form of enforcement (which could also be costly).

The counterplan is usually presented in the first negative constructive. It may be either extensive or skimpy. The negative might, for instance, adopt all the affirmative plan planks, except, of course, those that are topical and comparatively disadvantageous. The negative then presents topicality, competitiveness, and comparative merit arguments. Since all three of these issues must be carried to win the round, the second negative constructive speaker would be wise to pay them appropriate attention, perhaps dividing responsibility.

The final question to be answered in the area of counterplans concerns the very nature of the debate process. So far the discussion has assumed that the advocates in a given round ask the judge to share a commitment to mutually exclusive alternative futures. But suppose that a negative team presents multiple versions of possible futures, arguing that there are many alternatives to the affirmative case, many counterplans that might warrant acceptance. The negative using this strategy is not committed to any policy system, but is in effect saying, "Judge, you choose whatever policy will be better than the affirmative."

These "hypothetical counterplans" may be numerous, inconsistent, and nonrestrictive of disadvantages. Does this tactic give the negative a decisive edge? Some shallow thinkers believe so, fearing that perhaps dozens of counterplans would foreclose the affirmative's ability to deal with any counterplans in depth. But this is not the case. The affirmative really has the edge if all that is asked of the judge is a hypothetical judgment. If the negative need not be committed to any policy, then the affirmative need not be committed to any particular case. New examples of the resolution could be presented in constructives and the plan repaired (because it is only a hypothetical commitment) to obviate disadvantages. Moreover, the affirmative might claim that if any counterplan is found to be topical, then there exists a warrant for the resolution and under its aegis the resolution ought to be affirmed. Thus, the introduction of hypothetical alternatives may severely harm the negative position if the affirmative knows how to respond.

Selecting the Negative Position

In this chapter we have discussed the various options that are available to the negative. While it is extremely unlikely that the negative would want to use all of them in the same debate round, a combination of the various options can prove quite successful. What follows is an outline of the negative options.

A. *Straight Refutation:* the strategy that denies the truth of all affirmative contentions.
 1. The negative may question the degree of support backing the affirmative contentions.
 2. The negative may wish to introduce evidence that directly contradicts the affirmative contentions.
 3. The negative may deny claims made by the affirmative that the affirmative advantages are independent reasons to vote for the topic.
B. *Defense of the Present System:* refutation of affirmative claims of harms in the present system.

    1. Problems do not exist. Even if the negative cannot show that the problem doesn't exist, it may be able to show that the problem is not a governmental or social responsibility.

    2. The negative can minimize the likelihood of the problem's recurring.

    3. The negative may show that there are trends in the present system to solve the problem.

C. *Minor Repairs:* a change advocated in the present system that falls short of the resolution but gains the advantages claimed by the affirmative.

D. *Plan Meets Need:* the proposal cannot solve the harms or accrue the advantages outlined by the affirmative.

    1. The negative may choose to prove that the plan does not work.

    2. The negative may demonstrate that there are alternative causes for the affirmative harms that are dealt with in the affirmative proposal.

    3. The negative may show that the plan can be circumvented.

E. *Disadvantages:* the harmful effect, or series of effects, brought about by the affirmative plan.

    1. The negative may develop case-related disadvantages that illustrate the potentially bad consequences implied by the topic.

    2. The negative could choose to develop policy (generic) disadvantages that look at the affirmative case and its impact on society as a whole.

    3. The negative could develop a process disadvantage that focuses on flaws in the affirmative method of producing results.

F. *Counterplans:* although the affirmative analysis of the problem is correct, the negative can offer a better proposal for solving the problem.

    1. The negative must demonstrate that the counterplan is truly counter to the resolution.

    2. The negative must show that the counterplan does not implement the resolution when solving the affirmative problem.

    3. The negative needs to illustrate that the counterplan offers a net advantage over the affirmative proposal.

There are certainly a great variety of potential issues for any affirmative case. The common strategy exercised by most negative teams is to swarm the affirmative case with as many of these arguments as possible, hoping that something might be successful. This tactic is not intellectually sound and is not likely to be successful in the long run. The affirmative may be able to toss a lot of challenges (or presses), questions, and assertions right back. The inevitable result is a morass of confusion and low speaker points. Since no coherent position is left, the decision is a matter of more or less random chance.

Our own advice is to prepare to debate the negative side of the question as a good general would prepare to fight a campaign. The primary principle is to select the best arguments relevant to the kind of debating that will probably be encountered.

List All Possible Arguments

Do not worry at this point what areas of stock analysis these arguments fit into. Simply list as many pro and con issues as you can possibly think of for supporting and opposing a particular case on the resolution. If you have already met the affirmative case and are preparing to beat it the next time, lay out the arguments from your flow sheet and try to think of others. Incidentally, observing elimination rounds is an excellent way to expand your own scope of argument analysis.

Cluster Similar Arguments

These clusters should begin to fit under rubrics such as significance, harm, etc. Importantly, once the clusters are developed, discover which arguments are independent and which are interdependent. There may be several distinct harms or several alternate ways the case may be topical. Independence is important to establish, because it gives you a greater variety of selection.

Evaluate Strengths and Weaknesses

By now you should have the affirmative issues, the negative counter, and the affirmative extensions arranged under each stock issue heading. The third step involves evaluation of the strength and weakness of these arguments. First, arrange arguments within a cluster from strongest to weakest. For example, under the category of harm, look at what seems to be the most significant and irrefutable harm area that can be selected by the affirmative and then look at the weakest; arrange other possible harm areas in between. Second, examine which stock-issue area seems to be the most difficult for the affirmative to prove. Arrange the stock issues from strongest to weakest; the weakest stock-issue area thus becomes the primary focus for negative attack. Remember that the principle of evaluating arguments should be to minimize your own burdens and maximize the burdens of the opposing team.

Select the Right Combination

If you establish an important set of arguments most likely to win the round, it would be foolish to waste valuable time developing other arguments that are not likely to be relevant or winnable. It is important that the negative position should contain independent links and impacts and refutation and defenses to provide numerous options for winning the round. But extraneous argument should be kept to a minimum. The final step here is to double-check that the arguments are consistent, that there is no contradictory claim that can mar an otherwise successful attack.

Summary

At the outset of the chapter, the difficulty of debating the negative position was pointed out. The authors are hopeful that the various strategies suggested will alert negative debaters to potential constructive positions that maximize the chance of success. Past forever are the halcyon days when negative speakers could "muddle and dump" and meet with unwavering success. Affirmative tactics, theory, and strategy are far more sophisticated than in those days when some uncertainty about 100 percent solvency was enough to vote negative. Indeed, affirmative case-making seems to have gained the upper hand, taking advantage of relatively thoughtless shotgun tactics. Construction of sound negative positions may help to offset the temporary ascendancy of the affirmative.

Questions for Discussion

1. Does the negative team ever assume the burden of proof of the debate proposition? What burden of proof does it take on in the counterplan case or for minor repairs?

2. Why does the negative want to win at least one disadvantage in each

debate round? Does winning a disadvantage guarantee a win for the negative? Explain.

3. Discuss the differences between a link and an impact in a disadvantage.

4. What are the three types of disadvantages that the negative can develop? What is the use of each?

5. What are the five strategies the negative should consider when planning a strategy against the affirmative case?

6. There are three types of plan-meets-need arguments the negative can develop. What are they and how can they be developed? Is it necessary to provide evidence to win the argument? Why or why not?

7. When developing arguments against the affirmative plan, how does the negative guard against contradicting arguments made against the affirmative rationale for change?

8. Under what circumstances would the negative want to run a counterplan? What must the negative do to win the counterplan? In what speech should the counterplan be presented?

Activities

1. Using your notes from your affirmative speech in Activity 4 in Chapter 3, develop a two- to three-minute first negative speech. This should include evidence to support your arguments.

2. Using the plan you developed in Activity 6 in Chapter 3, develop disadvantages and plan-meets-need arguments (with evidence where appropriate).

3. Using a case developed by another student, write a counterplan and be prepared to defend its nontopicality and competitiveness.

4. Using the resolution chosen for the Activities in Chapters 3 and 4, develop with evidence policy (generic) disadvantages on the resolution.

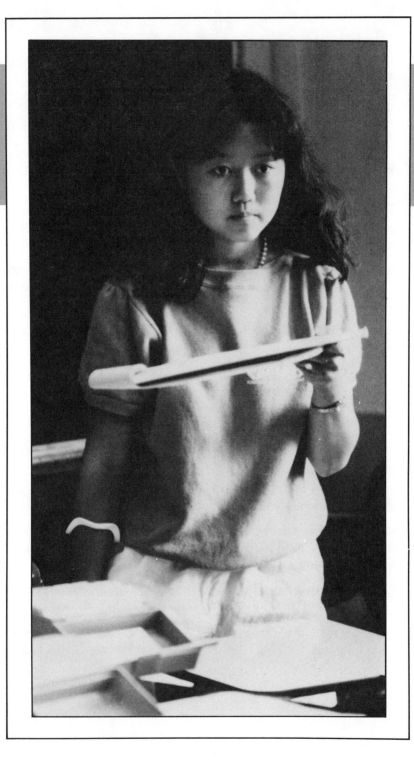

Chapter 5

Competitive Presentation

Objectives and Key Terms

After studying Chapter 5, you should be able

1. To explain strategies and tactics for upholding the affirmative burden of proof.

2. To explain and demonstrate how the affirmative maintains the offensive in a debate round.

3. To explain the strategies and tactics for effectively narrowing the debate as affirmative and as negative.

4. To demonstrate strategies and tactics the affirmative and negative can use for expanding the debate.

5. To explain the strategies and tactics the negative can use to uphold presumption.

6. To develop the ability to take the offensive edge from the affirmative or negative.

7. To explain how the affirmative and negative should respond to the strategies of the opposition.

8. To explain the strategies used when a debater responds to the negative counterplan.

9. To explain the obligations of each speaker in a cross-examination debate round.

10. To explain and demonstrate the objectives of the cross-examination period.

In order to implement the strategies and tactics discussed in this chapter, you will need to understand the following terms:

upholding the burden of proof	upholding presumption
parallel pattern of organization	counterargument
series pattern of organization	perspective
narrowing the debate	negative block
expanding the debate (spread case)	cross-examination debate

U p to now we have dealt only with the activities that are most important before a debate actually begins. The debater must understand the fundamentals, do a good job of research, and then build a constructive argument. Academic debate is not, however, a solitary activity. Its essence is the clash of ideas and evidence of speakers on two sides of a topic.

Like chess, debate is a matter of strategic attack and defense. It is characterized by tactical advances, shifts, and even retreats. Debaters, of course, do not use pawns and queens. The debater's weapons are arguments and counterarguments, all designed to achieve victory for their users. Through their preparation and practice in academic debate, debaters learn research and argumentation skills and acquire the ability to defend themselves against the verbal attacks of others.

This chapter discusses the major strategies and tactics of the presentation of the debate case during actual competition. Many debaters overlook this level of debate strategy and tactics because it is subtle and often takes years to learn from experience. In fact, it is usually only the very experienced debater who is aware of this level of debate. However, in discussing the competitive presentation, this text addresses itself not only to the experienced debater, but to debaters at all levels. There is no reason why even novice debaters cannot use the strategies and tactics of competitive presentation, just as they learn to use evidence cards. In fact, these tactics become more effective with practice and refinement.

Affirmative and Negative Competitive Approaches

When the typical debate begins, there usually are six people in the room. The judge is there to make a decision and to help the debaters by giving them feedback on their performance. The timekeeper, when available, serves as a chairperson, letting the individual speakers know how long they have spoken. In the preliminary rounds of most tournaments, there will not be enough timekeepers to go around. Usually, the judge will time the speeches, or each debater will keep time for his or her colleague, with the judge keeping track of prep time. The other four persons, the debaters, are there to present the pros and cons of the debate proposition.

For the duration of the debate itself, the debaters are closed-minded advocates who try to get the judge to agree with them. After the debate the students should analyze what they have learned and thereby restore debate to its educational perspective. The debater can improve only by analyzing each debate and determining what did or did not go well in a round. The strategies discussed here can work for the debater only with continual refinement and analysis. Successful debaters never stop researching the topic. They realize that an argument can be lost with outdated evidence. Tactics, too, must be researched and updated. But it is during the debate that the strategies of competition seem most important, at least in terms of the win or loss.

During the debate the major competitive strategies of both teams are analyzed. Just as chess players follow strategies of attack, debaters choose from proven "moves" that have been successful in the past. The strategies and tactics discussed here are some of the major moves that are available to debaters.

Affirmative Strategies and Tactics

Three fundamental affirmative strategies and one variation of these strategies have appeared in recent years. All the strategies are designed to put the affirmative in a position in which it can win the debate or to force the negative into a position in which it is likely to lose the debate. Although the strategies do not guarantee victory, they assure the affirmative that if it succeeds in implementing them, it will be more likely to win the debate.

Affirmative Strategies

- Upholding the burden of proof

- Maintaining the offensive

- Narrowing the debate

- Expanding the debate

Upholding the Burden of Proof

Debate fundamentals require that the affirmative prove that the proposition should be adopted. The **burden of proof** is satisfied if the affirmative presents a prima facie case and defends that case throughout the debate.

In the hands of a good debater, this fundamental becomes a definite affirmative strategy. To the nonthinking debater, on the other hand, the affirmative "burden of proof" may seem just a few words in a debate book that occasionally find their way onto a debate ballot. Good debaters, however, think in terms of burden of proof when the case is written, and they actively work to support their burden, in the mind of the judge, throughout the debate.

Writing the case involves three considerations. First, the debater analyzes the issues in the present system and picks the issues that will develop the strongest case for the adoption of the resolution. Second, he or she analyzes the judges most likely to hear the debate rounds in order to see what kinds of cases will be most acceptable to them. For instance, a student who debates in an area in which the judges are conservative would avoid the components case and would tend to use the comparative advantages case. Finally, the debater writes the case so that it will be obvious that the burden of proof has been met in the first affirmative. The wise debater does not hide the problem behind a mountain of evidence but highlights the evils in the present system and the effectiveness of the affirmative proposal so that even the least attentive judge will see and re-member them.

Tactics for Upholding the Burden of Proof

Analysis

The best way for the affirmative to uphold its burden of proof is to have a very strong constructive case. Some glib speakers can uphold a weak case against weak competition. But, if the affirmative case is strong, even the least experienced debater can hold his or her own against more experienced competition.

As you learned in Chapter 3, the affirmative team can develop the best analysis by choosing the best arguments it can find in forming its case. The affirmative should look for a problem in the present system that justifies a change. This problem should constitute a serious evil (the harms or problems should be significant), and it should result from a structural or attitudinal defect in the present system. The affirmative's plan for a change should correct the defect in the present system and thereby remedy the problem or go further toward remedying the problem than the present system can. Also, of course, the proposal should have other advantages, such as low cost and high efficiency.

This statement about the affirmative's analysis really is nothing new, nor does it amount to a tactic for upholding the affirmative's burden of proof. Thinking debaters turn this fundamental of debate theory into a tactic by the way in which they analyze the present system.

The debater should momentarily forget that he or she is a debater and analyze the case as an informed, critical thinker. Next, the case should be examined to see whether the analysis is really correct. That is, would the case as developed stand up in the real world? Is the problem really sufficient to justify a change? If adopted—by Congress, for example—would the proposal really remedy the situation? Would the advantages actually result in the real world?

Perhaps this tactic sounds like nonsense to some readers. If a debater can document the problem, the proposal, and the advantages with evi-dence, isn't the case necessarily adequate? The answer, unfortunately, often is "No!" Debaters are constantly fighting the difference between the world of words and the world of reality. So much opinion evidence is available on any policy question that almost any stand can be supported with a great deal of this type of evidence. Debaters often joke that if you look long enough and hard enough, you can find a person to say or prove just about anything.

Unfortunately for the affirmative, some analyses are as easy to defeat as they are to support. Frequently, not only the preponderance of evidence weighs against the analysis, but so does the judge's common sense. Whether or not a judge will "buy" an affirmative case idea is as important as having adequate evidence to support the affirmative. There is nothing more disheartening than reading a ballot that says the judge did not believe the affirmative case.

In 1972, prior to the OPEC oil embargo, college debaters found it all but impossible to persuade judges to vote for "stop oil imports" cases. In these affirmative cases, the affirmative argued that the United States imported too much oil from the Middle East. This dependence on imports made the government vulnerable to the whims and desires of a very shaky region of the world. The solution presented by the affirmative usually involved reducing imports to close to zero over time and implementing conservation programs while moving to new sources of energy. While the arguments and evidence were sound, the judges continually voted negative, indicating that they found the scenario unbelievable—that is, until October 1972, when the OPEC countries did in fact cut the supply of oil.

In another instance, a team developed an affirmative case on a foreign policy question that was based on repealing the Captive Nations Resolution. Several outstanding authorities argued that the "captive nations" philosophy represented the major threat to world peace. Therefore, the affirmative reasoned, if the Captive Nations Resolution were repealed, the cause of world peace would be significantly advanced. The team managed to win many debates because it was made up of outstanding debaters, but soon it began to have trouble upholding the burden of proof as the negative teams developed arguments against the case. Few judges felt that the affirmative's analysis was correct in the real world. Thus, it was easier for the negative team to win than it would have been if the affirmative had had a more sensible analysis.

Undoubtedly, this affirmative analysis was valid in the literal sense. The experts who were quoted knew what they were talking about when they said that, on a theoretical level, the Captive Nations Resolution represented a threat to world peace. But the debaters had failed to use the tactic of critically examining the analysis. As a result, all they acquired was a national reputation as "that funny team with the Captive Nations case."

Organization

Clearly, the organization of the affirmative has to grow out of the affirmative's analysis. The affirmative team should organize its arguments in the way that is the most logical for its particular approach to the proposition. The traditional need case usually begins with a presentation of the proposition and the definitions (if not incorporated in the plan), which is followed by the need-for-a-change argument, the proposal, and the advantages. The following is a typical organizational outline for a traditional need case:

Proposition: _____.
Definitions: _____.

   I. There is a need to change the present system.
     A. Problem.
     B. Inherent defect.
     C. Extent of harm.

  II. The affirmative has a proposal for change.
     Statement of proposal: _____.

 III. The affirmative proposal would be advantageous.
     A. It would remedy the problem.
     B. Additional advantage #1: _____.
     C. Additional advantage #2: _____.

Example of the Traditional Need Case

Proposition: *Resolved:* That the federal government should establish a comprehensive program to significantly increase the energy independence of the United States.
Definitions: Operationally defined in the plan.

   I. U.S. dependence for sources of energy is harmful.
     A. U.S. is dependent on foreign oil imports.
     B. This dependence causes inflation.
       1. Inflation causes unemployment.
       2. Inflation causes death and suffering.
       3. Inflation reduces economic output.
     C. The present system cannot solve because energy independence is not a goal of the present system.

  II. Fossil fuels will run out.
     A. Fossil fuels are finite.
     B. There is a need to develop alternative energy sources.
     C. The present system cannot develop alternative sources because it lacks a comprehensive national energy program.

Plan

1. A five-member energy board with all necessary powers will be created. All necessary staff and facilities will be provided. All members will be required to retire at age seventy, with a replacement to be appointed by the board.
2. Duties of the board.
   A. Oversee programs for solar energy.
   B. License buildings equipped for solar energy.
   C. Oversee research and development of alternative energy sources.
   D. Provide tax incentives for conservation.
   E. Provide tax incentive for insulation.
3. Funding will be by a mix of cutting tax loopholes, elimination of duplicative programs, and cutting defense.
4. Enforcement by fines and/or imprisonment.

Advantage

I. Solar energy is the best energy alternative.
   A. Solar energy is cheap.
   B. Solar energy is effective.
   C. Solar energy is renewable.
   D. Solar energy is technologically feasible.

The comparative advantage case also follows definite patterns of organization:

Proposition: _____.

Definitions: _____.

   I. Affirmative plan: _____.

  II. Comparative advantage I: _____.

 III. Comparative advantage II: _____.

 IV. Comparative advantage III: _____.

Example of a Comparative Advantages Case

Proposition: *Resolved:* That the federal government should guarantee comprehensive medical care for all citizens in the United States.

Definition: Operationally defined in the plan.

Plan

I. The Department of Health and Human Services will be mandated to carry out the following objectives:
   A. All United States citizens will be guaranteed comprehensive medical care as a legal right. All medical care, with the exception of nonreconstructive cosmetic surgery, will be provided free of charge.
   B. Doctors wishing to practice medicine in the United States must practice solely under the plan. All doctors will be exclusively salaried, ini-

initially 10% above their present averages and adjusted for inflation. Doctors will be mandated to work at minimum hours.

C. Financial incentives to encourage distribution of medical personnel, as necessary, will be provided; providing for the expansion of educational facilities as needed.

D. Medical care facilities will be built or reallocated as determined by community needs.

E. All necessary quality controls will be utilized, including a drug utilization review board.

F. Transportation, education, outreach, and emergency care will be provided.

G. Increased commitment to medical research.

H. Health professionals will be exempt from sovereign immunity.

II. Funding will be obtained from the optimal combination of independent trust funds based on the income tax, diversion of funds from medical care programs no longer needed because of the affirmative proposal, and cost controls where needed.

III. Violations of the letter or intent of the affirmative proposal are punishable by loss of license, fines, imprisonment, or loss of salary.

Advantage

I. The affirmative guarantees comprehensive medical care. (The comparative advantage)

A. Access to medical care is denied millions.

B. The dual system of medical care precludes access.

C. The federal government should guarantee comprehensive medical care.
1. Access to medical care should be guaranteed.
2. Denial of access leads to death and suffering.
3. Denial of access justifies federal intervention.

The criteria case can follow one or two patterns of organization, which are outlined below:

Comparative Advantages Approach

Proposition: _____.
Definitions: _____.

I. Criteria of the present system.

II. Affirmative plan.

III. Advantages of achieving the criteria.
A. Comparative advantage I.
B. Comparative advantage II.
C. Comparative advantage III.

Traditional Need Approach

Proposition: _____.
Definitions: _____.

I. Criteria of the present system.

II. Present system fails to meet the criteria.

III. Affirmative plan.

IV. Affirmative proposal does a better job of attaining the criteria.

Example of the Criteria Case

Proposition: *Resolved:* That the federal government should establish a comprehensive program to increase significantly the energy independence of the United States.

Definitions: Operationally defined in the plan.

Criteria

I.   Any energy source used should meet four criteria.
A. An energy source should be renewable.
B. An energy source should be as inexpensive as possible.
C. An energy source should be nonpolluting.
D. An energy source should be technologically feasible.

Plan

1.   An independent, self-perpetuating board will be established. All necessary staff, facilities, and funding will be provided. All board members will retire at age seventy.
2.   Methanol.
A. Farm land will be set aside for making methanol. Ongoing research will be provided to insure the maximum yields possible.
B. Insect infested trees will be used for methanol production.
C. Ten percent of forest preserves will be cultivated for methanol production.
D. Tax credits for methanol development will be given.
E. Beginning in 1990 all cars will be designed to use methanol fuel (10% methanol and 90% gasoline).
F. Where necessary, industry will be given incentives for retooling to use methanol fuel in place of oil or coal.
3.   Research and development of energy alternatives will be provided.
4.   Funding will be provided through a mix of closing corporate tax loopholes, elimination of federal paper waste, cutting defense, and a 10% tax on alcohol and cigarettes.
5.   Violations of the plan will be punishable by fines and/or imprisonment.

I.   Methanol is a renewable energy source.

II. Methanol is an inexpensive energy source.

III. Methanol is a nonpolluting energy source.

IV. Methanol has been proven to be technologically feasible.

The net benefits case can be organized in the following way:

Proposition: _____.
Definitions: (where needed)_____.

Affirmative plan.

Rationale:

I. Net benefits of present system.
   A. Costs.
   B. Benefits.

II. Net benefits of proposed affirmative system.
   A. Costs.
   B. Benefits.

III. Relative cost-benefit ratios favor affirmative plan.

Example of Net Benefits Case

Proposition: *Resolved:* That the United States should adopt a policy to increase political stability in Latin America.
Definitions: Operationally defined in the plan.
Affirmative plan:

1. An independent, self-perpetuating board will be established. All necessary staff, facilities, and funding will be provided. All board members will retire at age seventy.
2. Duties of the board.
   A. Impose sanctions on the Pinochet regime. The severity of sanctions to be determined by the board.
   B. Oversee and report on human rights practices in Chile.
   C. Where necessary provide incentives for compliance.
   D. Develop enforcement measures that will include but not be limited to fines and/or imprisonment.
3. Sanctions and progress on human rights to be reviewed biannually.

   I. Present system.
      A. Costs.
         1. Massive human rights violations plague the Pinochet regime.
         2. Violent overthrow is inevitable.
      B. Benefits.
         We justify support in the name of stability.

   II. Affirmative system.
      A. Costs.
         Pinochet may not like the plan.
      B. Benefits.
         1. Human rights abuses would be curbed.
         2. Violent overthrow of Pinochet would be disastrous.

   III. Affirmative is net-beneficial.
      A. Present policy is destined to fail.
      B. Affirmative policy guarantees maximization of both stability and human rights.

These organizational patterns are designed to demonstrate to the judge that the affirmative has upheld its burden of proof. The judge can easily follow the debater's organization to see what the affirmative's reasoning was. The good debater carefully emphasizes each major heading and subheading so that the judge can follow the organization.

Of course, in actual competition the affirmative does not phrase its contention in debate form. Instead of saying "Our first contention is that there is a need to change the present system," the speaker says, "Contention I: Current educational standards are lacking. Subpoint A. SAT scores are falling. . . ." The contention describes the affirmative analysis and the critic can see that the basic problem is the lack of educational standards.

The internal organization of the case also is a tactical matter. The team, from its analysis, should decide whether to use a **series** or **parallel pattern of organization**. A case that is organized in serial fashion is like the older type of Christmas tree lights: If one light bulb burns out, the whole string goes dark. Lately, the manufacturers have wired lights in parallel fashion: If one light burns out, the rest of the lights remain bright.

A case that is organized in series, then, is one in which each argument depends on the preceding argument for its support. If the negative can destroy an argument, the whole case or series of arguments falls. The following is an example of a serial organization on the crime topic.

If	(1) Police should stop crime,
And if	(2) Crime is increasing,
And if	(3) The crime increase is causing a significant loss of life and property,
And if	(4) The loss of life and property is widespread,
And if	(5) Police are handicapped by court decisions on confession;
Therefore	(6) Congress should pass legislation reversing the decisions of the court
Because	(7) Several advantages will follow:
	a. The crime increase will be stopped;
	b. The loss of life and property will be stopped.
Therefore	(8) The proposition should be adopted.

Going back carefully over the series of arguments, one can see that if any of the arguments is lost, the whole case falls.

Now let us suppose the analysis suggested a parallel organization to the affirmative, whose basis is contingency. The team argues that if any one of several contingencies is true, the proposition should be accepted. The example takes a different form.

I. If any one of the following arguments is correct, then school security should be significantly increased.

    If   (1) Violence occurs in the classroom and people are injured,

    Or if   (2) Juvenile delinquents consistently disrupt classes and intimidate teachers,

    Or if   (3) High school students destroy significant amounts of equipment and school property;

    Then   High school security should be increased

    Because (1) Crimes against students will decrease;

              (2) Classroom disruption will be discouraged;

              (3) Crimes against property will decrease.

In this case the negative team must defeat all three contingencies if it is to stop the affirmative from upholding its burden of proof.

Although the parallel style of organization is more difficult to defeat, it is not necessarily the best form. It does not allow an in-depth development of each contingency because there is not enough time for a lengthy documentation. Again, the thinking debater does not *automatically* use a particular style of organization. He or she analyzes the proposition carefully and then chooses the style of organization that best fits that analysis.

Presentation

There also are tactics for presenting the affirmative's case that help fulfill the affirmative's strategy of upholding the burden of proof. The affirmative team must remember that it is not enough for it to feel that it has upheld the burden of proof. It must make the judge feel that it has succeeded in doing this. The structure of the affirmative can be critical in convincing a judge that the proposition should be adopted. An affirmative team trying to convince a judge that sex education should be included in the curriculum of elementary and secondary schools would have greater success using the comparative advantages format as opposed to the traditional need/plan format.

Affirmative speakers should remind the judge that their case is adequate for justifying adoption of the resolution. Especially during the rebuttal period, each speaker should emphasize that the affirmative contentions stand, and therefore justify the adoption of the debate proposition. Without mentioning "burden of proof," the speakers can help the judge see that the proposition must be accepted.

Maintaining the Offensive

The affirmative has many obligations. It must analyze the proposition without begging the question. It has to meet the burden of proof because the affirmative side is presumed wrong until it presents a prima facie case. But the affirmative has a major strategic advantage that helps offset the weight of its obligations.

It can interpret the topic in any way that it chooses, as long as it doesn't unfairly interpret the question. It can present any organization it chooses and can use any argument it feels will support the proposition. When the debate begins, the affirmative team knows what the major arguments will be, while the negative team does not. When the high schools debated the foreign policy topic on Latin America, debaters discovered just how much of an advantage the affirmative can have. The affirmative could begin each round knowing the ins and outs of a particular Latin American country while the negative did not know if it would be debating Honduras, Guatemala, Nicaragua, Chile, Mexico, or any one of the other smaller countries in the region. The affirmative could argue that a change in any one of these countries would increase political stability in the entire region of Latin America. The negative would need to prepare arguments for each country without knowing from round to round which country would be debated.

The affirmative team, then, is on offense; the negative team is on defense. Experienced debaters know that this is a definite advantage for the affirmative team. The team that is on the offensive at the end of the debate often is the team that wins the round. The affirmative strategy, therefore, is to begin the debate on the offensive and to maintain it throughout the debate.

The tactics for maintaining the offensive are discussed later, after two strategic approaches are considered. First, the affirmative tries to make its own case the reference point for the entire debate. Because it has carefully and tightly constructed its case, the affirmative wants the argument to center around it, not around the negative case. Second, the affirmative does everything it can to fend off the negative's attempts to put it on the defensive. Even though it knows that a good defense is often a good offense, the affirmative avoids going to the negative's ground during the debate. Just as the affirmative's case is best for the affirmative, because the affirmative constructed it, it knows that the negative's ground is dangerous because it was constructed by the negative for its own advantage.

Tactics for Maintaining the Offensive

The affirmative strategy is to begin the debate on the offensive and try to stay in this posture. Four tactics help advance the affirmative's strategy: the case, the timing, the rebuttal, and the handling of the negative's constructive argument.

The Affirmative Case

If the affirmative's case is a good one, the affirmative will stand a good chance of maintaining its offensive position throughout the debate. On the other hand, some cases are so weak that even the first affirmative speaker is on the defensive.

The tactic here is for the affirmative to choose the strongest possible arguments. If it has a choice among many strong arguments, it should choose the arguments that will be most difficult for the negative to answer. Good debaters avoid contentions that can be answered in one sentence or with one quotation; they look for contentions that force the negative to build a total argument if it hopes to reply. It should take the opposition longer to answer an argument than it took the advocate to give it. If the negative has to spend most of its time on the affirmative's ground, it obviously will have a difficult time capturing the offensive.

Timing the Presentation of Partitions

At this stage the affirmative has arrived at the pattern of organization that is to its best tactical advantage. The speakers have not decided, though, when to say what. Careful timing often makes the difference between maintaining the offensive and losing it.

The affirmative team has two speeches in which it can present its constructive case, and it can present its entire case in the first speech or save part of the case for the second speaker. This amounts to a decision to present additional contentions or additive advantages in the second speech.

Typically, when using the traditional need case, the first affirmative presents the need-for-a-change contentions, the plan, and possibly its advantages. This does not allow the team a great deal of time to develop the need-for-a-change argument. Therefore, it is easier to answer and tends to allow the first negative speaker to take the offensive. When the affirmative puts its advantages in the second speech, the negative is given less time to think of arguments to the affirmative's advantages. Finally, if the debaters are relatively inexperienced, the second speaker feels more secure knowing that three or four minutes of his or her speech can be prepared ahead of time. Even though the affirmative may choose to present additional reasons for change in the second speech, the affirmative must still present a prima facie case in the first affirmative constructive speech.

Despite the advantages in dividing the constructive case between the first two speeches, more and more debaters prefer to present the entire case during the first speech. First, this makes it more likely that the critic will fully understand the affirmative's analysis. Second, although the affirmative has less time to develop each need-for-a-change contention in depth, it can wait to see which contentions the negative wishes to challenge. The affirmative, then, does not have to waste time and evidence on arguments that may become unimportant during the debate. Finally, because the whole case has been presented, the second affirmative can spend the entire constructive speech rebuilding the affirmative's case. Should the negative present a spread attack, this may be the most important reason for presenting all of the case in the first affirmative constructive speech. The second affirmative speaker may find it difficult to adequately answer eight minutes of negative attacks in only five minutes. If the second affirmative speaker can't uphold the affirmative case already presented, it would be of little use to present three more minutes of new case arguments.

In deciding which tactic to use, the debater should consider several factors. The nature of the case obviously is the prime factor. If the reason-for-change argument requires much time to develop well, the advantages obviously should be saved for the second speech. Also, the debater should consider what is normally done in debates in his or her area. If almost all affirmative teams present their complete cases in the first speech, it might even appear unethical to save it for the second speaker. Finally, the advocate must weigh possible negative attacks, which is largely a consideration of what the negative is expected to do during the negative block (the second negative constructive speech and the first negative rebuttal). If the negative is expected to develop a strong attack during the negative block, it usually is wise to present the advantages in the first speech. If the first negative doesn't mention the proposal and advantages in her or his speech, the affirmative can deduce that the negative is saving its attack for the time in the debate when the affirmative has the least time to answer the negative's objections.

Timing the presentation of the parts of the case is also an important factor if the affirmative has a comparative advantages case. Here the debater is usually expected to present the entire constructive case in the first speech. However, it is not unusual for the second affirmative constructive speaker to present one to three additive advantages at the beginning of the second affirmative constructive speech. The debater should keep in mind the same cautions mentioned earlier.

Rebuttal Techniques

It is easy to tell when the affirmative has lost its offensive advantage. During the speeches after the opening affirmative presentation, the affirmative speakers no longer talk about their own case. Instead, the speakers begin to reply to the negative's attacks on their case. They are now in the position of *defending* against the negative's arguments. In short, they are refuting, not rebuilding.

If the affirmative properly handles its rebuttal technique, each speech should be focused on an analysis of the status of the affirmative's case in the debate rather than of the negative argument. The debater should say: "Remember, our first contention was that 'crime is on the increase'; now what did the negative have to say about that?" Instead, the defensive affirmative says: "Well, the first negative argument was that 'crime is not increasing'; here's what we have to say about that."

The distinction may be subtle, but it is very important to the affirmative strategy. In the first illustration, the affirmative speaker is debating the merits of the *affirmative* case. In the second he or she is arguing the merits of the negative case. The judge is no longer in the position of deciding if the affirmative's case still stands at the end of the debate. Now the judge must decide if the negative case stands. This, clearly, is to the advantage of the negative.

The specific tactic in each affirmative speech usually is to begin with a point-by-point analysis of the basic affirmative case to see if it still stands. The debater should go through the following steps, asking and answering each question:

1. What was the affirmative's argument?
2. How did the negative reply to it (if at all)?
3. This is why the affirmative is correct.
4. Therefore the affirmative argument still stands.

The only time this procedure is changed is in response to the negative block, when the affirmative team often must go on the defensive for one or two minutes to answer the alleged disadvantages of the affirmative's plan. In the first affirmative rebuttal, the strategy is to go to the plan attacks first, answering them as distinctly as possible but also as quickly as possible. The first affirmative rebuttalist should group together any arguments possible, explaining why one answer applies to all the arguments. After adequately handling plan attacks, the affirmative returns to the case to rebuild in the areas where the most damage has been done. It is unlikely that the first affirmative rebuttalist will have time to cover all the case arguments, so selection is important. By ending the speech with case arguments, the affirmative ends on the offense. The same strategy should be used by the second affirmative rebuttalist.

Handling Negative Constructive Arguments

A good negative team often presents its own constructive case to support the presumption that goes with the present system. It frequently is difficult, or almost impossible, for the affirmative to reply to the negative's constructive case without becoming defensive. Of course, this is one of the reasons why the negative advances a constructive argument.

Frankly, the affirmative's tactic here is to refute the negative's constructive case, a defensive move, while maintaining an offensive psychology in its attack. This is not easy to do, and to do it well requires much careful thinking and practice. There is an applicable tactic, however, that many affirmative teams have found to be successful. As the affirmative speaker refutes the negative's constructive case, he or she should continually put the negative's arguments in the affirmative's perspective.

For example, the most common negative constructive attack follows the defense of the present system strategy. The negative builds a case that directly defends the presumption. The affirmative speaker should first point to the affirmative's indictment of the present system and then see how the negative's case affects this indictment. She or he should stress the validity of the *affirmative* analysis of the goals of the present program to demonstrate that the negative's analysis has been faulty.

Supposed disadvantages of the affirmative's proposal sometimes can be handled in the context of the affirmative's proposal. The disadvantages can be grouped under specific planks of the plan. If the affirmative has thoughtfully designed the proposal, it should be able to show that the disadvantages are not likely to occur.

Throughout the refutation of the negative constructive arguments, the affirmative should engage in rebuilding, not refuting. By placing the negative's arguments in the affirmative's perspective as often as possible, the affirmative remains at least psychologically on the offensive. Negative arguments should look like attacks on the affirmative case, not like independent constructive defenses.

Narrowing the Debate

Narrowing the debate builds on the strategy of maintaining the offensive. The affirmative team wants the debate to center on its own carefully prepared grounds—home ground is the safest ground. If its entire case constitutes safe ground, exposure in less than the whole case should provide even greater safety. Therefore the thinking affirmative usually tries to force the negative to deal with only two or three issues in its case. The affirmative does this by narrowing the range of arguments as the debate progresses.

If this strategy has been successful, the last affirmative rebuttal speaker should be able to identify two or three issues that still are important to the decision and can devote the whole speech to these issues. Inasmuch as the affirmative has the "last word," it should be able to establish a limited number of issues during the last speech. Therefore, it stands a good chance of winning the debate.

Tactics for Narrowing the Debate

Because the strategy of narrowing the debate stems from the strategy of remaining on the offensive, the tactics for remaining on offense usually are the best tactics for narrowing the debate. However, the affirmative speakers consciously try to narrow the range of the arguments they will have to defend during the course of the debate.

As the debate progresses, each affirmative speaker should add perspective to the debate at the end of each speech. He or she should analyze the debate for its basic issues, for these are the arguments on which the proof of the affirmative's case depends. By the end of the debate the affirmative should have narrowed the debate to two or three key issues that the last speaker can concentrate on to establish the affirmative's argument. In so doing the entire last speech can be devoted to these issues.

Expanding the Debate

Most affirmative teams prefer to operate under the strategy of narrowing the debate. If they are successful, they stand a much better chance of winning than if a large number of issues have been developed. The only problem is that the negative teams are aware of this affirmative strategy, and they have, in recent years, been effective in **expanding the debate**. As a result, a new affirmative strategy has arisen—the use of cases that deliberately expand the debate. Some debaters call this a "spread case."

The spread case is designed to catch the negative off guard and to expand the debate to a point from which the negative can't recover. The affirmative takes advantage of the negative's plan to capitalize on any chance to expand the argument. It allows the negative to expand the debate, but in such a way that the negative's attack is blunted on all points.

The second affirmative rebuttal speech, in this case, is quite different from that in the previous discussion. Using the spread case, the last speaker points to the large number of arguments the affirmative has presented. He or she points to the arguments the second negative rebuttalist didn't discuss, then refutes objections the negative raised.

It is obvious that the affirmative's strategy of expanding the debate is difficult to handle—the debater can be defeated by her or his own strategy. However, highly skilled debaters have found it a very effective approach.

Tactics for Expanding the Debate

Since the negative normally wants to expand the range of arguments that are important in the debate, usually it is not difficult for the affirmative to carry out this tactic if it is using the spread case affirmative. The affirmative case should be constructed in the parallel style, and there should be three or four major problems or contingencies under each contention. The affirmative argues that if any one of the contingencies still stands at the end of the debate, the affirmative's proposal should be adopted. As the debate progresses, each speaker stresses that all of the contentions are important and that nothing can be ignored by the negative.

Again, this strategy usually is effective only in the hands of a very skillful debater. It is very easy for the affirmative to "spread" itself so thin that it cannot rebuild its own case, much less answer the negative's case. If the judge feels that the negative has won most of the arguments, he or she is apt to give it the decision.

Negative Strategies and Tactics

If the affirmative strategies are successfully carried out in the debate, the affirmative will almost always win the decision. On paper, at least, it looks as if the affirmative should always win. But unfortunately for the affirmative, the negative team has ideas of its own on how to win a debate. There are counterstrategies and tactics that are designed to give the negative the chance to win. And this is what excites many people about academic debating. Debate is more than an accumulative stacking of opinion quotations; it involves the clash of arguments and ideas, of strategies and tactics. It involves an accumulation of experiences in research, creative thinking, and organization as well as the use and placement of arguments, strategies, and tactics.

Obviously, most of the negative's strategies are the opposite of the affirmative's. The negative tries to uphold its presumption, to take the offensive away from the affirmative, and to expand the debate in response to the typical affirmative's attempt to narrow it.

Negative Strategies

- Upholding presumption
- Taking away the offense
- Expanding the debate

Upholding Presumption

"The present system is innocent until it is proven guilty." This basic principle is a great asset to the negative team. The negative knows that if the affirmative cannot present an adequate indictment of the present system, the negative team should win the debate. Most negative teams, however, prefer not to leave their competitive lives in the hands of the affirmative and wait to see if the affirmative does an adequate job of maintaining the burden of proof. The thinking debater strives to support the present system when on the negative side. This is the negative's basic strategy.

The tactics of this strategy will be discussed later, but at this point it can be said that the negative's strategy for **upholding presumption** focuses on three areas. First, the debater thoughtfully analyzes the present system, trying to identify its goals and checking to see if it is efficient in arriving at those goals. Then the debater analyzes the judging in his or her area to see what the critics require of the affirmative to meet its burden of proof. If the judges tend to be traditional, the negative debater knows that presumption can best be upheld if the need-for-a-change issue or comparative advantages is stressed. If the judges are flexible and encourage components and goals cases as well as need cases, the negative must be prepared to uphold its presumption over the affirmative's indictment of the system. Third, the debater must focus on the presentation of the case. The negative argument should be highlighted to emphasize that it is upholding its presumption. Good negative teams do not leave it to the judge to see the impact of their arguments; they make sure the impact is seen by pointing to it throughout the debate.

Tactics for Upholding Presumption

In this case, the negative's tactics constitute a consideration of when to apply the various negative alternatives during the debate. Each of the alternatives, except the counterplan strategy, is designed to uphold the presumption that goes with the present system.

Refutation

The negative can uphold its presumption by refuting the affirmative's case. If the case does not "stand" at the end of the debate, the presumption has been maintained, the present system is found innocent, and the negative wins the debate.

As mentioned earlier, very few negative teams prefer to rely entirely on straight refutation; rather, they combine it with other attacks. Thus, part of each of the negative speeches—with the exception of the second constructive—is partly devoted to constructive argument and partly to the direct refutation of the arguments the affirmative team asserts.

The essence of this attack is, first, **counterargument**, and, second, **perspective**. The counterargument is designed to contradict a specific affirmative argument. The debater puts the argument in perspective by showing how the defeat of the particular argument affects the affirmative's case. After each counterargument the debater talks about the status of the burden of proof. The negative might stress that his or her refutation has weakened the need-for-a-change argument or that the argument proves that the affirmative's plan cannot correct the alleged evils in the present system. Presumption is maintained, then, by directly subverting the affirmative's strategy of upholding the burden of proof.

Defense of the Present System

Defending the present system has already been discussed, and it should be clear that it is one of the best—certainly the most direct—ways for the negative to uphold its presumption. If the present system is sound, there should be no reason to adopt any proposal, including the one the affirmative advances.

The defense-of-the-present-system argument should be advanced early in the first constructive speech by the negative team. It must then be carried through the entire debate. The affirmative makes every effort to keep the negative so busy with the affirmative's case that the latter drops its defense of the status quo. Obviously, the negative wants each affirmative speaker to deal with the negative's constructive case.

Present System and Disadvantages

When combined with refutation, this negative tactic is the best way for the team to maintain its presumption. The defense of the present system comes in the first negative constructive, and the disadvantages of the affirmative's proposal are stated and developed in the second constructive. The tactics of the negative block, which sets forth the disadvantages, are discussed in the next section.

Taking Away the Offense

The affirmative is the offensive team in a debate; the negative speakers know this and it worries them. They also know, because the affirmative begins the debate on the offensive, that it is likely to maintain the offensive role throughout the debate. If it does, the negative team, of course, is forced to defend against the affirmative's attack. Because good affirmative teams construct good affirmative cases, the negative knows that as long as it is on the defensive it can expect to have trouble stopping the affirmative, and it probably will lose the debate.

One of the fundamental negative strategies, therefore, is to take away the offense—to change roles with the affirmative. If it succeeds, the affirmative is forced to debate on the negative's ground, and the negative knows that this is to its advantage. As soon as the affirmative is put in the position of defending against negative arguments instead of rebuilding its own, the affirmative is arguing defensively and the negative has become the stronger contestant. The negative, therefore, is more apt to win the decision.

As was mentioned earlier, a psychological presumption attaches to being on the offensive. The team that advances an argument can phrase it to its best advantage and to the best advantage of its evidence. The team also is likely to have the best evidence inasmuch as the argument is its own. So the negative prefers to have the debate judged in the context of negative argument. It wants the critic to be thinking in terms of whether the negative argument is valid, not whether the affirmative case is sound.

Tactics for Taking Away the Offense

The tactics discussed in this section are the most powerful tools the debater can use when on the negative side of the question. Smart debaters can put the affirmative team so much on the defensive that only the best teams can hope to win against them. In fact, negative speakers have become so effective at utilizing these tactics that many debate coaches have experimented with new debate formats that are designed to overcome what they feel is a clear negative advantage in debate. The heart of this advantage lies in the negative block that is built on the first negative speech to put the affirmative solidly on the defense.

The First Constructive

When the negative commences its assault on the affirmative's offensive position, the negative speaker typically denies the affirmative's constructive argument through refutation and defense of the present system. The essence of this first attack is that the first negative speaker provides his or her own pattern of organization and analysis, one that the negative would like to see the affirmative follow. If the negative's attack is strong enough, the second affirmative constructive speaker may have to adopt the negative's organization. The following hypothetical flow sheet illustrates the way some negative debaters carry out this tactic.

The second affirmative speaker in the example abandoned the affirmative colleague's organization in favor of the contentions and subpoints of the negative team. The affirmative is already in trouble if it does this, because it has gone on the defensive. If the affirmative doesn't adopt the negative's organization, the latter needn't despair; the affirmative still has to face the negative block, the second negative constructive, and the first negative rebuttal speeches.

Tactics for the Second Constructive

The purpose of the second negative constructive speech is to tear down the plan. With this in mind, the second negative should not find it necessary to go over arguments pertaining to the case for the plan. In most cases, to do so would leave the negative rebuttalist with very little to say. There are times, however, when the second negative may want to begin his or her speech with a couple of observations about the case. The affirmative case could have developed in such a way that the negative has a new inherency or significance argument to offer. Or the negative might feel that the case is not topical. Since each of these would be a new argument in rebuttals if left for the first negative rebuttalist, they must be presented in the second negative constructive. Another time when the second negative might advance case arguments is when first negative has too many arguments to pull through and asks his or her colleague to pull them. Whatever the reason, case arguments offered in second negative are developed as observations and are presented before moving on to plan attacks.

In structuring plan attacks, the negative wants above all to be sure the judge understands the argument. To help insure this, the debater should divide the arguments into categories: solvency, workability, and disadvantages. Most second negatives present the arguments in this

The Negative Attack

First Affirmative	*First Negative*	*Second Affirmative*

Proposition:
Definitions:
I. Need for a change
    A._____
        X _____
        X _____
    B._____
        X _____
        X _____
    C._____
        X _____
        X _____
II. Proposal:
III. Advantages:
    A._____
    B._____
    C._____
	I. Aff. has misanalyzed
	    the present system.
	
	    A. Goals:
	    B. Effectiveness
	    C. What they have
	        asserted is untrue:
	
	    1. _____
	        X _____
	        X _____
	    2. _____
	        X _____
	        X _____
	    3. _____
	        X _____
	        X _____
	Therefore, we should
	reject the affirmative
	proposal.
		I. The Neg. claims we
		    have misanalyzed the
		    present system.
		    A._____
		    B._____
		    C. These arguments
		        against our case
		        are invalid.
		    1. _____
		        X _____
		    2. _____
		        X _____
		    3. _____
		        X _____
		Therefore, the prop-
		osition should be
		accepted.

or

First Affirmative	*First Negative*	*Second Affirmative*

Proposition
I. Need for change
    A. Needless death
        and suffering is
        characteristic of
        present system
        X_____
        X_____
    B. Harm is wide-
        spread
        X_____
        X_____
II. Harm is inherent
    A. Industry perpet-
        uates harm
    B. Government is
        doing nothing
III. Plan
IV. Advantages to the
    plan
    A.
    B.
    C.
	I. Concede that harm
	    exists but argue that
	    harm is overstated
	II. Concede inherency
	III. Plan-meets-need
	    arguments
	    A. Plan does not
	        result in advan-
	        tage A
	    B. Plan does not
	        result in advan-
	        tage B
	    C. Plan does not
	        result in advan-
	        tage C
		I. Negative claims that
		    harm is overstated.
		    A.
		    B.
		II. The plan does meet
		    the needs outlined.
		    A.
		    B.
		    C.

order, although it is not necessary to do so. Disadvantages usually carry the most weight (that is, their harmful effects will offset the affirmative advantages) and therefore are generally presented last. One word of caution here: The debater should be careful not to run out of time before getting to the most important disadvantages.

It is not necessary to advance solvency and workability arguments in every round. The negative may choose not to run solvency arguments so as to provide more impact to the disadvantages. Or the negative may have too many disadvantages to even bother with solvency or workability. On the other hand, though, one should always run at least one disadvantage to offset the affirmative advantages. Many judges feel that the negative must win at least one disadvantage to carry the debate. Knowing this, the negative should carefully structure each disadvantage as if it were preparing an affirmative case. Affirmative responses should be anticipated wherever possible, with answers incorporated into the disadvantage. Care should be taken to make each disadvantage independent of the others and to make it difficult for the affirmative to group disadvantages for quick answers.

Expanding the Debate

As the affirmative's strategy of narrowing the debate grows out of its desire to remain on the offensive, the negative's strategy of expanding the debate is based on its strategy of taking away the offensive. The negative knows that the affirmative team will advance only so many arguments during the course of the debate; further, the affirmative will try to condense all its arguments into two or three major issues by the time of the last affirmative rebuttal speech. Unless the negative significantly adds to the pool of arguments, it is not likely to take away the offense.

The first negative strategy, therefore, is to expand the debate by adding a significant number of arguments. Its sharpest focus is on the contentions. The second negative focuses on solvency, workability, and disadvantages. In some instances the second negative may be asked to pick up some of the first negative arguments (as discussed earlier). In the last negative speech, the second negative will choose those case and plan arguments that the negative feels are most important. So as not to appear to be dropping other arguments, the negative should explain why the debate is being narrowed to these particular arguments. This strategy will help to put the negative on the offensive.

The other element of this strategy is preventing the affirmative from reducing the case to a few major arguments of its choice. The negative has attempted in earlier speeches to make every affirmative argument seem shaky and therefore important. The affirmative, then, is forced to deal with its entire case and with the negative's arguments as well.

Tactics for Expanding the Debate

The **negative block** consists of the second negative constructive speech and the first negative rebuttal. Because these speeches are uninterrupted in standard debate, they provide the negative with twelve to fifteen minutes of argument (depending on the time limits). The affirmative has only a four or five minute speech in its first rebuttal (to counter the block), and for this reason most judges feel that a debate usually is won or lost in this period. If the negative wastes the block, it probably will lose. If it uses it well, the negative is likely to win.

The Second Constructive

Although some debaters habitually used this speech for refutation, the second negative constructive speech should be just that—a constructive speech. The negative hopes to present eight to ten minutes of arguments that will seriously undercut the affirmative's analysis. Because most negative teams indict the affirmative's case or reason for change in the first constructive, the second negative speaker focuses on the plan area. Good negatives know that this is a fruitful area for attack. The affirmative's case falls if its proposal can't solve the problems it is designed to correct or if it has serious side effects that are worse than the problems in the present system. Also, many affirmative teams (particularly less experienced teams) pay much less attention to their proposed plan than to their need-for-a-change argument. Therefore, their evidence and argumentation in the plan area are apt to be weaker. Finally, the negative side stands a good chance of taking away the offensive with plan objections because it uses the negative's own arguments, not just responses to the affirmative's case.

Plan objections are not developed haphazardly. The good negative carefully studies the affirmative proposals it expects to encounter and those it has already heard. First, the negative builds arguments that suggest the proposal will not remedy the problem. Second, it studies the workability and practicality of the proposal. Third, the negative looks for harmful side effects that are apt to result.

The plan-meets-need analysis is based on a careful consideration of causal relationships. The affirmative has identified a problem that it says exists in the present system and claims that the problem is caused by various structural defects in that system. The affirmative's plan, then, corrects the defects, and will—it says—eliminate the problem.

The negative now uses an "even if" argument. The debaters say that even if the problem exists (which they deny), the affirmative's plan is not the proper way to correct it. The negative accuses the affirmative of misanalyzing the causal relationship. It sets out to prove that the alleged defect could not have caused the problem, and, therefore, correcting the defect would not eliminate the problem. The negative then usually argues that even if the defect caused the problem, the affirmative's proposal would not correct the defect.

Suppose, for instance, that the affirmative claimed that an increase in crime is caused by court rulings on confessions. The negative could first suggest, using the sine qua non standard, that the crime rate would have increased regardless of the courts' decisions and that "doing something" about the decisions would not stop crime. But *even if* the court decisions have "created" crime, the affirmative's change would not guarantee more confessions.

Workability is the second area for negative emphasis in the second constructive speech. Again the negative bases its attack on an "even if" analysis. Even if a need for a change exists, and even if the affirmative's proposal could meet the need—even in theory—the affirmative's plan would be unworkable. And if it cannot function mechanically, obviously there is no reason to adopt it.

Workability objections, then, focus on the mechanics of the affirmative's proposal. Has the affirmative allowed for the repeal of legislation that might block its plan, and has it called for the legislation that would allow the plan to work? One team, for instance, advocated free trade between the United States and the communist countries. It had removed the trade embargoes but had forgotten to remove the high tariffs on communist products.

The negative also considers the practicality of the affirmative's plan. If the affirmative has recommended that free medical attention be provided all citizens, it must be able to show that there will be enough doctors to handle all the patients. The affirmative's plan is expected to be only hypothetical, but it must have reasonable probability of working in the real world. Before running solvency or workability arguments, the debater should first stop to consider if a disadvantage in the same area would have greater impact. For example, instead of arguing workability on the free medical care issue, the negative could emphasize the disadvantage that the shortage of doctors would cause death and suffering. That is, rather than arguing that there will be a doctor shortage that will preclude the advantage of free care, the negative argues that free care would increase the doctor shortage and people would die because of a lack of qualified personnel to provide the free care.

The last area, then, of plan analysis is the analysis of the affirmative's proposal for possibly harmful side effects, which usually are called the "disadvantages" of the affirmative's proposal. The negative block can really begin to gain momentum here, but often the affirmative can incorporate the opponent's plan attacks into its own case, thus staying on the offensive. Disadvantages, however, must be treated as separate negative contentions in the short first rebuttal speech of the affirmative.

The negative's tactic in the disadvantages area is to present several very reasonable side effects that it suspects will follow from the plan. The negative prefers to present three or four sound objections that will be difficult to answer, rather than a large number of superficial disadvantages that can be refuted in single sentences.

Typically, a disadvantage will include three parts. First, a causal link between the disadvantage and the affirmative proposal must be established. Second, the harms must be documented and shown to be significant. And finally, the disadvantage will include an explanation of why it is unique to the affirmative's proposal. This link is important because if the same harms occur in the present system but without the affirmative's advantages, there is no longer a disadvantage caused by the implementation of the plan and no reason not to give the proposal a try.

For example, one disadvantage to the proposal for energy independence is that third world countries would starve. The argument would be developed as follows. First, the third world is dependent on its exports of oil for money. Second, the U.S. imports one-half of its oil from these countries, as documented by the affirmative. And third, U.S. independence would significantly decrease third world income and cause mass starvation. The negative might also document other harms to the loss of income.

The reason why the good negative debater develops each disadvantage thoroughly is to force the affirmative to take at least as much time (preferably more) refuting the disadvantage as was taken giving it.

Therefore, the second negative points to a serious disadvantage, shows why it is inherent in the proposal, and then documents the position.

The Second Negative
Observations About Case or Plan
1.
2.
Plan-Meets-Need or Plan-Meets-Advantages
1.
2.
3.
Disadvantages
1.
A. Harm
B. Link
C. Impact
2.
A. Harm
B. Link
C. Impact
3.
A. Harm
B. Link
C. Impact

These, then, are the tactical areas that come into focus in the second negative constructive speech. Although the organization might vary from debater to debater, the basic points will change very little, regardless of the type of affirmative case.

The First Rebuttal

One way to judge the quality of the negative team is to watch what happens in the first rebuttal speech. Because the negative speakers follow each other, teamwork is extremely important. If the second constructive speaker has already said all there is to say about the affirmative's case, the first rebuttalist will have nothing to add to the debate. It is a sign of a weak team if the second negative constructive speaker merely summarizes what the previous speaker has said. Also, it's a sign of a weak team if the first negative rebuttalist has been left with too much to say in the short rebuttal speech.

Most good teams, however, find it relatively easy to solve the teamwork problem. The first rebuttal speaker simply restricts his or her speech to what the second affirmative constructive speaker had to say about the initial negative attack on the affirmative case. This makes sense for a number of reasons: (1) This speaker should do the best job of rebuilding the first negative analysis because she or he advanced it in the first place; (2) This arrangement leaves the second constructive speaker free to think about plan attacks before the second negative speech; and (3) The negative is guaranteed that the reason for a change attack will be resubstantiated early in the rebuttal period.

The first rebuttal speaker for the negative should go through the first negative attack on the affirmative's case to see what the affirmative said about it. The first negative rebuttalist has a choice in the way he or she decides to present the arguments in the first rebuttal. First, he or she could reply carefully to each affirmative argument with counterarguments and evidence. Next, he or she could point out the negative arguments that the second affirmative speaker overlooked, explain their importance, and ask for the affirmative's reply. Or the first negative rebuttalist could choose to take the offensive. This involves picking five to eight arguments that have been made by the affirmative and the negative on the case. These arguments would then be presented in a format to the advantage of the negative. These arguments would include such things as negative philosophy, inherency, significance, and minor repairs. This leaves the first affirmative rebuttalist with a very difficult decision. She or he can either follow the negative structure and debate on the defense or try to pull the negative structure back into the case structure. In many instances the first affirmative rebuttalist will choose to follow the negative structure because of time pressures. The following chart shows how the entire negative block should look.

Essence of the Negative Block

This phase of the negative attack is, in essence, one long negative speech. Its strategic goal is to overwhelm the affirmative rebuttal speakers by presenting a great deal of very damaging data. The tactic is to present carefully worked out constructive arguments and good rebuttal arguments and to avoid duplication between the two speakers.

Both of the speakers lend perspective to their arguments by showing how the affirmative's case has been affected, but the end of the first rebuttal is the only time at which a summary occurs during the negative block. Nonthinking debaters seem to feel a compulsion to summarize the debate as it has come down so far at the beginning and end of every speech. The wise negative team begins the second constructive with a short forecast of what is to come during the negative block and ends the block with a single summary at the end of the rebuttal.

The Negative Block	
Second Negative Constructive	*First Negative Rebuttal*

Forecast of negative block
Even if there were a need for a
change in the present system . . .
Observations about case or plan
1.
2.
Plan-Meets-Need
1.
2.
3.
Disadvantages
1.
  A. Harm
  B. Link
  C. Impact
2.
  A. Harm
  B. Link
  C. Impact
3.
  A. Harm
  B. Link
  C. Impact
	The affirmative has misanalyzed the
	present system
	1. Goals
	  Aff. reply:
	  Neg. answer:
	2. Effectiveness
	  Aff. reply:
	  Neg. answer:
	3. What they have asserted is untrue
	  A.
	    Aff. reply:
	    Neg. answer:
	  B.
	    Aff. reply:
	    Neg. answer:
	  C.
	    Aff. reply:
	    Neg. answer:
	Summary and perspective

The negative block is a strong strategic force in the debate because it is uninterrupted. And, more important, the affirmative team has only two short speeches in which to reply to it. The bulk of this reply obviously must come in the first affirmative rebuttal.

Narrowing the Debate

This is relevant only as a response to the affirmative spread strategy, and the spread case depends (in theory) on the negative speakers being nonthinking debaters. If they are, they'll repeat their habitual strategy and spread themselves so thin that the affirmative will win.

The tactics of responding to the spread case are complex, but the strategy is simple. The negative must narrow the affirmative's case so that it can put a great deal of evidence into a few arguments that truly penetrate the affirmative's analysis. At the same time, the negative advances its own arguments, particularly by centering on the disadvantages of the affirmative's plan. The idea is to defeat the affirmative with its own strategy. If the negative is successful, the debate ends with the negative maintaining a consolidated case and the affirmative hopelessly trying to defend a case that has spread out into an array of difficult arguments.

Tactics for Narrowing the Debate

The main negative strategies for facing the affirmative spread case are to narrow the range of arguments and concentrate on the disadvantages of the affirmative's proposal. The tactical burden for carrying out the first strategy falls on the first negative constructive speaker; the burden for the second strategy falls on the second speaker.

When the first negative speaker turns to the analysis of the first affirmative speech, he or she will find that the affirmative has presented a contingency argument, arranged in parallel fashion. The affirmative has asserted that if any one of several things is true, the affirmative's proposal should be adopted. The first thing the speaker should do is try to destroy the contingency analysis. The first negative should argue that the contentions do not represent contingencies and that the negative has to prove that any one of them is true to win the argument.

For example, a spread case on the Vietnam issue asserted that the United States should withdraw from Vietnam if: (1) the United States could not win politically; or (2) the United States could not win militarily; or (3) a victory in Vietnam would not stop further communist aggression. Many negative teams simply turned the contingency case back on the affirmative by arguing that if any of the arguments were valid, the United States should continue its involvement in Vietnam.

The second negative tactic comes into focus during the second negative constructive speech. Presenting the normal disadvantages attack, the second speaker can demonstrate that even if the contingency argument were valid, the affirmative's proposal should be rejected because of its inherent disadvantages. Even if the affirmative succeeded in spreading the negative arguments too thin, the disadvantages argument would justify the rejection of the proposition.

Responding to Opposition Strategies

Affirmative Responses to the Negative Block

Because of the power of the negative block, the prospects for an affirmative team seem rather dim. However, teams manage to win debates even when they are on the affirmative side. In recent years affirmatives have begun to win more often than negatives. The years of "When given the choice, choose negative" are gone. Most elimination rounds find the team winning the toss choosing to be affirmative. The authors have noticed at tournament after tournament that the teams that make it through the preliminary rounds to the elimination rounds are about as good as other teams on the negative, but they excel on the affirmative side. This probably means that the better teams have learned to overcome the weight of the negative block.

The key affirmative speech with which to counter the negative block is the first affirmative rebuttal. Although traditionally the first speaker position has been that of the weaker team member, most debaters and coaches now realize that a debate is won or lost in the first affirmative rebuttal. Therefore, the first speaker must be an excellent, thinking debater with a solid knowledge of debate strategy and tactics.

The strategies of the first rebuttal are the same as the general affirmative strategies that were mentioned earlier. The speaker wants to end the speech having upheld the burden of proof. He or she wants the affirmative to be on the offensive; that is, to deal in the context of the affirmative's case. Ideally, the range of arguments in the debate should be as narrow as possible. The tactics for doing this are rather easy to describe but hard to put into practice.

First, the affirmative rebuttal speaker wants to cover all of the material that was presented in the negative block. This always means going to the plan attacks presented in the second negative constructive speech first. Obviously, the first affirmative rebuttalist cannot begin to provide detailed answers to the many arguments that were presented, but he or she can utilize tactics that will make it possible to talk about everything in just a few minutes.

1. *Prepare answers to negative plan objections.* This is where the affirmative rebuttal sheet (discussed in the next chapter) becomes very important. The debater should carefully prepare—ahead of time—to

answer negative objections. All the anticipated objections should be listed, and the shortest possible replies should be developed. Preferably, the first rebuttalist should be able to give a one-sentence counterargument that refutes the objections, along with a brief, powerful quotation to support the counterargument. Hours of preparation are spent here to save valuable seconds in debate, but the good first affirmative rebuttal speaker knows that the time is well spent. The difference between winning and losing a debate can be thirty seconds that were wasted during this rebuttal.

2. *Adapt the proposal to negative plan objections.* The best way to answer negative plan objections is to have a plan that does not allow the disadvantages to result. Thinking affirmative teams carefully adjust their proposals as the season progresses to account for negative objections.

For example, if the affirmative's proposal on the crime topic says that a lawyer need not be present for a confession to be valid, negative objections might be that: (1) The civil rights of citizens would be abridged; (2) Coercion could cause innocent people to plead guilty; and (3) People could confess to first-degree murder although they were guilty only of manslaughter. If the affirmative's proposal is adjusted to contain a provision for state-appointed neutral observers at all confessions, all of these objections could be answered in one sentence. The observer could inform the judge of the manner in which the interrogation proceeded and the judge could decide if the defendant's civil rights were violated, if the defendant had been coerced, or if he or she was led to plead guilty to the wrong crime.

The important point is that negative teams often do not listen carefully to the details of the affirmative's proposal. In this example the negative might present the standard objection to a confession case without accounting for the specific provisions of the affirmative's plan. Wise affirmative teams adjust their proposals to take care of standard objections.

3. *Consolidate negative arguments.* There are few debates in which the negative fails to leave the first speaker with eight or ten objections to answer. If the first affirmative rebuttalist talked about every plan objection, the whole speech would be gone without ever returning to the affirmative's case. Fortunately for the affirmative, there are few debates in which the negative plan objections cannot be consolidated, and the tactic for doing this is to take several objections and point out that all of them result from the same supposed flaw in the

affirmative's proposal. Often, two or three counterarguments can answer the negative plan objections.

4. *Return to the affirmative case.* After answering the negative plan objections, the first affirmative rebuttal speaker should return to the basic affirmative case. This means that she or he will review the basic affirmative rationale for change, incorporating the negative arguments of the first rebuttal. The strategy is to put the affirmative case back into the debate showing that the negative's attacks on the reason-for-change argument really do not apply or are invalid. The last part of the speech, then, should be devoted to the affirmative case.

5. *Pull the important affirmative arguments through the negative block and into the affirmative rebuttal.* One of the major reasons why many affirmative teams seem to be winning the debate during the constructive speeches, only to lose the round in the rebuttals, is that the important affirmative issues got lost after the negative block. Of course, this is one of the tactics of the negative team. It wants the affirmative to come over to the negative case, which seems overwhelming after the two back-to-back speeches.

However, the negative tactic can easily be upset if the first affirmative rebuttalist pulls the affirmative issues through the block into his or her speech. The first affirmative rebuttalist should try to narrow the debate on the affirmative's ground. Typically, all that has to be said is: "There are three issues that have been really important in this debate. It is clear, at this point, that we must accept the affirmative proposal unless the next negative speaker can show that we are wrong. Those issues, remember, are. . . ."

By choosing important affirmative issues, such as whether a structural defect exists, the affirmative knows that it will be arguing where it is strongest. It hopes that the second negative rebuttal speaker will devote his or her time to those issues and that the judge will expect that that will be done. If the first affirmative rebuttalist comes back to affirmative ground, the negative block will have been successfully overcome. If not, the judge may penalize the affirmative.

In addition to covering all of the affirmative case, the affirmative may pull issues (usually more of a summary than an analysis). A better strategy would be to narrow the debate down to the issues the affirmative wants to pull. Most first affirmative rebuttalists will be facing time problems. It is much better to cover several key issues well than to run out of time halfway through the case or merely repeat each part of the case.

The five tactics for dealing with the negative block may sound easy, but they are rather hard to carry out. There is no question that the affirmative faces a difficult task in overcoming the negative block, but, lest panic set in, the first affirmative rebuttalist should remember that the judge is well aware of the problem. In fact, the critic probably has tried the first affirmative rebuttal position at one time or another, and if the speaker does not cover every negative argument in this short speech, the critic is likely to understand. Whether or not the judge will be very upset if some of the arguments are saved for the last rebuttal will depend on the importance of the issues left for the last rebuttal.

The important thing is that the debater get to tactics 4 and 5. The first affirmative rebuttalist must return to the affirmative case and pull the important affirmative arguments into the rebuttal. If he or she fails to do this, having the most understanding critic in the world won't help. The debate, then, will center on the validity of the negative case, and the affirmative constructive case may never be mentioned with force again. Few affirmatives can hope to be successful if this happens.

Affirmative Responses to the Counterplan

As Chapter 4 suggested, the counterplan is becoming a more common negative strategy. Every debater can expect to meet a counterplan a few times during a debate season—but it has been the authors' experience that few affirmative teams know what to do to respond to the counterplan. This brief section presents the guidelines for that response. If the suggestions are followed, negative teams will think twice before they take the counterplan approach.

First, it is necessary to recall the fundamentals of the counterplan strategy. The negative team surrenders its presumption, admitting that there is a need to make a change in the present system. The negative argues that its proposal, which is different from the one implied by the debate topic, is the change that should be made. The affirmative team still has the burden of proof of the proposition, and it has the obligation to show that the proposal implied in the proposition would be better than the negative counterplan.

The first step in responding to the counterplan is to keep the same basic affirmative strategies that operate under other negative attacks.

The affirmative still upholds its burden of proof, maintains the offense, and narrows the debate. The affirmative, then, should not change its basic attack. The worst thing that can happen is for the affirmative to assume suddenly that its obligations are different; for instance, that it no longer has the burden of proof of the proposition.

For a better understanding of the affirmative's tactics, the debater can turn to the second affirmative constructive speech to see what the tactics of that speech are. The first affirmative has already presented the normal affirmative case, and the first negative speaker has responded by saying that the negative agrees that there is a need for a change—but the affirmative's proposal is not the change to adopt. Also, the first negative has presented the counterplan, which, the negative alleges, is the better approach to the problems of the present system.

The second affirmative should begin by reviewing the affirmative's analysis of the problems in the present system. He or she should put particular emphasis on the structural defect that makes the problems inherent in the system. Because the negative has conceded that the problems are evil and widespread, the second affirmative constructive speaker need do no more than explain the affirmative's analysis of the need for a change.

The negative counterplan must solve the problems the affirmative defines, and the debate centers in the area on the structural defect. The negative is likely to deny the affirmative's analysis here or to suggest further defects that the affirmative is supposed to have overlooked. If the negative team has suggested that there are other defects in the present system, the affirmative should either deny that the defects exist or suggest that the present system is taking care of them. Further, it is possible that if the alleged defects exist, they in no way affect the ability of the affirmative's plan to solve the problems of the present system as the affirmative defined them.

After this groundwork, which is necessary to uphold the affirmative's burden of proof and to lay the basis for later attacks on the counterplan, the affirmative speaker is ready to move on to a direct comparison of the affirmative and negative proposals. The debate now becomes one of comparative advantages. The basic question is: Should the affirmative proposal or the negative counterplan be adopted to solve the problems of the present system?

The first criterion for answering this is to see which plan best "meets the need." This is where most counterplans fall short, because good affirmative teams build such tight cases that only their specific proposals can remedy the inherent problems of the present system. The affirmative speaker should carefully compare the proposals, stressing the ability of the affirmative plan to do the job and the inability of the counterplan to correct the defect. If the case has been structured properly, inability should be inherent in the counterplan because the only way the negative could solve the defect is by presenting the same proposal.

The next tactic is less important, but it can be very damaging to the counterplan. The speaker should compare the relative costs, workability, practicality, and efficiency of the two proposals. Even if both proposals would solve the problem, which plan would be better? If the affirmative can demonstrate that its plan is better, its attack on the counterplan is complete.

Even though it looks as if the affirmative has a definite advantage in the counterplan debate, there are several ways in which it can lose.

1. *Misanalyze the proposition.* If the affirmative proposal does not really correct the defects of the present system, the counterplan that is designed to do this will win. This error most often takes the form of the affirmative's choosing a problem that would fit well in some other debate topic but not in the topic it is debating.

2. *Forget to uphold the burden of proof.* Many debaters think that a counterplan debate is just a debate between two plans, but this is not true. The affirmative still must present a prima facie case for the resolution. The second negative rebuttalist can legitimately argue that *even if the counterplan were rejected,* the affirmative's proposal should not be accepted because the affirmative has failed to support it adequately.

3. *Let the negative shift its ground.* The only legitimate counterplan is one that is very different from the affirmative's proposal but nevertheless corrects the same problems. The affirmative has the right to define the problems, or there would be two different, unrelated debates, with no clash between them. Some negative teams, however, get confused and present counterplans that are designed to remedy entirely different problems in the present system. If the affirmative then tries to show that its plan will correct the negative's problems, the affirmative is taking on more than it has to and may well confuse the debate enough to lose it.

4. *Lose the offensive in the debate.* If the affirmative lets itself get into the position of defending against the negative counterplan, it may easily

lose the debate. Instead, the affirmative's case must be at the front of the judge's mind. The negative must be kept in the position of defending against it.

Cross-Examination Debating

Thus far our discussion has focused only on the strategies and tactics that are used in the traditional debate format. Other strategies and tactics, however, become important when the debater participates in cross-examination debating.

Cross-examination heightens the clash of ideas and arguments in a debate.

Nature and Purpose of Cross-Examination Debating

In a traditional debate, the two debate teams never talk directly to each other; they discuss the other team and its arguments, in the third person, with the judge. In **cross-examination debate**, however, each of the four constructive speeches is followed by question-and-answer periods in which the speaker who has just spoken is questioned by a member of the opposing team. In traditional debate, because the two teams never directly confront each other, the participants can go through an entire debate without clashing with each other as individuals. One team asks a question, which the other team ignores, misinterprets, or fails to answer for lack of time.

Cross-examination, on the other hand, is designed to heighten the clash of ideas and arguments, giving each team the chance to penetrate ever deeper into the ideas and analyses of the opposition. For this reason many coaches prefer good cross-examination debating to good traditional debating. Nobody, however, seems to enjoy cross-examination debate when the debaters do not know how to handle cross-examination. The purpose of this section is to provide a few insights into cross-examination debates, which the authors, at least, would like to see become more popular.

Strategic Purpose of the Questions

Even though debaters are given much freedom during the cross-examination period, there are basically three purposes for asking direct questions of the opponent. The questions should be designed to provide clarification, gain an admission, or provide data for later speeches.

Clarification

One of the great advantages of cross-examination debating is that the debaters have the opportunity to clarify their opponent's stand. If a debater wishes, he or she can ask to have anything that the other team has said repeated or explained. Detailed documentation can be requested, or the debater can pursue the implications of various arguments.

Admissions

It is difficult to get a debater to admit anything, especially that something might be wrong with his or her logic, but the skilled examiner can often use the opposition as evidence against himself or herself. Logicians have suggested for more than two thousand years that evidence from a reluctant witness is very good evidence for an advocate. If the debater can get the opposition to admit flaws in its own case, little additional evidence will be needed to prove the debater's points. One of the purposes of cross-examination, therefore, is to gain an admission from the opponent that will damage its case. (The tactics for doing this are discussed a little later.)

Obtain Data for Later Speeches

This purpose obviously overlaps the two that were mentioned above. The debater must remember, though, that cross-examination does not take place in a vacuum. The real purpose of examining the opponent is to get material that will be useful in subsequent constructive and rebuttal speeches. One of the things that irritates critics in poor cross-examination debating is that debaters rarely follow through on the answers they get; in fact, the questions often seem totally unrelated to the debate. The debater should realize that many judges feel that admissions or points won during cross-examination do not apply to the decisions until they are mentioned during a formal debate speech.

Cross-Examination Tactics

Tactics of the Examiner

What follows is a relatively short list of tactics the debater can follow when in the role of the examiner.

1. *The examiner should begin with careful, analytical preparation.* Anyone who is even slightly familiar with legal strategy knows that cross-examination is a vital part of the trial. Legal cross-examination is not an unplanned, extemporaneous affair but a carefully prepared and reasoned approach to witnesses. The good attorney avoids asking questions of a witness if ignorant of how the witness will answer. The same is true of cross-examination in debate.

   The first tactic, then, for the examiner is to carefully analyze the case he or she expects to hear. Then, being ready to account for what the opposition actually says in the debate, he or she should prepare specific questions that contribute to his or her attack. Each question should lead to a point of clarification or of admission. The examiner should be fairly certain of the answer that will be given to the question being asked. Few things are more damaging than a surprise answer that helps the opponent.

2. *The examiner should develop simple questions.* The purpose of the question is to get an answer, not to confuse the opponent. Each question should be direct and simple so that the examinee cannot fail to

understand it. If the examinee then tries to be evasive by pretending to misunderstand, the judge will quickly see through this ploy.

The examiner should be particularly careful not to ask complex or negative questions. A complex question is one that requires two answers. A negative question is characterized by "Is it not true that . . . ?" and is too difficult to understand and answer.

3. *The examiner should develop limited questions.* Because the examinee knows the purpose of cross-examination, the examiner can be assured that he or she will be on guard. No debater will make large admissions that will damage the case. However, the skillful debater can lead the examinee in little steps that do not *seem* dangerous. One of the authors witnessed the example that follows in a debate on the censorship of books. The examinee was on the affirmative side, in favor of eliminating all censorship, and the examiner wanted the examinee to contradict his argument that no book is a corrupting influence. He knew that the whole affirmative case rested on this argument, and the examinee would be very careful in his answers, but limited questions prevented the examinee from seeing the implications of the questions.

EXAMINER: "Are you a religious person?"

EXAMINEE: "Well, yes."

EXAMINER: "Would you recommend the Bible to people who want to become more religious?"

EXAMINEE: "Yes."

EXAMINER: "Would you recommend it, say, to a children's Sunday school class?"

EXAMINEE: "Of course."

EXAMINER: "Do you think the Bible might make the children more religious?"

EXAMINEE: "Yes."

EXAMINER: "Now, turning to a different subject, do you believe in education?"

EXAMINEE: "Yes."

EXAMINER: "Do you believe in using textbooks and movies to supplement class work?"

EXAMINEE: "Yes."

EXAMINER: "Why?"

EXAMINEE: "Well, because they help the student. This seems like a waste of time. What's your point?"

EXAMINER: "My point is this. If children can be influenced religiously by the Bible and educationally by books and movies, how can you argue that pornographic books have no influence?"

EXAMINEE: "Well . . ."

4. *The examiner should ask worthwhile questions.* There is no rule in debate that says the examiner must use all of the cross-examination time (or all of the speaking time for that matter). Each question should be worthwhile, or it should not be asked. Debaters who use cross-examination poorly often ask a question just to hear the opponent say yes. The answer may never be used for any purpose, or the question may not even pertain to the debate.

   The wise examiner directs questions at topics that are most important to the opponent's case. Questions of clarification are about relevant items, not unimportant details. Questions to gain admission often focus on the points of the opponent's case that bear heavily on the burden of proof or presumption.

5. *The examiner should use the answer in later speeches.* This point has already been made but it should be stressed again. The skillful debater refers to the questions and answers at the first opportunity during a constructive or rebuttal speech. This guarantees that the critic will see the relevance of the cross-examination period to the debate.

6. *The examiner should ask questions fairly and honestly.* This, in many ways, is the most important point of all. Although the examiner is in control of the question period and has a great deal of latitude in what he or she does, the examiner should be honest with and considerate of his or her opponent. It should be remembered that the examinee is *not* required to give yes or no answers, has the right to ask for clarification of the questions, and can be expected to avoid dangerous admissions. The debater who remains honest and cool-headed can expect to be successful at cross-examination debating.

Tactics of the Examinee

The examinee, like the examiner, can follow a set of tactics to improve his or her ability to answer questions without being afraid of destroying his or her own case.

1. *The examinee should analyze and prepare for questions.* The thinking debater prepares for the role as carefully as he or she prepares to ask questions. The case should be carefully analyzed, both affirmative and negative, to see what questions would be most likely for the opponent to ask. Answers should be carefully prepared or the case adjusted so that the questions are no longer relevant.

   Many debaters take advantage of intensive practice to sharpen their ability to answer questions, and practice debates with fellow squad members can be very useful. Also, colleagues should practice questioning each other. Usually, they are very familiar with the strengths and weaknesses of the case, and their questions should be "better" than those any opponent can be expected to ask.

2. *The examinee should think ahead.* In answering each question, the examinee should carefully think of the implications of the answers. The examinee in the censorship example should have seen where the examiner was leading him. He could have avoided the trap by saying that the Bible could make children more religious only if they are already religious, that books and movies can help students learn only if they are ready to learn. Correspondingly, he could have argued that pornographic books could influence only those who are already perverted.

3. *The examinee should answer questions honestly and fairly.* As the last chapter of this text indicates, the credibility of the debater often is a major element in his or her effectiveness. Only by answering questions fairly and honestly can the debater maintain credibility. Critics are as upset by debaters who avoid answering questions or who fill up time with long answers as they are by the unethical examiner.

What Cross-Examination Is Not

1. *It is not a time to present arguments.* One of the rules of cross-examination debating is that the cross-examination period consists of questions and answers. Debate critics usually are very severe in en-

forcing this requirement, and they watch carefully for violations, such as questions that begin "Are you aware of the fact that . . . ?"

2. *It is not a time to perform.* One of the reasons that many people become disenchanted with cross-examination debating is that for some strange reason debaters think the examination period is a time to show off their skills as fledgling attorneys. Doing a poor imitation of Perry Mason, the performing debater will shout at his or her opponent and strut back and forth with thumbs dramatically hooked in the vest. Such behavior, clearly, is to be avoided.

3. *It is not a place for trickery.* It has been mentioned several times that the best way to handle cross-examination is honestly and fairly. However, the authors have been amazed at the number of immature debaters who look to gimmicks for getting the best of their opponents. There are two reasons for not trying to trick the opponent during cross-examination. First, trickery is unethical and inconsistent with debate, which is formal argumentation that is based on reasoning and evidence. Second, *there are no effective tricks.* Inexperienced debaters often think that the only difference between them and champion debaters is that the latter know the "tricks of the trade." They soon find out that the only "trick" that really works is taking the path of most resistance to achieve superior research, organizational, and competitive skills. Debaters who try to use other tactics soon find that they lose more debates than they win.

Summary

The students who have carefully read this chapter have covered a great deal of difficult ground. They have looked at the major strategies and tactics, affirmative and negative, that come into play during a round of debate. Even though the strategies of competitive presentation often are subtle and difficult to understand, debaters must learn them. They are as much a part of good debating as the speaker's stand or the evidence cards. Students who fail to study the strategies shortchange themselves competitively and—more important—lose one of the most important educational advantages of debating.

Questions for Discussion

1. What is the difference between using a series and a parallel form of organization? Discuss the strategic advantages of using each.

2. The affirmative has the strategic option to expand or narrow a debate. In what circumstances should the affirmative try to expand the debate?

3. How does the affirmative decide what to include in the first affirmative speech?

4. When maintaining the offensive, the affirmative will usually begin with a point-by-point analysis of the case to see if it stands. The exception is the first affirmative rebuttal. What procedure should the first affirmative rebuttal use in response to the negative block?

5. For the negative, what is the value of the negative block? How can the affirmative overcome the negative block?

6. Why does the negative want to take away the affirmative offense?

7. What tactics can the negative use to maintain presumption?

8. In cross-examination the examiner and examinee have certain responsibilities (or tactics) they should fulfill. Discuss each of these.

Activities

1. Before debating, detail (in writing) the strategies to be used and the tactics that will help carry them out. This exercise should be done prior to your practice debate.

2. Listen to a debate. Follow the debaters as they carry out the strategies of their side of the proposition. Outline the strategies used. How did the teams do in fulfilling the strategies? How could they improve?

3. Using your affirmative case, outline the analysis in both a parallel and a series pattern of organization. Which would be best for your affirmative case area? Why?

4. Using an affirmative plan from Chapter 3, Activity 6, outline workability, solvency, and disadvantage arguments. Assess the impact of each. List the arguments in terms of the priority of their impact on an affirmative.

5. Using the flow of a debate, rework the first affirmative rebuttal. How could the affirmative better consolidate the negative arguments?

6. In the last three chapters, you have been outlining affirmative and negative arguments. Take these arguments and work out possible cross-examination questions. Next, provide answers to the questions.

Chapter 6

Strategic Refutation and Rebuttal

Objectives and Key Terms

After studying Chapter 6, you should be able

1. To recognize the logical fallacies of argumentation. These include fallacies of factual arguments, of value arguments, and of causal arguments, as well as analytical fallacies in debate.

2. To explain the strategies and tactics of refutation and rebuttal. This includes how to anticipate possible arguments by using a rebuttal sheet and how to prepare for actual arguments.

3. To explain the tactics of refutation and rebuttal during the debate round.

4. To think through and prepare with evidence affirmative and negative briefs.

5. To produce a clear, understandable flow of a debate.

6. To explain and demonstrate how to answer an argument in a debate round. This skill includes the statement, counterargument, evidence, and perspective.

In order to fulfill the objectives in this chapter, you will need to understand the following terms:

logical fallacies

fallacies of factual arguments

fallacies of value arguments

fallacies of causal arguments

analytical fallacies

debate brief

flow sheeting

T hus far you have examined theories, strategies, and tactics that lay the groundwork for successful debating. Yet, there is still much more to be learned about debating.

The student must be able to do more than merely guide his or her own attack through research, constructive argument, and competitive strategies. He or she must be able to penetrate the argument of the opposition and to defend against the opponent's refutation. In order to carry an argument through an entire debate, the debater must master the tools of attack and defense.

Attack and defense are the major considerations of this chapter. Refutation, or attack, may be defined as the process by which your opponent's arguments are challenged. Rebuttal, or defense, is the process by which your own arguments are rebuilt. Although the strategy and tactics of refutation and rebuttal are the main items of concern here, the first topic for discussion is the logic of attack and defense. Just as constructive argument involves the logic of building arguments, refutation and rebuttal have their own logical bases: the logic of fallacies.

The Logic of Refutation and Rebuttal

This section deals with the **logical fallacies** of argumentation and analysis. By thoroughly understanding the "illogical possibilities," a debater can become very effective at refutation and rebuttal.

An argument is fallacious if its conclusion is not justified by the evidence that has been presented in support of it. For example, the evidence might be correct, and a conclusion might be perfectly true, but the logic of the argument itself may not justify the conclusion. Or the logic of an argument might be valid, but the evidence may be faulty. A fallacy can be deliberate or accidental, but the result is faulty reasoning.

Fallacies of Factual Arguments

As you learned in Chapter 1, a **factual argument** has as its conclusion a statement of fact. The advocate maintains that something exists or does not exist or is or is not true. Further, there are three general sources of evidence for factual arguments: experiences that the debater and judge have had in common, reliable statistics, or authoritative opinion.

Personal Experience

When using personal experience to demonstrate that a factual argument is true, the debater risks creating a fallacious argument on at least two levels. Personal experience may simply be invalid, or one's generalizations from that experience may be faulty.

A debater once argued that no poverty existed in his home town, Colorado Springs; the student suggested that he had lived there all his life and had never seen a poor person. Certainly, some people had more money than others, but nobody was really poor. The debater hoped that his argument would stand as an example of one place in which a general poverty program would be unnecessary, but his argument could be regarded as fallacious on either of the two levels mentioned above.

Perhaps the debater's report of his experience was untrue—a young man from an upper middle-class home might not recognize poverty. It could be reasoned that less fortunate classmates skipped lunch because they were dieting. Also, rundown neighborhoods could be discounted because "that kind of people just don't take care of their homes." Or perhaps the generalization was faulty—one student's experience may not justify a generalization about an entire city. The latter was likely in this case, because the debater's environment may well have been limited to the best areas of town.

Statistics*

Almost everyone has heard the expression "Figures don't lie but liars figure." Prime Minister Disraeli put it even stronger when he said, "There are three kinds of lies: lies, damned lies, and statistics." These cynical comments do not mean that statistics should always be distrusted, but they indicate that statistics are subject to fallacies.

Strictly speaking, a statistic is a tool that allows a researcher to make inferences about the nature of reality. Figures are manipulated through mathematical procedures to yield more data than are already known. For instance, "average" is a statistic that yields more information than a long column of figures. Sophisticated statistical techniques can tell us a good deal more about the nature of reality.

A statistical argument can be fallacious for many different reasons, but three problems are most common: the fallacious sample, the nature

---

*The authors recommend that *every* debater read the excellent book on this subject by Darrell Huff, *How to Lie with Statistics* (New York: W. W. Norton, 1954).

of material that is left out of the statistical report, and the nature of the process of reasoning from statistics to conclusion (the non sequitur).

1. *The Fallacious Sample.* Many of the statistics that debaters use are sampling statistics. The principle involved in sampling is that a look at one part of the population will yield information about the population as a whole. For example, to determine the average class size at a particular school, one might determine the average size of ten classes chosen at random. If the sample was valid, it could be assumed that the average obtained was valid for the school. Public opinion pollsters don't interview everyone in the country. They carefully sample a few thousand persons and often can accurately predict the outcome of an election.

   But the sampling process can go astray if, for instance, the sample does not represent the whole. This was the case in the 1936 presidential poll mentioned earlier. The *Literary Digest* assumed that a sample of telephone subscribers was representative of the electorate. What they overlooked was the fact that many people—in this case Democrats—couldn't afford telephones during the Depression. A more recent example can be found in the 1980 presidential election. The weekend before the election, the race was being described as "extremely close." Yet, on election day Ronald Reagan won by one of the largest landslides ever.

   Other problems also can arise, even if the sample is legitimate. Statistics frequently are gathered through questionnaires, but researchers know that only 10 to 15 percent of those who receive questionnaires can be expected to answer them. Accordingly, a poll of a sample of police chiefs that tried to determine police effectiveness received answers only from those who were satisfied with their departments. Those who weren't satisfied were reluctant to admit it.

   People sometimes lie to interviewers. A famous study revealed that *Harper's* magazine was one of the most popular in the United States, but the number of subscribers, as projected by the poll, was several million more than the figures *Harper's* reported. Because they wanted to appear "cultured" to the interviewers, many people simply lied about the magazines they read.

2. *Material Left Out of a Report.* Debaters should be very careful of the unlabeled graph and the statistical table that do not detail the methods used therein and the kinds of statistics being reported. Liars can

"figure" by choosing the kind of average that best fits their bias. By not reporting the *kind* of average they used, they leave their readers in the position of accepting an argument that may be fallacious.

There are three kinds of averages: the mean, the median, and the mode. The mean is the arithmetic average, the total divided by the number of scores. The median is the point below and above which 50 percent of the scores fall. The mode is simply the score that appears most frequently.

The following table shows how one can choose the best statistic to support one's bias and not report the average used.

Income in "Magic City" Subdivision
Family A earns $30,000 per year
Family B earns $20,000 per year   Mean = $17,785.71
Family C earns $19,000 per year
Family D earns $15,000 per year   Median = $15,000.00
Family E earns $13,500 per year
Family F earns $13,500 per year   Mode = $13,500.00
Family G earns $13,500 per year

An unscrupulous person could manipulate these averages to suit a particular cause. In an effort to attract new business, one might say that the average (mean) family income in Magic City is $17,785.71 per year. Or one could quote the median, $15,000, to show that Magic City is the "average American city." On the other hand, it could be argued that the poor citizens of Magic City just can't afford to pay taxes: Their average income is only $13,500 per year (mode). Using the mode would make a stronger argument against high property taxes than, say, the mean.

Researchers who are ethical carefully label their statistics so that the reader can see what the statistics actually mean. Fallacies can be expected, especially in unlabeled statistics and in statistics that are provided by sources with vested interests.

3. *The Non Sequitur.* The Latin phrase *non sequitur* applies to many kinds of argument besides statistically based factual arguments. Non sequitur stands for "does not follow" and is used by logicians to describe any fallacious argument in which the conclusion does not follow from the evidence. Non sequitur arguments also are heard every day. A petulant sweetheart might say, "You never give me presents!

You don't love me!" A debater might say, "I'm due to win; I've lost three debates in a row." Or a debater might argue, "The public schools no longer need to spend large sums of money on sex education in secondary schools because teenage pregnancy has dropped by 50 percent."

Statistical non sequiturs usually take the form of the last example: the statistics are valid, but the evidence and the conclusion pertain to two different things. Therefore, one cannot say that the conclusion follows from the evidence, even if the evidence and the conclusion separately are valid.

Many non sequiturs are easy to identify. If the advocate suggests that poverty is disappearing in the United States because the gross national product has reached more than $700 billion, it should be obvious that the conclusion does not follow from the data. However, some fallacies are more subtle. If crime statistics seem to indicate that crime is on the increase but the definition of crime has changed from one year to the next, the crime rate may not be increasing. The advocate who uses such statistics has been talking about two different things when comparing the statistics from two different years. Similarly, one could argue that the incidence of cancer has increased in the last fifty years, but the argument would be fallacious simply because doctors did not readily identify the disease until fairly recently.

Authority

Clearly, the opinion quotation is the most common form of support for factual arguments in debate. If an advocate cites an expert who offers the opinion that something exists or does not exist, one or two common fallacies may exist here. The individual author may be suspect, which is a matter of external criticism, or the "facts" reported may simply be untrue, which is a matter of internal criticism.

A fallacy of unreliable authority most often takes the form of the biased authority who reports something to support his or her cause. A person who opposes the foreign aid program may present evidence to prove that the program is ineffective, while the opposition may select the available information to validate a counterstand. One might say that the program is a failure 30 percent of the time, while the other might argue that it is 70 percent effective.

The debater looking for fallacious arguments in this area should turn to the standards for judging an authority that were detailed in Chapter 2.

Is the authority an expert? Is the source free from bias? How was the information obtained? What is the date of the information?

Another kind of authority fallacy is the untrue "fact." A hardware store advertised a gigantic end-of-the-year sale and boasted that many of the items on sale had been reduced as much as 100 percent. Certainly, it is the best authority on its prices, but is the statement true—does it really make sense? A 100 percent discount would mean that the total cost of the product had been eliminated; in short, that the hardware store was giving things away. Unfortunately, it is unlikely that any merchant is going to give the merchandise away, much less pay the customer to take the product—as is implied by other sales that advertise 150 to 200 percent discounts.

In debate, this fallacy usually is not as easy to identify in the evidence used by debaters. The best procedure for the debater to follow is to see if the evidence is consistent with other known information. Do other authorities agree? How was the information derived? Does it make sense? The advocate should be especially wary of a startling new fact that only one authority reports.

Fallacies of Value Arguments

A **value argument** is one in which the advocate wants the audience to agree that a positive or a negative value should be attached to a particular situation. The situation itself has been established through a factual argument, and the next step is to assign it a value. After showing that poverty exists, for instance, the debater will want the judge to agree that poverty is bad. After proving that crime is increasing, another advocate may want the critic to decide that such a situation is a social evil.

The three most common methods that are used for proving value arguments were outlined in Chapter 3. The debater can argue from criteria or from authority. The criteria arguments are based on standards that have been officially established, on examples, or on the debater's personal experience. The authoritative support involves the reading of a quotation from an expert who has expressed her or his own value judgment in print. The fallacies that are connected with each of these are simply the problems that arise from inadequate support for an argument.

Recorded Criteria

In searching for recorded criteria, the debater looks for a written statement of the goals and interests of the principal party in the debate topic. One might turn to the Charter of the United Nations, the Constitution of the United States, or the policy statements of the president. Fallacious arguments arise when a written statement does not agree with actual practice or when the statement has been misinterpreted.

One might agree, for example, that dictatorship should be abolished in the Soviet Union because the constitution of that country guarantees freedom of speech, press, and religion. It certainly does, but these criteria apparently are not the ones that are in operation. Or one might argue against war and for peace because the policy of almost every country is said to be peace-loving. But if such criteria represented the real interests of all nations, there could be no war. Apparently, ideology and sovereignty are more important than high-sounding policy statements.

Example

A value argument from example clearly depends on a very high degree of similarity between two situations. When socialized medicine was debated, negative teams were fond of pointing to difficulties in Great Britain to show why the affirmative's proposal would be bad. The affirmative countered by "pointing with pride" to elements of the system that worked well in Great Britain.

Both arguments are likely to be fallacious. There are many more differences than similarities between the United States and Great Britain, and usually there were significant differences between the proposal the affirmative suggested and the British system of national health care.

Unless an example compares very favorably in every important way with the situation to which it is being compared, the argument from example probably is fallacious.

Authority

The discussion of faulty authoritative arguments also applies to value judgments. A value argument probably will be fallacious if the authority does not meet the criteria. The source must be an expert. He or she should not be biased. The information should have been gathered carefully and should be recent enough that the debater can be sure that no new developments have affected the validity of the argument.

Fallacies of Causal Arguments

Causal arguments have already been identified as the most difficult arguments to prove. Because of this it is very easy to show that a causal argument is fallacious. Three major fallacies of causal arguments are discussed below: the post hoc fallacy, the fallacy of the hidden cause, and—again—the fallacy of the inadequate authority.

Post Hoc

This fallacy is so common in argument that some logicians feel if they could just educate people about its dangers, they would have done all they need do in the way of logical training. The phrase *post hoc* is short for the Latin phrase *post hoc ergo propter hoc*, or "after this, therefore because of this." Because one event is closely followed by another event, the first is assumed to have been the cause of the second.

Superstitions usually are based on post hoc reasoning. Someone, a long time ago, had bad luck just after walking under a ladder. Somebody had trouble all day on Friday the 13th. A baseball player noticed that he got a hit just after he touched his right hand to his left heel. From then on, the first person avoided the ladders, the second stayed home in bed on Friday the 13th, and the baseball player always touched his left heel before going to bat.

Such fallacies, however, also appear in less frivolous kinds of thinking. The stock market falls if the president is slightly ill, because investors remember that the last time the president had a serious illness a recession followed. Reformers say that Rome fell—and everyone knows this happened—because it had the same fault they are trying to reform.

The logician's argument for countering such thinking is that *correlation is not causality*. That two events change simultaneously or are close to each other in time does not mean that one caused the other.

The best test for the post hoc fallacy is the sine qua non criterion from law: would the second event have occurred if the first had not occurred? One study proved that the salaries of Baptist ministers had a high correlation with Cuban rum prices, but few people would argue that the rum prices wouldn't have gone up if the ministers hadn't been given a raise.

Hidden Cause

Teachers, including the authors, are fond of "selling" the values of education to students. One of the most common arguments they make is that the longer students remain in school the more money they will make later. People with an eighth-grade education can expect to make, say, $675,000 during a lifetime; high school graduates might make $900,000; and college graduates might make $1,350,000. The cause may be good, but the argument is fallacious.

It may be true that a degree or a diploma is required for many positions, but it doesn't appear true that education is necessarily the cause of higher salaries for the more educated citizens. Hidden causes probably have operated that result in both a higher level of education and higher salaries. Highly motivated and intelligent persons are more likely to go farther in school and are more likely to be highly regarded in their work. To see that a hidden cause probably is more important in such cases, one need only look at the self-made millionaire who went no farther than the second grade or at the Ph.D. who makes less than the millionaire, even after obtaining a great deal of formal education.

Often the hidden cause fallacy is very difficult to uncover. Only through careful experimental research and detailed application of the sine qua non and proximity standards can one be sure that some hidden cause is not operating.

Authority

Again, many debaters find it easy to turn to the opinion of an expert to "prove" that causal relationships exist. Experts, however, are not immune to fallacious thinking. The critical debater should carefully examine what experts say to discover post hoc thinking and hidden causes. If such fallacies seem to be operating, or if the authorities fail to meet the criteria for establishing their expertise, any argument that is based on their opinions will be fallacious.

Analytical Fallacies

Besides looking for specific logical fallacies, the debater should examine case constructions and presentations for **analytical fallacies**. Frequently, the beginning debater overlooks the larger problems when searching for specific points of attack.

Begging the Question

This, basically, is a fallacy of the affirmative constructive argument. Although the affirmative has the right to its own analysis of the debate proposition, it is obligated to interpret it within reasonable limits. Some teams try to narrow or expand their analyses, thus misinterpreting the proposition, so that their opposition has a much more difficult time attacking their case.

Limiting the question is the most common form of begging the question. For example, on the topic RESOLVED: *That the United States should substantially reduce its foreign policy commitment*, one team felt that it could not support a substantial reduction; therefore, it advocated withdrawing the United States' commitment to import goods from Monaco. Few negative teams could argue with this, but every judge who heard the team felt that it was begging the question.

Another team, which was debating the same topic, suggested world disarmament as the solution to the world's problems. The case was so general and philosophical that it was very difficult for negative teams to defeat it. Again, most critics felt that the affirmative had expanded the proposal so that it wouldn't have to debate the real issues. It was begging the question.

Even though begging the question is primarily an affirmative fallacy (derived from stretching or constricting the debate topic), the negative also can be guilty of this fallacy. Any time the negative—or the affirmative, for that matter—answers an argument of the other team by limiting or expanding its implications, it is committing the fallacy of begging the question.

Faulty Assumptions

Wise debaters carefully examine the assumptions that underlie the opponent's case. They try to discover the premises on which the case is built. If the argument derives from a faulty assumption, the whole case may be one large fallacy. For instance, on the topic RESOLVED: *That the federal government should establish minimal educational standards for elementary and secondary schools in the United States*, several affirmative teams advocated that minimum competency testing be instituted in secondary schools to guarantee future increases in college enrollments. However, the case was predicated on the assumption that minimum competency testing was designed to increase college enrollment. Negative teams that could show that the assumption was faulty could defeat the case.

Non Sequitur Need for Change

In the traditional affirmative need case, there usually are four arguments that form the evidence for the conclusion that the present system should be changed. They are, of course, that a problem exists in the present system and that the problem is inherent, evil, and sufficiently widespread to justify a change. Occasionally, though, the conclusion does not follow from the specific contentions that the affirmative develops.

For instance, does the existence of minor waste in the foreign aid program justify a structural change in the present system? Perhaps the problem calls for adjustments to eliminate waste, but it does not necessarily follow that the program should be discontinued.

Non Sequitur Proposal

Intelligent negative teams ask themselves whether the affirmative's proposal follows from the need-for-a-change argument. One team, for example, argued for free trade in the western hemisphere because of the growth of communism in Latin America. Certainly, if such a problem exists, a change may be warranted, but does this analysis justify free trade between Canada and the United States? Does it even follow that the United States should engage in free trade with Latin America?

Non Sequitur Advantages

This analytical fallacy arises when the affirmative's advantages do not follow from its analysis of the present system and from its proposal. In the free trade example, does it follow that the affirmative can claim the advantage of being able to stop the communist menace? Could it even argue that free trade would help the poorest Latin American nations? If they are underdeveloped nations with little to trade, lower tariff barriers would do little good.

Inconsistent Attack

The affirmative and the negative suggest opposing ultimate arguments in a debate. That is, the affirmative argues for the debate proposition, while the negative argues that the proposal should not be adopted. All the arguments for both sides become evidence for these ultimate claims. Therefore, each team is responsible not only for its specific arguments, but for the way these arguments relate to each other. It is on this level that many teams commit the inconsistency fallacy. An experienced debate team watches for inconsistent argumentation.

On the affirmative side, many teams want to maximize the need-for-a-change argument while minimizing the cost of their proposal. If they go too far in either direction, the case becomes inconsistent. In a debate on compulsory health insurance, the affirmative said there was dramatic need for a change because 7 million elderly persons were without adequate medical attention every year. Clearly, this was a serious problem, but the same team said that its plan would cost only $50 million a year to operate. This sounds good, but was it consistent? Does it seem reasonable that $7.00 per person is adequate for solving such a drastic problem? Or perhaps the $50 million figure was accurate, and the need argument was exaggerated. Through such inconsistency the affirmative worked itself into a very common affirmative dilemma.

A common negative fallacy, on the other hand, is to argue first that the present system is working beautifully and that the affirmative's proposal is terrible, and then to turn and argue that the affirmative hasn't met its obligations because the plan it proposes is just like the present system. Such reasoning causes a judge to question the entire negative analysis.

Emotional Appeal
In most kinds of public speaking, emotional appeals are acceptable and even desirable as evidence. They are not acceptable, however, in competitive debate. Therefore, an argument that is based on religious or patriotic appeals is considered fallacious by most debate judges. More subtle, but just as fallacious, are arguments that discuss a "spreading, cancerous growth" in the present system or that compare the affirmative's case with communism.

Ad Hominem
The ad hominem attack is an old standby of the propagandist and the unscrupulous advocate. Instead of attacking a person's arguments, it's easier to attack her or him personally. Although such arguments may make entertaining politics, they are not considered legitimate in debate.

Although debaters rarely call each other names, students should be very cautious of a very common mistake in which debaters, especially "old hands," seem to enjoy giving critiques of their opposition's debating skill. They point out how illogical the latter are, how poorly they have developed their case, and even what poor speakers they are. This is simply a sophisticated form of the ad hominem fallacy.

It is, of course, perfectly legitimate for a debater to point out a weakness in an opponent's case. One must not, however, criticize the other team members as individuals. A debater must attack the argument, not the person who presents it.

Writing Briefs

To be successful, a debater must research important arguments. Only with current, expert evidence can a debater hope to prove points critical to her or his position in a round. However, researching evidence is not enough to insure victory.

Debate requires that the advocate arrange evidence in a useful manner so that arguments can be effectively presented in the round. A common device for organizing arguments and evidence is the **debate brief**. A debate brief is generally a page of arguments and evidence that can be read as the need arises in a given round. The brief is different from a prepared speech in several ways. First, the arguments are not entirely written out. A first affirmative speech permits a polished oration. Because the other speeches in the round depend on precise responses to opposing argumentation, a brief must be prepared so that it can be used flexibly. Therefore, the debater should arrange arguments so that relevant objections can be entered into the round. Second, a brief does not speak to a number of major issues. Each brief concerns only one major issue pertinent to the defense of a case or an attack. For example, the negative may

Writing briefs is one way to prepare for debate rounds.

have a variety of plan-meets-need objections to an affirmative case. Each one should be briefed out separately so that the arguments that best pertain can be selected for delivery and the others held in reserve. Finally, briefs contain multiple pieces of evidence, not all of which are read in every round of debate. If you expect that a particular argument is crucial for your case, you may wish to have two, three, or four quotations on the brief. It is not necessary to read all the evidence to prove the argument, at least initially. But if the argument becomes the focus of contention later on, the backup evidence will be useful in further establishing the point.

Affirmative Briefs

The affirmative briefs may be divided into those pertaining to the defense of the case and those pertaining to the defense of the plan. Case briefs should be fashioned to counter the most likely negative objections to the affirmative contentions. For instance, if the affirmative is contending that discrimination has three separate harms—unemployment, diminished productivity in the economy, and perpetuation of the psychology of poverty—briefs should be constructed to further establish the significance of each harm. If the affirmative is aware of important negative evidence, in this case the Presidential Commissions on Homelessness and on Hunger, individual briefs should be constructed to attack the credibility of the negative position.

Plan briefs should be constructed so as to anticipate workability arguments and disadvantages. Plan briefs are similar to case briefs with a couple of important exceptions. Plan briefs designed for the first affirmative rebuttalist must be more compact. Because the first affirmative rebuttal only allows five minutes for refuting plan and case attacks, briefs must contain only essential objections and critical evidence. It does little good to read a long brief on a single disadvantage if the brief takes up all the time available for speaking. The affirmative may wish to write a longer version of plan responses, just in case the negative concentrates on a single issue.

Negative Briefs

Negative briefs are divided into case and plan attacks. Case briefs are like affirmative briefs, except that they anticipate likely case contentions and work to diminish significance or inherency of the affirmative position. A negative brief on the case typically works to undermine the credibility of affirmative studies or the cogency of the rationale behind the arguments. The negative brief might also be constructed to add more considerations in defense of the status quo. Because the affirmative will usually pick on aspects of policy that do not work or examples that suggest policy has failed, the negative should be prepared to examine the status quo's successes and to put its failures into context.

Negative briefs on the plan are constructed a bit differently. A disadvantage is really the inverse of an affirmative case. A disadvantage must be carefully written to anticipate objections that would dismiss it as irrelevant, trivial, or contradictory in terms of the overall negative position. A disadvantage brief must include a statement of the relationship of the plan to its ill effects on the status quo, a statement proving that the consequences of the plan are significantly evil, an argument that proves that only the plan will cause the disadvantage and not status quo policies, and an overall comparison between the plan's virtues and vices. Unless a disadvantage brief contains all these arguments, the negative position can be discarded by a judge on the grounds that it is not pertinent to an evaluation of the affirmative case. Similarly, the negative position on topicality should be well prepared so that any steps that a plan might take beyond the scope of the resolution can be countered. Otherwise the affirmative might be able to preemptively anticipate disadvantages.

Checklist

Briefs are useful tools. However, there are certain dangers to using them. The following checklist can help you ensure that you are writing and using briefs correctly.

1. *Are statements precise and clear?* If arguments are written out and are too lengthy, then it may be difficult to adapt the issue to the specific arguments of a given round. If arguments are not written out and the brief contains only catch phrases or labels and evidence, then the judge may not understand the nature or the importance of an argument. An argument on a brief must be concise, and yet it must explain the issue clearly.

2. *Does the evidence match the argument?* A debater should put the strongest quotations in the brief, and these quotations should prove what the argument claims. Evidence that is slightly off point, not

credible, or out-of-date does little good. One inappropriate use of evidence weakens the credibility of all the rest of the arguments. It is better not to make an argument than to deploy one with weak evidence.

3. *Is the brief flexible?* If a brief is too long and its positions are too complicated, then a debater will misallocate time. On the other hand, if the brief is superficial, then when an issue is extended over a number of speeches, the debater is left with nothing more than repeating earlier statements and proof. Preparation should include an organizational scheme that anticipates use in situations that call for initiating a beginning position and extended refutation. Unless a brief can accommodate such uses, it may hinder good debating.

4. *Is the brief current?* Arguments must be continually revised throughout the course of a debate season. There is an unfortunate tendency among some debaters to leave the brief the same once it is written. This is a tragic mistake. A brief that worked well one time may not work the next. Briefs should be reviewed. New evidence should be added. Weak arguments should be discarded and better arguments constructed.

5. *What briefs are compatible?* It is important that colleagues work out a consistent position. Debaters should think through the implications of using various combinations of arguments. Implications are not always obvious. Make sure that the briefs defending the status quo do not contradict briefs that suggest disadvantages to any movement toward resolving status quo problems.

Sample Briefs

The following are example briefs taken from actual debate files. Study their composition and see if you can improve on them.

Affirmative Brief

This brief is part of a defense for an affirmative case that changes NATO defense strategy. Part of the change is the elimination of chemical weapons. This brief shows why chemical weapons are harmful from several different vantage points. Note that the brief is constructed by putting together arguments on the same issue. A piece of evidence supports each argument.

(1) Chemical weapons do not deter war.

Weickhardt 86: November, Bulletin of the Atomic Scientists, p. 28.

"Possession of chemical weapons is claimed only to deter the use of chemical weapons once a war is under way—not the war itself."

(2) NATO has no policy governing the use of chemical weapons.

Weickhardt 86: November, Bulletin of the Atomic Scientists, p. 30.

"Be that as it may, the inherent ambiguity of the policy on retaliation in kind has prevented NATO from developing a comprehensive policy or procedures for the use of chemical weapons."

Ember 80: Chemical and Engineering News, December 15, p. 26.

"Arking agrees with Mikulak. For one thing, he does not see how building up a binary capability will significantly improve U.S. offensive capability because we don't integrate chemical weapons into our forces anyhow."

(3) NATO integrates chemical weapons into its military posture, war-time use is assured.

Blackaby 82: June/July, Bulletin of the Atomic Scientists, p. 27.

"And possession of poison gas, it is argued, is simply to deter the other side from using it. However, once these weapons have been integrated into the force structure—which is necessary if they are to fulfill their reputed deterrence function—the military will undoubtedly begin to look beyond deterrence to scenarios in which the no-first-use policy is abandoned."

(4) An integrated NATO policy would impair the deterrent value of chemical weapons.

Spiers 86: Chemical Warfare, p. 203.

"If air-delivered against targets in the Warsaw Pact's rear, retaliation could risk the possibility of escalation. In view of these risks, authorising chemical release could prove politically contentious within the alliance and cause serious delays in NATO's decision making."

Negative Brief

The following brief may be used against a case that bans NATO's use of chemical weapons. Like the affirmative brief, the negative brief is constructed of arguments and evidence. The explanation of the argument is reduced to a short, clear statement of the issue.

(1) Only chemical weapons can deter the Soviet use of chemical weapons.

Abshire 86: Binary Chemical Weapons, p. 10.

"The probability that the Soviets might use their massive chemical attack capability was assessed by the Chemical Warfare Review Commission, headed by Ambassador Stoessel. The Commission concluded that it found 'no reason, other than fear of retaliation, to assume that the Soviets would not use chemical warfare if they judged it to their advantage to do so.' "

Spiers 86, Chemical Warfare, p. 201.

"Only the threat of retaliation in kind can reduce the possibility of an aggressor exploiting the imbalance caused by degradation. As Harold Brown, the former Secretary of Defense, explained, it would be a 'read deterrent balance,' threatening to force the Soviets into a degraded mode of operations and thereby reducing their incentive to launch a chemical attack. Defense spokesmen, under successive administrations, have underlined the centrality of this assumption."

(2) Threatened retaliation makes the costs of Soviet chemical use too high.

Roberts 87: Chemical Warfighting Policy, p. 26.

"According to another participant, chemical weapons retaliation by the West would impose costs on so many Soviet warfighting goals that any Soviet decision to initiate chemical warfare would have to be weighed carefully as long as they face any serious prospect of retaliation."

(3) Historically, chemical weapons have been deterred by threatened use of chemical weapons in retaliation.

  Adelman 86: Fall, Orbis, p. 451.

    "From the standpoint of deterring chemical weapons use, the
risks of delaying the restoration of an effective U.S. deterrent capability are not negligible. In light of the Western experience in the
years before and during World War II, it should be clear that without
a credible deterrent or retaliatory capability, there is very little prospect that stipulated prohibitions on chemical warfare would hold fast
in the event of a conflict."

Preparation for Refutation and Rebuttal

Refutation and rebuttal, of course, are different processes. Refutation involves attacking the arguments of the opponent. Rebuttal means rebuilding arguments that the opponent has attacked. Nevertheless, the
two procedures are treated here as one; distinctions are made only when
there is truly a difference in a strategy or tactic to be used.

    Many beginning debaters do not think of preparation as part of refu-
tation and rebuttal. They seem to feel that the time to come up with their
attack and defense is during the debate, while they are sitting at their
desks or even while they are speaking. Such a notion can only lead to disaster. Careful preparation is one of the most important parts of attack
and defense in debate.

Strategy

The experienced debater knows that effective refutation and rebuttal require almost as much preparation as constructive argument; in fact, the
strategy demands it. The strategy of the debater is *never be unprepared for
an argument of the opposition or for an attack on your case*. The good
debater may occasionally be surprised by a new attack but should never
be surprised a second time by the same argument.

Tactics

Such a strategy sounds very good, but it is not easy to fulfill. It requires that the debater take the path of most resistance. Possible arguments and attacks must be anticipated, and new approaches encountered during the year must be immediately researched. A former debater brought home the last point very forcefully. She had lost a semifinal round one weekend because she was completely surprised by a negative attack against her affirmative case. The next week she lost again, to the same team, because of the same argument. She said that, as soon as she heard the argument the second time, she realized that she had meant to do something about it during the intervening week. This debater was "twice surprised," but she never forgot again.

Three tactics can help overcome such surprises. The first is anticipating arguments before a competition. The second is preparing for arguments that develop during the season. The third involves careful self-assessment.

Anticipate Possible Arguments

This procedure will vary slightly, depending on whether the student is preparing for refutation or rebuttal. To prepare for rebuttal, the debater must carefully analyze the affirmative and negative constructive cases. With the help of the coach and fellow debaters, he or she should critically analyze the cases to see what arguments would be the best to use against them. The various answers to the counterarguments should then be carefully researched.

The same sort of process can be used to prepare for refutation. The probable affirmative and negative cases should be outlined, and the specific counterarguments should be developed and researched. Frequently, debaters have meetings with several other teams to pool their ideas about possible cases, and the labor is divided up to facilitate research.

At this point many of the best debaters use rebuttal sheets, which is a simple way of formalizing their preparation. The arguments most likely to arise are listed, along with the replies and the best evidence. Rebuttal sheets can also be made without specific reference to pieces of evidence. During a debate, the speaker can quickly refer to the rebuttal sheet for a summary of the research. (A typical rebuttal sheet is shown below.) Rebuttal sheets should be continually updated. As teams change and modify their affirmative cases during the year, rebuttal sheets will prove to be of little value if they are not updated.

Rebuttal Sheet—Negative Arguments		
Argument	*Answer*	*Evidence* *(this column optional)*
NATO is effective.	Yes, it does appear to work, but only because there is no longer a threat of aggression.	6A13, 6A14, 6A15, 6A16

Prepare for Actual Arguments

Again, most debaters deliberately prepare arguments against cases they have heard or attacks that have already been made against them. Because debate tournaments typically take place on weekends, many debate groups meet early in the week to review the past tournament. Each team relates the affirmative cases it heard, recalling how it replied to the case and asking for suggestions for improvement. Each team also reports on the attacks it received on its affirmative case. By pooling experiences, every debater can develop a large backlog of refutation and rebuttal material. Such information can be committed to rebuttal sheets for ready reference.

If some readers think that such sharing of information may border on unethical behavior, the authors would argue that there is nothing unethical about avoiding surprise. Careful preparation, moreover, often teaches more than anything else. But preparation done in a vacuum gains very little. Rather than repeating mistakes week after week, the thinking debater can sharpen his or her logical and research skills by constantly looking for feedback. This is not to argue that squads should mass-produce affirmative and negative blocks. But there is nothing wrong with starting with someone else's block and developing it into an argument uniquely your own.

On the other hand, there is nothing sadder or more boring than listening to a debate in which the debaters are reading someone else's block with little understanding of what it means, much less how to apply or extend the argument. *Under no circumstances* should a coach write a block for a debater. While to do so *might* win a particular debate, it does not help the debater learn to think through arguments and apply them with extensions in a rebuttal.

Personal Assessment

This aspect of the rebuttal tactics is probably the most difficult. Some debaters seem to be endowed with such unshakable self-confidence that they can't objectively examine their own abilities, but a careful assessment at least of the team's strengths and weaknesses is an important part of preparation for refutation and rebuttal.

Debaters should carefully analyze their own case and their repertoire of arguments and evidence. They should detail their weaknesses as well as their strengths. Surely, a team cannot expect to do a good job of rebuttal if it uses one or two weak arguments or if it does not have the highest-quality evidence to support its assertions.

Refutation and Rebuttal During a Debate

Preparing for refutation and rebuttal is just the first step. All of the preparation won't help if debaters can't put what they know into effect during a debate. The data provided in Chapter 5 on the presentation of arguments are applicable here, and several special strategic features of the presentation of refutation and rebuttal material also apply.

Strategy

It should be obvious that the overall strategy of both the affirmative and the negative is to overcome all the important arguments that their opposition presents during a debate. Also, the three strategies of competitive presentation are important here.

The affirmative seeks to overcome the negative's attempts to maintain its presumption. The affirmative also tries to keep the negative on the defensive, to maintain the offensive. And the final affirmative strategy may be to narrow the debate as much as possible, countering the negative's attempts to expand the range of arguments. (In some cases the affirmative may choose to counterspread.)

Naturally, the negative's strategies take the opposite form. The negative team wants to overcome all affirmative assaults on its case for the present system. The negative does its best to take away the offensive and put the affirmative on the defensive. Finally, the negative refutation and rebuttal are designed to counter the affirmative's attempts to narrow the range of arguments that are important in the debate. In rebuttals the negative may find it more advantageous to narrow the debate to the negative's strongest points.

Tactics

The actual process of refutation and rebuttal during a debate is one of the most exciting elements of the whole activity. The debater has only a few minutes, after hearing an argument, to prepare an attack or defense. It is essential to prepare and react quickly. This section follows the process from the time the advocate hears the argument to the time a response is made.

Flow Sheets

The most basic tactic in refutation and rebuttal is to remember what has been said during the round. Surprisingly, many debaters simply don't listen carefully to the arguments of their opponents and, as a result, miss many of the subtleties of the case and often misinterpret the opponent's arguments. The first step, then, is to develop a system for taking notes that will guarantee that the debater hears the arguments and later can report them accurately to the judge.

Flow sheeting is the term that many debaters use to describe the process of taking notes during a debate. The goal is to follow the flow of the debate and accurately record all of the principal arguments of the debaters involved in the round. This can be done on a single sheet so that the student can easily see the flow of the arguments for any particular debate. When using a single sheet, the debate's plan and plan arguments flow onto the back of the sheet. Although using a single sheet of paper per debate is economical, most debaters and judges find it easier to use multiple sheets of paper.

Typically, notes are taken on two large pads.* Many debaters use legal-size pads, and others prefer large, spiral-bound sketch pads. The sketch pad probably is best because it provides the most space and because old flow sheets can be kept in the pad for later reference. When using a legal pad or art pad most speakers partition the pad ahead of time and allow one section for each speech in the debate.

---

*Large pads, preprinted in black and red to distinguish affirmative and negative entries, are available from National Textbook Company, Lincolnwood, Illinois.

The Large Case Flow						
1st Aff. Construc- tive	*1st Neg. Construc- tive*	*2nd Aff. Construc- tive*	*1st Neg. Rebuttal*	*1st Aff. Rebuttal*	*2nd Neg. Rebuttal*	*2nd Aff. Rebuttal*

The Large Plan Flow				
Aff. Plan	*2nd Neg. Constructive*	*1st Aff. Rebuttal*	*2nd Neg. Rebuttal*	*2nd Aff. Rebuttal*

Of course, the debater should accurately record what is said during the debate. Most speakers develop abbreviation systems that allow them to record information very quickly. The authors have seen championship debaters who were so proficient at flow sheeting that they could record the source, date, and page of each quotation that was used during the round. They did not develop this skill by chance, however. They carefully practiced accurate flow sheeting during many practice rounds.

🕊 **NTC CASE ARGUMENTS**

Tournament:_____

Round:___2____

First Affirmative Constructive	First Negative Constructive	Second Affirmative Constructive	First Negative Rebuttal
OBS: REAGAN HATES FIDEL		EXTEND U.S. INTERV.	
CHR. CENT '84		DROPPED	
— TIME FOR CHANGE			
WILLIAMS '84			
POL. UNDERM.			
RADIO MARTI EXACERB.			
KENZIE '87			
CITED IN BREAKDOWN			
OF IMMIG.			
CUBA FEARS INVASION			
LEO GRANDE '86			
AGREEMT W/ SOVIET UNION			
SS			
ADM. OFF. THREATEN	1. CLOSE TIES W/ SOV.	1. RECENT EVENTS DISPROVE	1. IRREL. TO RELATIONS
TO GO TO SOURCE OF	PREV. NEGO.	CASTRO NOT ATTENDING	2. NO ANALYSIS
INSTAB.	CR '84	ST FUNCT. →	3. SOV'S CONTOL CUBA
		SIDNEY '87	ECO
ADV I ↑ POL. STAB.	2. STRONG TIES		COW '85
	CR '84	2. US. ACTION FORCE	BATES '87
A. US SEEKS TO LIMIT		CASTRO TO USSR	
CUBA/SOVIET INFLU.	3. RELATIONS IMPR.	KNIGHT '86	→
	SMITH '87		
SMITH '87		3. CONTAINMENT BAD →	DA ANSWERS
US CONTAINMT. POL			
HARMS WLD. PEACE		4. DOESN'T ASSUME →	NO ANALYSIS
		WAR IN INTERM	
LEO GRANDE '86			
MAKES ATTACK MORE			
LIKELY			
CASTRO '83			
WILL COMPRO.			
ROBERTS '83			
FORCES MOSCOW TO			
ABANDON CUBA			

Affirmative: _34 A_

Negative: _12 A_

Affirmative Rebuttal	Second Negative Rebuttal	Second Affirmative Rebuttal
NTERV. INDEP.		EXTEND U.S. INVADES CUBA IF VOTES NEG.
ND #2: U.S. ON FORCE CASTRO	1. RELATIONS IMPROV. → IRRELEVANT W/ SOVS	
	2. SOVIET CONTROLS → U.S. FORCED CUBA CUBAN ECO.	
OPPED	3. CLD. PREV. CASTRO → 1. NEW FROM NEGO	2. NO EVID. 3. SOVS WANT IMPROVED
ACTIONS CAUSE ND CONTAIN BAD →	NO ANALYSIS	US/USSR REL. NATION '87
		U.S. ACTIONS DETERMINE

©1986 National Textbook Company • Lincolnwood, Illinois 60646 U.S.A.

Symbols and Abbreviations

T	topicality
Inh	inherency
DA	disadvantage
PMA	plan-meets-advantage
PMN	plan-meets need
Circ	circumvention
PS	present system
SQ	status quo
TA	turnaround
CP	counterplan
Sig	significance
OBS	observation
U	unique
NU	non-unique
thr	threshold
$	dollars, money, finance, revenue, funding
MR	minor repair
EXT	extratopicality
x	dropped argument
NE	no evidence used
??	(used before an argument or card to show you're not sure you flowed it correctly)
CX	statement from cross-ex.
>	greater than
<	less than
↑	increase
↓	decrease
→	causes
↛	does not cause
=	equals, is
≠	does not equal, is not
w/	with
w/o	without
w/in	within
b/c	because
avg	average

CASE ARGUMENTS

Tournament:_____

Round:_____

First Affirmative Constructive	First Negative Constructive	Second Affirmative Constructive	First Negative Rebuttal
B. CUBA KEY TO LA PEACE	4. CASTRO WON'T NEGO.	1. WE UPDATE (1983)	1. DOES NOT WANT
GREEN '83	LA RP '83	2. NOT ASSUME RADIO	
US. HAS STAKE IN		MARTI	2. CRANE EVID. TAKES
PEACE	5. WON'T GIVE UP		THIS OUT
	LEADERSHIP	3. AFF. WON'T HARM	
HANSON '78	CR '84	CASTRO'S 30 WLD ROLE	
FUTURE DEP. ON OUT-			
COME IN CUBA	6. CAN'T IMPROVE RELA.	4. CASTRO WANTS ——→	DOES NOT ASSUME
	WOOD '87	NORMALIZATION.	AFF. ACTION
		NYT '87	
	7. WON'T DISCUSS		
	SIGAL '87	5. EXTEND SOLV.	
C. SOLVENCY			
	8. US. HOSTILITY NOT→	1. RADIO MARTI ——→	ABOVE
THAYER '84	AFFECT DEC. TO NEGO	2. THREAT OF INTERV.	
CAN ELIM. THREAT	CRANE '86	X ——————→	CASTRO DOES NOT PERC.
		3. WE'RE UPDATING ——→	IRREV.
LEO GRANDE '86	9. SOVIETS SUPPORT		
CUBA WILL END ALL	CUBA	1. IRREV.	
INVOLVE IF US. DOES	JONES '87	2. FEEDS CASE	
SS		US POL. ↑ SOV. INFL.	
KEY TO PEACE	10. NO SOLVENCY ——→	EXTEND C SUBPT. ——→	NOT SOLVE IF CASTRO
		SNOW '85	WON'T NEGO.
		CRABTREE '86	

Affirmative:_____				
Negative:_____				

irst Affirmative Rebuttal	**Second Negative Rebuttal**	**Second Affirmative Rebuttal**
S. ACTIONS-RADIO ARTI INTERV. DROPPED IE POST DATE		
	CASTRO WON'T NEGO. —> ABOVE PEACE	
IE NORMALIZE		
A BOVE ————————>		——> EXTEND CUBA KEY TO REGION
A BOVE ————————>		——> EXTEND SOLVENCY

©1986 National Textbook Company • Lincolnwood, Illinois 60646 U.S.A.

Symbols and Abbreviations

T	topicality
Inh	inherency
DA	disadvantage
PMA	plan-meets-advantage
PMN	plan-meets need
Circ	circumvention
PS	present system
SQ	status quo
TA	turnaround
CP	counterplan
Sig	significance
OBS	observation
U	unique
NU	non-unique
thr	threshold
$	dollars, money, finance, revenue, funding
MR	minor repair
EXT	extratopicality
x	dropped argument
NE	no evidence used
??	(used before an argument or card to show you're not sure you flowed it correctly)
CX	statement from cross-ex.
>	greater than
<	less than
↑	increase
↓	decrease
→	causes
↛	does not cause
=	equals, is
≠	does not equal, is not
w/	with
w/o	without
w/in	within
b/c	because
avg	average

Debaters must record the arguments accurately because the first thing they have to do in refutation and rebuttal is tell the critic which of their opponent's arguments they are talking about. If this argument is misquoted or exaggerated to its disadvantage, many good judges penalize the speaker. They feel that a debater should defeat an opponent through reasoning and evidence, not by changing the arguments for the worse.

As a debate progresses, flow charts serve to show debaters what they will have to discuss during their speeches. A debater wants to spend time on the arguments that have been connected with important issues and to point out any important arguments that the opponent has failed to discuss. In the sample flow sheets, you can see that some arguments might be stressed because they have received strong attack and others because they have been ignored by the opposition. (The Xs indicate where evidence was read or will be read.)

From a flow sheet, then, the debater can identify the major issues that require refutation or rebuttal. Some arguments are even visually obvious, because the flow sheet might show that they have been talked about often or at length. Other arguments should be analytically obvious. Contentions that penetrate the need-for-a-change argument, the plan-meets-need argument, the affirmative advantages, or the negative presumption certainly are worthy of discussion.

Answering the Argument

Once the debater has decided which arguments to attack or rebuild, four specific tactics come into play: (1) The argument to be discussed should be presented; (2) The counterargument should be presented; (3) Evidence should be presented to support the argument; and (4) The argument should be placed in perspective.

1. *Statement.* It seems clear—to the authors, at least—that before one can defeat an argument presented by the opposition, one must first direct the judge and the opposition to the argument being attacked and explain why it applies to the opposition's case. Basic though this may seem, many debaters often overlook it. They proceed through a speech and merely present arguments that they think apply to their opponent's case, leaving it to the judge to see the relationship. Experienced debaters know that the judge cannot always be trusted to see a connection that seems very clear to the debater. Typically, debaters who fail to indicate specifically which argument they are refuting or how their argument fits into their opponent's case discover that

judges complain (on the ballot) that there was no clash in the debate. Debaters forget that their judges have not done the extensive research into the topic that they have. What may seem crystal clear to the debater and even the opposition might not make sense to the judge. It never hurts to provide everyone with a verbal roadmap.

The statement need not be extensive or lengthy, and it should fairly represent the opposition's argument. The following is an example for a debate that dealt with the crime topic.

> The affirmative has suggested that there is a need to change the way we currently handle confessions because crime is on the increase in the United States. If I can show that crime is not increasing, then there is no need for a change.

2. *Counterargument.* The counterargument is the key to refutation and rebuttal. If it is properly derived, it defeats the opposition. If it does not truly run counter to the argument, however, it should not be given. Again, some debaters omit this tactic. They might simply say, "About the need argument, here's what J. Edgar Hoover has to say." This type of statement does little to identify which specific need-for-a-change argument is being discussed, nor does it show the judge what conclusion the evidence is supposed to support. Evidence does not make an argument, nor does an unsubstantiated conclusion. A counterargument can be claimed only when a speaker presents evidence, a conclusion, and an explanation of how she or he reasoned from one to the other.

A counterargument can legitimately focus on any one of the three elements in an argument. First, the speaker can maintain that the opposition's assertion is fallacious because the evidence is faulty. The conclusion might not be true, but one can't tell from the evidence cited. Second, the speaker can argue that the logical relationship is fallacious. The debater can suggest that the evidence might or might not be true and the conclusion valid or invalid; the alternatives do not matter, because there is no way the conclusion can be derived logically from the evidence. Third, a counterargument can legitimately focus on the conclusion. The debater suggests that, regardless of the evidence and reasoning, the conclusion is invalid. In the example of the illiteracy statistics, the speaker could suggest that the increase is not a true increase.

Statement	Counterargument
The affirmative has argued for a change because reading scores show that illiteracy is increasing. If I can show that illiteracy is not increasing, there is no need to change the present system.	There has really been no increase in illiteracy. There has just been an increase in the number of students taking reading tests.

3. *Evidence.* Like any other argument, the counterargument is not complete until it has been supported by evidence, and the debater can use any kind of evidence that meets the logical requirements of proof. It could be anything from personal experience to external sources, such as observational data or authoritative opinion.

In a counterargument that is designed to question the opposition's evidence, the debater frequently questions the external validity of that evidence. It might be argued that the source from which it was drawn is biased or is not in a proper position to comment on, say, minimum competency testing. When challenging evidence the debater might question the qualifications of the author or produce evidence showing that the opposition's evidence is faulty. One debater, for instance, quoted Chief Parker to show that apparent crime increases in Los Angeles were due to changes in the method of reporting.

To question reasoning, debaters must generally depend on their own resources for proof. When questioning the reasoning behind an argument, the debater must show the logical fallacy. The types of fallacies can be found at the beginning of this chapter. If a fallacy is blatantly obvious, the debater need merely point this out. For example, observational data that show a high crime rate do not prove that crime is increasing.

A counterargument that is designed to overcome the conclusion of an argument usually requires evidence that simply supports the opposite point of view. Inasmuch as most of the issues involved in a debate topic are highly controversial, this is a very common type of attack. The debater seeks more and better evidence to support the contention, for instance, that illiteracy is not increasing or—in the current example—that the increase in illiteracy is due to an increase in the number of students taking reading tests.

Statement	Counterargument	Evidence
The affirmative has argued for a change because reading scores show that illiteracy is increasing. If I can show that illiteracy is not increasing, there is no need to change the present system.	There has really been no increase in illiteracy. There has just been an increase in the number of students taking reading tests.	X_____ _____ _____

4. *Restatement for perspective.* To complete the clash with the opposition's argument, the debater must put the entire development into perspective for the judge. The debater should review the argument that has been attacked and show, again, how the counterargument affects it. It is important to show how the debate is affected if the counterargument is valid. In the case of rebuttal, the conclusion from the advocate would be that his or her argument still stands; therefore, the case is still strong. For refutation the debater must show how the attack has hurt the opposition. In the example we have been using, this perspective would focus on the affirmative's need-for-a-change argument. If the problem suggested by the affirmative is not a problem, there is no need to change the present system.

Statement	Counterargument	Evidence	Perspective
The affirmative has argued for a change because reading scores show that illiteracy is increasing. If I can show that illiteracy is not increasing, there is no need to change the present system.	There has really been no increase in illiteracy. There has just been an increase in the number of students taking reading tests.	X_____ _____ _____	Therefore, if there is no problem, there is no need for a change. If there is none, the proposition should be rejected.

Summary

Although attack and defense tactics of refutation and rebuttal require a great deal of skill, they look like fairly easy processes. The advocate need only understand the logical fallacies, develop sound strategies for attack and defense, and then proceed to attack and defend.

Refutation and rebuttal skills, however, are much easier to talk about than to learn and practice. This, probably, is why many good public speakers have difficulty speaking fluently when they first learn to debate. Only after hard and careful practice can they become proficient debaters.

Questions for Discussion

1. What is a fallacy?

2. How do you detect fallacies in factual arguments?

3. How do you detect fallacies in value arguments?

4. How do you detect fallacies in causal arguments?

5. Differentiate between begging the question and a faulty assumption.

6. Differentiate the role non sequitur plays in need-plan and comparative advantage arguments.

7. What happens to an argument when it is found to be inconsistent with another argument advocated by the same team?

8. How does the fallacy of emotional appeal differ from that of ad hominem?

9. What roles does refutation play in debate?

10. How should a debater select arguments for refutation?

Activities

1. Write an affirmative brief. Give the brief to a fellow debater and ask for a critique. Rewrite the brief to improve the quality of argument and evidence.

2. Make a list of arguments that embody the fallacies listed in the chapter. See if your colleagues can guess which fallacies you are trying to illustrate. Have your colleagues guess which fallacy the argument illustrates. Work to create good or valid versions of the same arguments.

3. Attend a tournament and, with some of your colleagues, flow elimination round debates. Save the flow sheets. Compare notes in debate class. Who has the best flow? What arguments present the best refutation?

4. Take the current high school debate resolution and predict what are likely to be important affirmative cases. Prepare a set of arguments that can be used to object to these cases. Discuss the strategic merits of the position you construct.

DUSABLE HIGH SCHOOL

DEBATE

Chapter 7

Lincoln-Douglas Debate

Objectives and Key Terms

After studying Chapter 7, you should be able

1. To identify the differences between Lincoln-Douglas debate and policy debate.

2. To explain how debating a proposition of policy differs from debating a proposition of value.

3. To identify the differences between value comparison and value assertion debates.

4. To explain value exclusivity.

5. To explain an on balance judgment.

6. To identify a value premise.

To participate in Lincoln-Douglas debate, you will need to understand the following terms:

proposition of value

proposition of policy

value comparison

value assertion

value exclusivity

residues case

on balance judgment

value premise

One strength of contemporary forensics is the variety of formats it makes available to debaters. Lincoln-Douglas is a format of increasing popularity among students. Like individual events, it offers the opportunity for persuasive speaking and one-on-one competition. Like team debating, it offers an opportunity to demonstrate analytical skills. While all the material concerning argumentation and debate discussed in earlier chapters is relevant to Lincoln-Douglas debating, there are key differences. These differences are covered in this chapter so that the advocate may acquire a better strategic sense of the activity.

Format

Lincoln-Douglas debates are modeled after the namesake for the activity. In an Illinois election of the mid-1800s, Abraham Lincoln and Stephen A. Douglas debated before audiences in different towns around the state. This has been the model for similar political debate in more recent times. Unlike Lincoln-Douglas debates, which featured lengthy speeches, the modern forensic event is regulated by a tight time format.

Although formats may vary somewhat, standard practice includes the following:

Affirmative Constructive	6 minutes
Negative Cross-Examination	3 minutes
Negative Constructive	7 minutes
Affirmative Cross-Examination	3 minutes
Affirmative Rebuttal	4 minutes
Negative Rebuttal	6 minutes
Affirmative Rebuttal	3 minutes

Notice that there are some similarities with standard debate. The affirmative speaker has the first and last opportunity to plead the case. The negative has more interior speeches, including a block of eleven minutes that is interrupted by only three minutes of affirmative questioning and a short rebuttal. Notice, too, that the total time allocated to each side is equal. This undoubtedly is a fairness condition for the debate. It must be said, though, that the dissimilarities are significant enough to alter strategic considerations.

The first dissimilarity is that the burden of debating is placed on the single speaker. Whereas in two-person debate an advocate can specialize in case or plan, depending on speaker position, in Lincoln-Douglas the speaker must be acquainted with all facets of the proposition under consideration. Note, too, that the participants are involved throughout the debate and cannot take a rebuttal break when their speeches are finished.

On the affirmative side of the ledger, such a format has significant implications for constructing the opening position. Because the first affirmative constructive speech is considerably shorter than that permitted either in standard or cross-examination debate, the speech must emphasize core evidence and arguments. Yet, it must permit room for the expansion of ideas throughout the discussion. The affirmative gets only one constructive speech. Consequently, the constructive should have as many well-developed *independent* subissues as possible. (The nature of independent arguments on a value proposition will be considered momentarily.) Although it is vital to craft a strong first affirmative, it is also important for the affirmative to develop flexible rebuttal skills because the affirmative speaker has more time and opportunity at the end of the debate.

On the negative side, it should be noted that there are fewer speeches, but more time is given to each speech. In a sense, the negative has a great opportunity, if she or he is prepared to carry the debate into areas not identified by the affirmative but relevant to the value question at hand. Even if the negative spends as much time talking about the affirmative case as the affirmative did in the first constructive, the negative still has a minute more. And even if the negative talks about all the issues that the affirmative covered in its four-minute first rebuttal, the negative still has two additional minutes to extend the discussion. Thus, the negative has the opportunity to widen the ground of argument. Of course, the affirmative still speaks last and can use the opportunity to point out why negative considerations are not relevant. Still, it would seem that as long as the negative is inventive and relevant it should be able to use the time advantage to its maximum strategic value.

Both the affirmative and negative are more involved in cross-examination than they are in other debate formats. Cross-examination becomes a more significant feature to the extent that it is useful in generating positions, testing evidence, and separating relevant from irrelevant considerations. Even more significant, the debate is between only two people, and the rapport established in cross-examination influences the tone and style of the activity. Unlike team debate, which has a corporate or legal style, Lincoln-Douglas depends on social grace, friendliness, and appropriate behavior—that is, on the character of the individuals involved—to create an interesting, productive dispute. Cross-examination should still be pointed, but it needs to be reasonable and interesting.

Debating Value Propositions

The factor that makes Lincoln-Douglas most interesting, apart from its unusual format, is the nature of the proposition to be discussed. Lincoln-Douglas debate pertains to **propositions of value**, which may be defined as statements that express preference. Statements of preference are an almost infinite class. One can prefer classical music to rock and roll, Ronald Reagan to Ted Kennedy, vegetables to meat, debate to football.

What makes value statements worthy of debate? Perhaps the best way to understand the nature of a debatable value question is to contrast propositions of value to propositions of policy. A **proposition of policy** always states a question of future conduct that is being proposed. Presumption resides with the negative because the affirmative asks for a change. Debate takes place because the proposal is, on its face, a request to do something different. The result is that the affirmative has the burden to show cause—a significant harm that cannot be remedied by the status quo and can be remedied, or at least mitigated, by an alternative.

The primary similarity between both types of proposition is that opinion in each type is unsettled on a matter of some concern. If everyone agreed that a policy was good or, alternatively, that a value was an absolute norm, then there would be no reason for discussion. However, beyond this similarity the responsibilities for discussion are quite different. Note that a value question does not call for the advocates to debate possible futures that will be influenced by present choices of conduct. Rather, a value question focuses exclusively on the present and asks the debaters to resolve a matter as to how the community (represented by the judge) feels about a question of common concern. Thus, the value proposition asks the debaters to place a concern in a context of appreciation or understanding. There are many different ways of doing this, and the framing of the value question will determine what the contextual obligation of the affirmative and negative will be.

The Question of Comparative Values

A **comparative value proposition** is structured along the lines of the statement *x is better than y*. Such values can be abstract (for example, freedom is better than equality), or they can be concrete (for example, the Latin Americans are better trading partners than the Europeans). A good comparative value proposition is one that takes two values that are of relatively equal strength but clearly different and asks for support.

The affirmative in a comparative value proposition has to show that under most or all circumstances the proposition is true. If the values under consideration are abstract, as in the proposition "Competition is of greater value than cooperation," the affirmative needs to develop concrete examples that demonstrate the truth of the statement. In this case, the affirmative might show that the resources necessary for a society to operate are maximized to the extent that individuals are motivated and that motivation depends on competition. The affirmative might also say that artistically and intellectually competition moves people to think harder and perform better than does a cooperative system, which breeds complacency and inspires an excessive concern for fairness. Note that the examples are developed by (1) stating why the value of competition is a positive good and (2) stating that the good is better because it is antecedent to or trades off favorably with its competitor. If competition is not proven valuable per se, then there is no reason to think that it is a good value in the first place. If competition is proven to be good, but it is *not* shown that it trades off favorably with cooperation, then there is no reason to think that it is better than cooperation.

Comparative propositions are often concrete rather than abstract. For example, a proposition might say, "It is better to cut government spending than it is to raise taxes." Note that the implied time frame is the present. Neither the negative nor the affirmative has the right to assume that the word *always* is implied in a value proposition when it is not there. In instances of concrete comparison, then, the affirmative examines current circumstances and evaluates the alternatives available. In many instances concrete comparisons may have implications for policy.

If it is unwise to raise taxes, then a plan of action could, for example, re-quire a balanced federal budget. But in value debate, the affirmative does *not* have the duty to defend alternative, future policies. Rather, the af-firmative burden is limited to evaluating the options put under consider-ation by the resolution. Still, such a debate involves policy issues insofar as one is looking to the consequences or outcomes of choices. In this case, the affirmative and negative argue much as they do in a counterplan debate by comparing the merits of policy. Contentions for such debating should be developed as comparisons.

The negative position in a comparative value argument may be con-structed on one of three grounds. The first position is to argue the in-verse of the affirmative. If the affirmative contends that duty is better than pursuit of private happiness, the negative argues that pursuit of pri-vate happiness is a higher value than performance of duty. If the affirma-tive argues that privately funded retirement plans are better than forced contributions to social security, the affirmative defends the reverse. In such instances, the negative must not only object to the affirmative's characterization of its side as a defense of the superior value, it also must advance constructive arguments defending the worth of its own position.

The second position is to argue that the two values are equivalent. Here, the negative might argue, for example, that Faulkner and Bellow are both fine authors and that while each is different, neither is necessar-ily better. Such a position is advanced by demonstrating the unique con-text that makes a comparative evaluation inappropriate. For instance, it might be said that, although Faulkner deals with Southern culture and Bellow represents Chicago, both are regional writers who did the most with their material. The point is that there are no reasonable grounds on which to assign a value of comparative merit. To win this argument, the negative must undermine the affirmative standards of comparison—in this particular example, the status of absolute artistic quality.

The third position available to a negative is to argue that not enough is known about the question to make a decision at this time. The nega-tive asks for a ballot on the grounds that any evaluation would be the product of ignorance, prejudice, or parochialism. Such an attack would (1) emphasize all the possible areas of value comparison that must be re-solved before a well-founded judgment can be rendered and (2) point to the fact that the affirmative has either failed to consider all the values in question or that no answer is possible because of limiting factors on re-search at the present time. In the comparison of Faulkner and Bellow, it might be pointed out that literary criticism is itself in a state of disagreement as to what constitutes a good work or a significant contribution. Note that if the negative takes this position, it is precluded from arguing the first and second positions. If not enough appropriate information exists at this time, then the reverse of the proposition cannot be asserted.

Value Assertions

Value assertion propositions are categorical judgments stated as positive or negative judgments. A positive value assertion states that some person, belief, custom, practice, event, or instrument is good. "Good" can be variously described by the proposition as right, just, valuable, beneficial, or beautiful. A negative value assertion states the reverse, depicting "bad" as unjust, worthless, detrimental, or harmful. Unlike a policy proposition, which is required to be stated in the positive manner, a value assertion may be either positive or negative. Like a policy proposition, the value assertion proposition clearly delineates grounds for debate.

Value assertions may be either concrete or abstract. A concrete value assertion identifies a person, thing, event, or custom to be evaluated. The value assertion may refer to a class or a specific event. For instance, a value assertion referring to a class would state, "The Olympic movement has been worthwhile for sports." This proposition would obtain greater specificity by saying, "The Los Angeles Olympics was worthwhile for sports." If the value statement refers to a class, then the affirmative case is constructed by showing examples chosen from the class and drawing a generalization. In this case, the affirmative would argue that the Olympics in Japan, West Germany, Moscow, Los Angeles, and Seoul were good for sports. The burden of the affirmative analysis is to show that all members of the class have the same essential qualities—stimulating competition, drawing publicity, featuring fair and sportsmanlike play. The affirmative must be prepared to show why counterexamples—that is, Olympic events that were unsuccessful—were atypical. Moreover, the affirmative must be prepared to show why the harmful consequences of Olympics for sports (say, in giving a stage for nationalism or terrorism) are either accidental qualities of only some Olympics or do not outweigh the good features.

In a value assertion referring to a specific person, event, or custom, the affirmative must be thoroughly acquainted with the unique qualities of the instance in question. For example, in debating the qualities of the Los Angeles Olympics, it might be pointed out that the free enterprise system of holding events made that particular event a success for sports. Whereas other Olympics burdened cities and left large debts, the Los Angeles games helped the city by generating revenue and increasing civic spiritedness and showed that large sporting events could help the public, thereby making international sports more viable. Note that the burden of the affirmative here is a bit different. The affirmative must show why a member of a class has unique features that make it of noteworthy value.

The negative position in a debate over value assertion is variable. The negative may wish simply to deny the proposition. In that case the negative has two options. The first option is to say that the link between the valued instance and class is simply not true. Consider the abstract proposition "The two-party system is detrimental to democratic ideals." If the affirmative argues that the reason for detriment is that two parties tend not to reflect the range of public sentiment, monopolize office, and provide inadequate choices, the negative can respond that the parties are diverse, that choices exist within the range of party opinion, and that such a system guarantees discussion and debate. Here the negative simply argues the reverse of the affirmative.

On the other hand, the negative might choose to say that the value as defined by the affirmative is misrepresented. Here the negative would show that democracy does not mean fragmented, diverse, chaotic speech but requires organized, meaningful representation of government by the people. If the negative utilizes this position, it might agree with the characterization of the party system advanced by the affirmative but show that the value in question has been inappropriately represented. Strategically, it might make sense to argue that the affirmative has inappropriately characterized the class or thing in question *and* has misdefined the value that is being applied as a criterion. However, the negative must first make sure that no contradiction appears. In the above example, the negative position would be inconsistent if both the value of representative democracy and the nonrepresentative nature of the party system were contended in the same debate.

Apart from straight refutation, the negative has the option of maintaining that there is not enough certainty or evidence to suggest that a judgment can be made. Suppose a proposition was stated thus: "United States defense spending is excessive." Certainly, there have been a lot of arguments pro and con on this issue. But it may be the case that in the present situation, when the United States cannot be sure of Soviet intentions, a judgment cannot be made. Surely, the Soviets have made peace gestures, agreed to reduce intermediate-range nuclear weapons, generally followed the ABM treaty, reduced nuclear testing, and conceded on some human rights issues. But they also have increased their total number of nuclear weapons, supported third-world wars of liberation, continue to violate human rights, and so on. By balancing conflicting signals, the negative sets up a context that implies that no judgment can be rendered at this time. To the extent that the negative can show that the relevant context of judgment suggests substantial uncertainty—equal reasons for a favorable or unfavorable judgment—it undercuts the affirmative rationale for a resulting affirmation of the value assertion.

Value Exclusivity

One of the more interesting calls for evaluation is that which challenges advocates to come up with ultimate commitments. Just as adjectives permit people to make routine judgments about the positive (good), the comparative (better), and the superlative (best), value propositions enable debaters to refine their thinking and to move toward refined judgments of discrimination. Value propositions that ask for exclusive judgments ask that a certain person, event, thing, custom, belief, practice, or class be put above all competitors. Sometimes such a proposition puts an unfair burden on the affirmative, especially when it calls for defense of exclusivity when there are a number of near competitors. For instance, if the proposition said that Billy Graham was the best preacher in the United States, the affirmative would not have a hard time defending the fact that his work is good, important, even outstanding. But given that the United States contains many good preachers, it would be hard to defend one against the many alternatives that could be advanced by the negative. On the other hand, questions of value exclusivity can be fairly advanced when there is a small group of options. The proposition can be worded so as to provide the context for judgment. Such a proposition might read, "The Los Angeles Lakers are the best professional basketball team." Because there are only a limited number of basketball teams and an even more limited number of professional basketball teams, and because there are only one or two competitors, the exclusivity of the proposition does not put an unfair burden on the affirmative.

An affirmative case that argues for an exclusive value judgment often proceeds by process of elimination. The technical term for this case structure is a **residues case**. A residues case is one that eliminates all alternatives except for the one that the affirmative desires. In the instance of the Los Angeles Lakers, the affirmative might draw comparisons in the following way. Teams that have not been to the championship finals cannot be considered as good because they have lost in the early rounds of competition. Of those teams that have been to the finals in recent years, none has as consistent a record as the Lakers. The Rockets beat the Lakers once, but they have not returned to the finals. The Celtics beat the Lakers more than once, but they have not won as many championships in the 1980s. The Los Angeles Lakers have the best record. Because there is a relatively small class for comparison, this case structure is relatively easy to define. However, the affirmative should be prepared to argue that other examples offered by the negative are not appropriate or adequate competitors.

The negative has several options. The first option is straight refutation. Here the negative might choose to say that one or all of the class in question are superior or equal to that defended by the affirmative. If the negative chooses one example, the debate evolves into a straight comparison. In the above instance, the negative might wish to defend the Celtics on the grounds that their losses to the Lakers have been the product of more injuries rather than less talent. Moreover, issues other than the NBA finals might be considered in evaluating the quality of a team. The negative may choose to defend multiple examples that are better in different ways than the affirmative example. For instance, in addition to defending the Celtics as a matter of past record, the negative might wish to look at future potential and argue that the Mavericks have younger, stronger, quicker, more talented players and are likely to be the best team at this time. The strategic value of arguing a single example is that the negative can focus in depth on a single comparison; multiple examples make the round more complex but also permit the negative some latitude of extension in concentrating rebuttal arguments.

In advancing straight refutation, the negative might wish to expand the pool of examples competing for the judgment of best in the field. In the above example, the affirmative obviously wants to discuss record, while the negative moves beyond consideration of record to an alternative criterion—present prospects. Expanding the grounds for argument is a useful negative strategy because the affirmative is likely to pick the strongest value criterion to define its judgment. If the negative expands the grounds of debate, however, it must show why its criteria are relevant, important, and superior to others for assessing the proposition. In this case the quality of talent is of obvious relevance, and it is important to assessing team strength, but it is *not* self-evident why it is a superior rationale for evaluating the proposition. After all, the Mavericks have had great talent for a number of years and have been unable to beat the Lakers consistently. Record matters more, the affirmative says. The negative must be able to clash at this level and show why record matters less than its own standards. Unless the negative is able to clash at the level of criteria for evaluation, it cannot reasonably widen the grounds of debate.

The final option for the negative is to show that there is not enough information to make a superlative judgment. Here the negative might suggest that all competitors for the superlative status are relatively equal, that the differences are not decisive, or that conditions are in a state of flux and that the possibility of judgment is therefore impaired.

On Balance Judgment

Frequently, value propositions are linked to decisions about what is good, better, or best. These propositions induce people to argue about what is good or bad, better or worse, at the top or only near it. Another kind of value argument centers on questions that invite debaters to consider mixed affairs on the whole. The locus of clash focuses on how a person, event, situation, custom, or belief that has had a checkered career can be assessed as a whole. The balanced judgment value proposition is framed by asking for a qualified assessment.

The following example has provoked much controversy: "On the whole, television has been good for society." Note that the framing of this proposition implicitly acknowledges that television has been extensively criticized and even that it may have done some harm. The affirmative is not expected to prove that television has always been good, that it is better than other media, or that it is the best thing that could have filled the public airwaves. Rather, the proposition permits the affirmative to acknowledge, even to argue, that television has not always worked well. It asks the affirmative to take the good and bad into consideration and to show how the former offsets the latter.

For instance, it may be the case that television does create bad health habits by advertising unwholesome food to children. But it is also the case that television alerts the public to health hazards, provides aerobics and exercise shows, and informs the public about new medical advances. The affirmative argument proceeds to show why studies of television's negative influence on nutrition are unreliable or why TV's positive influences are better for the nation as a whole or in the long run. It also may be the case that television wastes a lot of time, diverting attention from studying and encouraging sedentary habits. The affirmative might acknowledge these complaints but show that the recent expansion of cable TV gives people access to arts and sciences that are not otherwise available. Seen this way, television, including network and cable, makes worthwhile viewing available. The responsibility for mindlessly watching bad programming is the viewers'. In this particular instance, the affirmative asks for a judgment on the grounds that the possibilities offered by TV as a whole outweigh the defects in the intelligence and taste of the viewers.

Affirmative cases that make an on balance judgment must have two components. The first component establishes the criteria on which judgment ought to be rendered. In the case of television, the criteria might be based on either actual effects (as in the health example) or potential consequences (as in the consumer habits example). The affirmative must be prepared to defend its choice of criteria and to clash with others that the negative might advance. The second component of the case shows why the criteria, when applied, demonstrate the affirmative's claim. In the above example, the affirmative claims that cultural potential is the best way to assess a contribution to society. By showing that the arts, sciences, and other events are made uniquely accessible by television, the affirmative demonstrates that television has a positive benefit. By showing that greater numbers of people are attending to quality programs and that people who watch bad television probably would waste their time anyway, the positive impact of such potential is demonstrated on the whole to be better for society.

The negative has a complex task in debating the question of on balance values. The negative must initiate its position by choosing either to accept, deny, or amend the affirmative's criteria for making an on balance judgment. If the criteria are accepted, then the debate focuses on whether the affirmative proves its case. If the criteria are denied, then the negative must show why the affirmative criteria are wrong. In the above example, the negative might say the relative grounds of judgment are not whether television itself has been good or can be good, but whether it has appropriately interacted with other artistic, educational, and cultural forums. By taking the social point of view, the negative might argue that television has displaced traditional lines of authority, minimized individual creative opportunity and talent, disrupted family life, and substituted real, human interaction with a false sense of communication. The criteria of social value and displacement opens up another line of thinking on an overall evaluation. It is not enough, however, to open up alternative criteria. The negative must show why its own criteria are superior to those of the affirmative.

One strategy that may make the negative task a bit easier is to distinguish between true and false instances of the value in question. In the above case, the negative might wish to separate cable television from television per se. It does seem that the core of the affirmative's argument depends on the special services that cable TV has offered. It could be argued that TV offered little variety in programming beyond cops and robbers, crime news and weather, talk and game shows before cable. Although cable TV might have future potential, the assessment of the cumulative effect, the on balance judgment, ought to refer to network television. By distinguishing between a true and a false representative of the class, the negative undercuts affirmative ground. It can be conceded that cable is on balance good if the negative persuades that what the proposition calls for is a judgment on network television.

Debates that call for on balance judgments are certainly the most complex value discussions. Potentially, such debates can have the best results, as many value questions are complex and do require factoring in the good and bad. On the other hand, if criteria are not clearly delineated and discussed, debates can evolve into mere assertions of opposing points of view. When that happens, the side that has the most clearly articulated presumption should win. Unlike policy debate, Lincoln-Douglas offers no natural position for presumption. A judge could assign presumption to the negative simply because he or she believes that all statements are not presumed true until proven so. It is not clear that this approach has a rational basis. A judge could assign presumption to the affirmative simply because the affirmative holds a commitment, and the negative spreads confusion without being clear about anything. It is not clear that this approach is rational, either. Presumption could be argued by teams insofar as the position advocated is agreed on by the many or the elite or is closest to other precedents and values held by society. This approach has much merit; however, a team might argue that self-determination of values is important to the individual as a social, ethical agent. In this instance, the value scheme that gave greatest latitude to the judge's own responsibility for choice would reflect presumption.

Style in Lincoln-Douglas Debate

Lincoln-Douglas debate has a unique style and educational values. The advocate should take the event as an opportunity to cultivate skills different from those required in policy debate. If Lincoln-Douglas is taken as an opportunity for policy debate by other means, then much of its potential contribution to your own career as a skillful advocate will be lost.

Proof

Policy debate requires quite a bit of evidence. Especially regarding questions of national scope, the main influence on the judge's decision is the evidence used to support a position. Values debate requires just as much proof, but the evidence is fundamentally different. First, much of the proof depends on the **character** of the speaker. Statements of value are always personal to some extent. They represent who you are, what you believe, and what you feel is reasonable and important enough to encourage others to agree with. Therefore, the speaker must find the right means of expressing his or her feelings about a question rather than rattling off objective evidence. Careful word choice and well-articulated arguments are essential to linking the character of your own concern with the quality of proof. Second, questions of value move people into concerns beyond the immediate. Here the quality of **opinion** is important, and one of the tests of quality is its ability to endure over time. Since values are the product of human opinion, predilection, or a feeling for the infinite, it stands to reason that those thinkers or leaders who have been time-honored should be given some deference. In policy debate, Aristotle and Plato are out of date. In a values debate, they can provide relevant proof. This is not to say that contemporary opinion is not prized where appropriate. It is to say that the range of evidence is greater.

Organization

Lincoln-Douglas debate has yet to develop a rigid, standard form of presentation. This is good insofar as it permits greater creativity for arguers. Yet, customs evolve and the debater would be wise to follow what is locally approved. Here are some organizational devices that might help speakers.

Careful flowing in Lincoln-Douglas debate insures that you won't drop any important arguments.

Affirmative Constructive

I. Statement of Proposition

II. Definition of Terms
  A. Define what is being evaluated by either a formal definition if the term is abstract (good, bad, liberty, justice) or an ostensive definition if the term is concrete (military spending, health benefits, rock and roll).

  B. State criteria for reaching a judgment about the proposition in the round (calling for a comparative, exclusive, assertive, or on balance judgment). State how such a judgment can be reached in the round of debate.

III. Value Link Contention
  A. Show how an abstract value is related to a concrete value.

  B. Show support for the link.
    1. Historical precedent
    2. Public opinion consensus
    3. Expert or experienced opinion

IV. Example Contentions
   A. Show how the example pertains to the general value.

   B. Show that the example is important.

V. Offset Contentions
   A. Show how alternative links are untrue.

   B. Show how alternative opinion is wrong or misdirected.

   C. Show how counterexamples are unimportant.

Example: "The American space program is a success."

   I. Definition: Space program: NASA space effort from inception to present. Success: Ability to accomplish substantial, important goals.

   II. Criteria: Success should be measured by achievement, and in the context of a space program achievement is measured in terms of making the best of scientific research in the pursuit of exploration.

   III. Value Link Contention: NASA has made significant achievements.
   A. NASA accomplishments have significantly increased humankind's ability to travel into and explore outer space. We can travel farther, see more, and understand more about the universe.

   B. Support: Examples, testimony.

   IV. Offset Contention: Challenger disaster is not a sign of failure.
   A. Risk is an inherent feature of scientific research. Such a failure should not tarnish the program, given the complexity of bringing about success.

   B. Challenger was atypical.

   C. NASA will continue to be supported, and space exploration will proceed.

Note that in this particular case the affirmative chose to offset negative contentions. Although such offsets may give the impression of defensiveness to the judge, sometimes they are desirable—especially when the affirmative is able to predict likely negative objections.

Negative Constructive

The negative constructive speech has several options. It can focus its attack on the definition of terms, criteria for evaluation, link contention, or offsets. It also can advance alternative constructive arguments. The following outline delineates negative options, but remember that the negative need not make all these arguments. Its position will vary with its own strategic options.

   I. Definition of Terms: The affirmative definition is accepted or debated. If debated, the negative may wish to show why the affirmative definition is on the whole unreasonable or why it needs to be significantly amended so that discussion centers on the proposition at hand and not on side issues.

  II. Value Criteria: The negative either accepts, disputes, or amends the criteria. If the latter two choices are made, then the negative must show why its own criteria for assessing value are superior. A negative that disputes the affirmative criteria for judgment yet offers none of its own fails to present a prima facie objection, unless it advances the position that there is not enough known about the subject to render a decision.

 III. Value Link Disagreement

   A. The negative can show that the instances of value advanced by the affirmative are not linked to criteria for judgment; that the qualities of the instance under evaluation are not in line with the affirmative evaluation; and that the examples are not relevant, complete, or as the affirmative represents.

   B. The negative can show that supporting opinion is unreasonably prejudiced, unqualified, or irrelevant to the discussion at hand.

 IV. Value Offset Argument

   A. The negative can advance counterexamples that weigh into consideration.

B. The negative can show an alternative example that meets its own criteria for making an evaluation of the proposition.

C. The negative can either refute or ignore, as appropriate, affirmative offset arguments.

Consider how these arguments might apply to the case supporting the proposition "The American space program is a success."

I. Definition: The negative might agree that the space program is equal to the NASA effort. The negative might amend the definition of success by saying that program goals are not necessarily the only determinants of success. A successful public policy is one that contributes to the welfare of the citizenry in proportion to its costs.

II. Criteria: The negative might agree that success equals achievement but further argue that achievement must be evaluated in terms of contribution to society over the long term. Any program has small achievements. The criterion for making a judgment on NASA should be its overall contribution.

III. Value Link Contention: NASA has made modest achievements in recent years.

A. The early part of the space program was a success. The negative could concede some obviously true examples: putting men and women in orbit, landing on the moon, launching deep exploration vehicles.

B. The more recent part of the program has been a failure. The focus of attack is commitment to space vehicles rather than rockets. It could be argued that the shuttle system is expensive, unreliable, and more of a public relations program than a scientific mission.

C. The negative offers testimony that deviation from the original intentions of NASA has left it a failure in terms of future prospects of scientific achievement.

IV. Offset Arguments

A. The Challenger was an unnecessary disaster.

B. The Challenger weakened political support for NASA and has blocked further scientific research.

Note that the negative tries to make the Challenger example relevant and indicative of the present state of collapse for NASA. The affirmative, on the other hand, tries to minimize the example and in further extension of the argument would point to the necessity for manned space explorations. This argument would be supported by plans for a space station. The affirmative would wish to show its feasibility and value.

Rebuttals

Lincoln-Douglas rebuttal periods are similar to those in policy debate. The stock issues are different, of course. The aim of rebuttals is to narrow the number of arguments to those that are the most relevant and crucial to the debate. Each side must resupport its own position on the appropriate criteria on which to make a value assessment of the proposition. In clashing on criteria, debaters uncover value premises. A **value premise** is a supporting assumption on which a criterion for evaluation is based. In the space program example, a value assumption that underlies the negative position is that the quality of a program must be based on its current state of contribution and its future potential. The affirmative can identify this as a premise and make the counterargument that a program can be a success if it makes a unique, outstanding contribution—and that NASA has done so. The negative might respond that the value premise on which this argument is based is that a program is considered worthwhile even if its history ultimately ends up leaving the situation worse off rather than better. Thus, the negative might say that public policy ought to be judged on pragmatic grounds of continuing contribution. The debate could be further extended, but it is important to generate clash by stipulating unexamined value premises and then showing why they are not sufficient to support criteria of judgment.

Delivery

Delivery is a very important component of Lincoln-Douglas debate. Constructive speeches should receive substantial polishing. Speeches ought to be concise, vivid, and worded with care. Although there is always pressure to speak faster and say more, debaters ought to practice clearing out irrelevant arguments so that those that count receive greater explanation, support, and careful delivery. Since organization is quite complex, debaters should practice arguments quite frequently before tournament participation.

Judging Lincoln-Douglas Debate

The following suggestions constitute NFL guidelines for judging Lincoln-Douglas debate. Advocates should follow these guidelines and adapt strategic arguments to meet the goals of the activity. Interpretation and application of these rules will vary with customs in specific regions. However, these rules suggest good practices for formulating and responding to arguments.

A decision should be based upon:

1. Clear use of values argumentation throughout the round.
   a. Establishment of a values premise to support the debater's position in the round.
   b. Establishment of values criteria based upon the values premise.
   c. Clash in the debate based on the values criteria and the values premise.

2. Application of the values presented to the specific topic at hand.
   a. Validity of logic in relation to the values as applied to the specific logic.
   b. Logical chain of reasoning, using the values, which leads to the conclusions of the affirmative or negative position.
   c. Clear explanation of the relation of the values to the specific topic with adequate explanation and a moderate degree of authoritative opinion for support.

3. Crystallization and condensation of the issues so that there is no need on the part of the listener to feel compelled to "flow" the arguments.

4. Presentation of contextual definitions by both debaters with justification presented by the negative if he or she presents a challenge to the affirmative definitions.

5. Debating of the resolution in its entirety. Neither the affirmative nor the negative are to debate their positions from the standpoint of isolated examples.

6. Effectiveness of delivery, using oral communication skills to persuade the listener with logic, analysis, and mode of delivery. The speaking should approximate superior speaking to community groups.

7. Overall presentation. Isolated "dropped" arguments are not enough to give a speaker a loss in the round.

8. Objectivity must be a primary goal of the Lincoln-Douglas debate judge.

9. Persuasiveness and logic should be the primary considerations. Analysts of values agree that values cannot be "proven" through factual, statistical evidence nor through isolated examples. As such, the judge should disregard attempts on the part of the debater to distort the nature of this event by relying on the above-mentioned. The Lincoln-Douglas debater should be encouraged to develop the use of authoritative opinion as evidence when needed.

10. Judges are encouraged to render a decision on the basis of what they hear, not on the basis of "outlined" arguments.

11. There are no prescribed burdens in Lincoln-Douglas. Neither the affirmative nor the negative has presumption or burden of proof. There is no status quo. Both sides should present the judge with a basic value position which is applied throughout the round and used to refute the resolution.

Summary

Lincoln-Douglas debate offers forensics students a unique opportunity for one-on-one competition. Debating propositions of value requires a special approach and the development of skills not often used in standard policy debate. Lincoln-Douglas debate is also judged by a somewhat different set of criteria. Debaters should familiarize themselves with these criteria as part of their preparation for competition.

Questions for Discussion

1. What are the differences between Lincoln-Douglas debate and two-person policy debate?

2. How does debating a proposition of policy differ from debating a value proposition?

3. What is required to debate value comparisons?

4. What is required to debate value extensions?

5. What is required to debate value exclusivity?

6. What is required to debate on balance judgments about values?

Activities

1. Construct examples of the different types of value propositions and evaluate the "debatability" of the propositions.

2. Discuss the requirements for value topic debating and differentiate the requirements from those of policy debate.

3. Conduct a Lincoln-Douglas debate among class members. Exchange constructive briefs beforehand so that the grounds of argument are defined.

Chapter 8

Forensic Tournaments

Objectives and Key Terms

After studying Chapter 8, you should be able

1. To understand the nature of a forensic tournament.
2. To anticipate the types of judges used at tournaments.
3. To prepare for a forensic tournament.
4. To organize your materials for competition.
5. To look ahead and prepare for future tournaments.
6. To understand the work of hosting a tournament.

To participate in a tournament, you will need to understand the following terms:

preliminary round

preset match

power-matched rounds

elimination round

expert judge

coach judge

lay judge

student judge

ballot

pairing

tabulation room

One of the joys of learning forensics is attending tournaments. Each year hundreds of tournaments are held across the United States. Some of these events are hosted by national organizations like the National Forensic League and the Federation of High Schools. Others are held by universities, either as part of a summer institute program or by special invitation. Still others are sponsored by local high schools as part of a season of forensic activities. In most areas of the United States, the high school forensic student has a range of choices for attending tournaments.

The key element that makes tournaments exciting is competition. When you enter debate or an individual event, you will be competing against students from other schools and perhaps other parts of the country. Such a situation allows you to test your skill and preparation. Tournaments are designed so that participants encounter increasingly difficult levels of competition as they continue competing. There are few more intense or exciting moments than awaiting the results of a close quarterfinal round of competition. Unlike classroom activity that occurs in rounds of lectures and tests, forensics always provides an intense, highly motivated, memorable experience. Competition can bring out the best of your own activities.

This chapter is designed to help you understand what makes up a forensic contest and to help you get the most out of the tournaments you will attend. You should approach every tournament with the assumption that it will be a good learning experience. In later life, you will encounter situations just as intense and important as those you encounter at a tournament. If you learn well how to master the situation of tournament competition, you will be able to handle other pressure activities later on.

What Is a Forensic Tournament?

The first thing to understand is that no two tournaments are exactly alike. The debate squad or speech program that chooses to host a tournament does so because it wants to provide a good environment for the forensic community's activities. A tournament is always an expression of how the hosts see the values of speech activities. Hence, each tournament has different activities, schedules of events, rules for participation, and practices concerning the use of judging and the matching of contestants. Generally, such diversity is a good idea. If all tournaments were alike, the activities might become routine and dull. Diversity permits students to adapt to the situation at hand, which is required in all good public speaking.

The debater and coach should read carefully each tournament invitation to see what special rules or procedures operate at a tournament they wish to attend. Too much diversity would leave students in the position of not knowing what to expect at all. Fortunately, most tournaments have several features in common, which will be discussed in the following pages.

Competition

Tournaments usually divide activities into preliminary and elimination rounds. A preliminary round matches competition randomly or through some preassigned seating system.

In debate, **preliminary rounds** are divided into preset matches and power matches. A **preset match** is made by the tournament hosts before competition begins. Two teams are assigned to debate each other—one on the affirmative and the other on the negative. A tournament may preset the majority or all of the preliminary rounds. **Power-matched rounds** are those in which matches are created based upon the accumulated record of teams at the tournament. If you have won all of your preset rounds, for example, you will meet another team that has won all of its rounds. If you have lost one round, then you will meet a team that also has one loss. Preliminary rounds usually consist of four, six, or eight matches per team, with each team alternating sides between affirmative and negative. The teams with the best record advance to the elimination rounds.

In individual events, preliminary rounds may be divided up into preset and power-matched events. Of course, such events do not involve teams, but sections in which individual speakers either give orations, do extemporaneous speaking, or participate in some other contest event. The judge of an individual event does not give a win or a loss, as in a round of debate. Rather, the judge ranks and rates the speakers. A rating is based on a point system that assigns a quality value to the performance. Ranking is based on a judgment as to the comparative merits of the speakers. Those with the best ratings get the highest rankings. The one or two best speakers in a section will be chosen to advance to the semifinal or final round of the individual events.

Elimination rounds in debate match teams with the best records in a bracket. Depending on tournament size, the bracket could begin with double octofinals, octofinals, quarterfinals, or even semifinal rounds. A single loss in a tournament elimination round eliminates a team from the tournament, while the winner goes on to the next higher level of competition. In preliminary rounds, there is usually only one judge. In elimination rounds, there are usually multiple judges. The team that wins persuades the majority of judges of its position. In some cases, a particular debate may not be held if the teams meeting are from the same school and the tournament has chosen not to rearrange the bracket to accommodate such a circumstance. In this case, the team with the better record typically advances.

Elimination rounds in individual events are comprised of those speakers who had the best ranking and rating in preliminary rounds. The number of elimination and preliminary rounds at a tournament will depend on the number of entrants and the tournament schedule. At a minimum, though, there is one preliminary round and one elimination (final) round. The winner of an individual event competition is usually determined by multiple judges in the final round. Sometimes the winner is determined on a cumulative rating and ranking assessment that includes performances in the early competition in the tournament. Individual events participants should always consult the tournament schedule to see how events are being evaluated.

Judging

Forensic tournaments always involve judges who make decisions concerning the outcome and quality of events. The judge is the person who stands in for a larger audience and who renders a decision in accordance with tournament custom and good educational practices. As in any speaking situation, it is up to the speaker to adapt to the level of expertise and needs of a judge. The following description of alternative judging pools should give you some clues about the kinds of judging to expect at forensic tournaments.

Expert Judge

Often, tournament events are judged by students who have recently graduated or gone on to college. Because these students are familiar with the latest forensic theory and practices, they are regarded as experts. **Expert judges** require less explanation in order to comprehend the nature and weight of an argument. They should also be less prone to general persuasive rhetoric as they understand and are concerned with the technical issues involved in debate and individual events. Expert judges may wish to "intervene" more in the round because they know the material and may see implications in arguments that the debater misses.

Coach Judge

In some areas of the country, the **coach** of a school may be asked to judge. Coaches often make for good judges because they are trained in debate and know the issues. They also have the objectivity necessary to see how arguments develop on their own terms. While a coach appreciates the issues involved in a debate, she or he may also wish to see signs of good public presentation. After all, the larger purpose of debate is to enable students to become skilled advocates.

Lay Judge

Some tournaments invite **lay judges** from the community. While these people are interested in current affairs and have various levels of intellectual accomplishment, they are not specialists in debate theory or in the topic under discussion. Speakers need to take this into account and to explain issues in greater detail and show why particular issues are important to the outcome of a round of debate. Although debaters tend to prefer the expert judge, the student should appreciate the lay judge. Remember that if you try a case before a jury in later life, the outcome will depend not on your ability to use legal jargon, but on your ability to persuade people of good sense that your position is correct.

Student Judge

A few tournaments use students in the judging process. If you are asked to judge, remember that you must be absolutely fair in rendering a decision. No real friend would ask you to play favorites. Also, when you write a ballot, remember that the purpose of commenting on a debate or individual event is to be constructive—to help another person improve. Just as you want to learn from ballots that are written to you, you should want to help other people learn from the ballots that you write.

Events

A forensic tournament involves a variety of different events. The tournament invitation indicates what events are available, lists the specific rules or guidelines that govern the events, and gives the schedule for competition. Some tournaments offer both debate and individual events. Others do not. The student and coach should decide together well in advance which events will be undertaken.

Tournaments often have different levels of competition. Novice divisions are for beginners who enter the tournament for the first time or are just beginning their forensic career. Senior debate is for those who are more experienced. Sometimes a tournament will have an open division that mixes beginners and advanced students. The level of competition should be determined by the degree of readiness a student achieves before the tournament. If you have been able to conduct research, have practice rounds, and prepare a number of briefs, then you are ready to compete. If this is your second year of debate, then you are ready to compete at a senior level. Premature entrance into advanced debate is not always beneficial. You may not understand the arguments well enough to challenge another team successfully. Staying too long at a lower level of competition is not wise either. When competition becomes too easy, there is little to be learned.

There is no easy rule for determining what kinds of events you should participate in. Some students enjoy a break from debate and see extemporaneous speaking as a way to add to their understanding of current affairs and improve their speaking skills. Other students like to write speeches and use original oratory as a way to talk about issues of a broader and more elevated nature than those that come up during policy debate. If the schedule permits both individual events and debate, then entry into this competition is advised. On the other hand, debate can be so intense that individual events become a distraction. It is important to get the agreement of your coach and colleague on the range of tournament participation.

Special rules govern all events. Individual events rules, for example, cover time limits, nature of authorship, subject matter, and the use of manuscripts. Debate rules govern evidence citation, time constraints on speaking, preparation time during rounds, and procedures for forfeitures. Pay special attention to these rules before entering the tournament. They will guide your preparation and provide a code of conduct at the tournament.

Special Awards

Tournaments often formally recognize outstanding individual and collective efforts. Debate tournaments offer speaker awards, which are granted to contestants who have accumulated the greatest number of quality points during the preliminary rounds. Ties for speaker awards are often broken by comparing ranks. Of course, debaters should welcome official recognition of their achievement, but they should not lose sight of the importance of team effort in winning debates. Many forensic tournaments offer sweepstakes awards. In general, such recognition goes to the schools that have had the best performance at a tournament. There is no generally accepted way of choosing sweepstakes winners because the award depends on weighing the outcome of debate and individual events activities. The tournament invitation will indicate how the winner of the award is determined.

Preparing for a Forensic Tournament

Once you have an idea of the rules, regulations, and nature of an upcoming tournament and have assessed the kind of judging and competition that will be available, you can begin preparing for a tournament. Preparation falls into four stages.

The first stage of preparation involves discussing the goals for the tournament. If you approach a tournament by simply saying that you need to do everything you possibly can do to get ready, you will raise your state of anxiety but will not get much accomplished. No one is ever fully prepared for a tournament. The debate topics are so broad as to involve, potentially, a career of research and thinking. Moreover, you and your colleague will inevitably be working under time constraints. Remember, schoolwork always comes first. Forensics is a supplement to learning and not a replacement for it. Given a great number of competing time demands, you need to establish a set of minimum goals that you want to accomplish in preparing for the tournament.

The first goal should be based on the kind of personal achievement you want to strive for at the tournament. One kind of achievement might be the development of a new idea that you think is worth testing or introducing to the forensic community. Is there a new, exciting argument that deserves to be heard? Another kind of goal is the development of a particular skill. For instance, cross-examination requires careful planning and can be an exciting activity. Perhaps a tournament can be a testing ground for a novel use of questioning in relation to your ability to conduct refutation. Whether you are thinking about substantive ideas, skills, or special strategies, it is important to agree with your coach and colleague on a set of productive goals for a tournament and to use the tournament as a way of achieving those goals.

Another kind of goal involves looking at the minimum number of activities you must perform to get ready for a tournament. All debate teams should have a completed and practiced first affirmative constructive. Some second-line affirmative arguments are needed to defend the case. This is the highest priority. On the negative side of the ledger, it is essential that a team develop one or two disadvantages against the general thrust of the topic. These can be adapted to suit specific cases. As the season progresses and you attend more tournaments, these minimum goals will be divided between repairing the arguments that need more evidence and developing new positions. Keep adding to your repertoire over the year.

The second stage of preparation involves practicing the material you have prepared. It does little good to research a lot of evidence or write many arguments if you are unfamiliar with them when you reach the tournament. Rather, it is necessary to speak—and speak again—before the tournament. If you can engage in practice debates with your colleague or another team on the debate squad, you can try out arguments and repair them. This permits you to reduce the possibility of making costly mistakes in the debate round.

Preparation is important at this stage because it enables you to simulate the debate round experience. Often debaters who do not practice speaking find themselves rusty at the beginning of a tournament. If you read your speech or practice arguing from briefs before the tournament, you will be able to spend more energy thinking up arguments on the spot at the tournament. Do not be discouraged if the arguments do not sound good. It is difficult to capture the excitement of tournament competition when you are speaking in front of your squad members who doubtless have heard the arguments before. But such speaking is vital to a good tournament.

The third stage of preparation involves sorting out materials for the tournament competition. It does a debater little good to have the best evidence, briefs, and arguments if he or she can't find them at the tournament. Debaters who do the best usually have an efficient filing and flowing system that permits them to lay their hands on appropriate materials at the right time.

One way to organize your material is to color code the briefs. If you use blue paper, for example, in all the speeches and briefs pertaining to the affirmative case, then you can easily sort out what is relevant to an affirmative debate. Different colors can also be used for different sets of negative arguments. Another way to organize material is to distinguish high priority evidence, which is likely to be used in every round of debate, from low priority material, which will be held in reserve. High priority evidence should be kept together, while backup material can be sorted out by topic, each placed in separate folders. (Incidentally, it is a good idea to leave a photocopy of your affirmative case and briefs with your coach. Many debaters have lost rounds because this vital information was misplaced.)

The final stage of preparation for the tournament involves setting up a schedule for the tournament itself. At any tournament, there will be times of intense competition and times for socializing with friends. The strategic debater will use some of the socializing time to make adjustments in arguments. Work out a schedule with your colleague so that after a given round both of you can go over the debate and determine what worked and what did not. Given that a tournament is an intense experience, you will have to schedule such work sessions carefully. Otherwise, on-the-spot adjustments will be difficult. However, if you and the rest of the squad develop a working rhythm at tournaments, such coordination will be invaluable.

The Tournament Experience

The tournament offers a complex set of experiences. Like any other event, it involves people whom you are very close to and people who seem indifferent or even a bit unfriendly to you. Especially when competition is keen, feelings run high. For this reason it is important to keep the tournament experience in perspective. Remember that later in life you will be in equally competitive situations. If you can learn to keep your cool at forensic contests and perform with grace and style under pressure there, you should be able to keep your head in difficult argument situations later on. The following are some suggestions for developing a perspective on the activity. The suggestions are derived from the authors' own experiences as students and coaches at tournaments, so they have some basis in experience. But we strongly believe that you will have to decide on the meaning of the experience and your own values.

The primary requirement for gaining a perspective on tournament experience is to remember that your work and not you are being evaluated. When someone criticizes your work negatively, it is difficult not to take such a criticism personally. Some debaters get depressed when they lose because they think that the loss means they have failed and that they are not as smart as their opponents. Others get angry and want to blame the judge or their colleague for a loss. Neither attitude is very productive. Indeed, viewing a loss as a matter of blame undercuts your ability to see arguments objectively and to search for improvement. So, too, a win does not mean that you are smarter than another person; indeed, it is possible that a win deserves criticism because the arguments could have been better. In some situations a loss may be the

A tournament elimination round is likely to draw many interested observers.

best that could have been done with a particular position or set of arguments. You should try to develop a perspective that permits you to evaluate your own arguments and the criticisms of others objectively. Pay attention to critiques. After a tournament, go through the arguments that you made and try to assess the strongest and the weakest and decide on new strategies. Only by maintaining an orientation to the arguments themselves will you be able to improve.

While a tournament is held to advance the quality of argument, it is also intended to help you understand how conflict is conducted and resolved with other people. If a debater wins a round by tricking the other side with an unusual affirmative or a strange strategy, the question must be raised as to whether that is a good thing to do to opponents who are also friends in a way. Remember, argument takes cooperation. Tournaments are held because people are dedicated to a process of learning through contention and clash. Certainly, clever strategies are part of debating, but a debater needs to develop personal standards of fairness and scholarship. These standards are based on recognizing that competitors deserve the best ideas and evidence to consider rather than strategic guile.

One of the key features of a tournament is cooperation with your fellow squad members. Tournaments are pressure situations. In each round choices have to be made, and not all the choices will be under your control. Given that slight mistakes sometimes have consequences for the outcome of a round, there is a tendency for debaters to debate their own colleagues—before, during, and after rounds—about the arguments to be used. At a tournament, you need to find a way to develop reciprocal trust and keep communication open. When things are going well, it is easy to be on good terms with a colleague. When things are tense or a disappointing loss has been incurred, it is more difficult. In such situations it is very important to find a way to work out differences, to continue a give and take in planning new positions, to find a way to maximize cooperation. Just as you will be asked to work with colleagues in future life, you will be well served by learning how to work in tense situations with colleagues in debate.

Finally, the tournament experience is a social experience. Occasionally, debaters use the excuse of intense competition to justify rude behavior. However, politeness is important. If you are debating inexperienced debaters, it does no good to make fun of them. You were once inexperienced. If you dislike a judge or think a tournament is poorly administered, it does little good to complain. Few people will listen willingly to a debater's rendition of how she or he thought a debate was unfairly decided. Although it is understandable that you wish to talk with friends, exclusive cliques simply make the experience less than it would be if you knew people from other programs. Debate tournaments require civility. Precisely because they are so intensely competitive they require mature, polite, and deferential behavior. You will find your self-control tested at times. The best debater is in complete self-control at all times.

Post-Tournament Work

After you have been eliminated from a tournament, the most important work of the tournament begins!

Debaters often underestimate the value of watching elimination rounds. Tired, discouraged, and ready to go home, debaters conclude that once they have been eliminated there is no need for further participation. But watching events can be extremely valuable. When you are debating, it is difficult to get the perspective of a judge who hears all the arguments and who has to sort out the significance of each issue. By watching a round and carefully flowing arguments, you will be able to develop a judge's perspective. Listening to a round enables you to hear ideas that you have not thought of, record new sources for evidence, and analyze extensions to arguments different from your own. More important, if you try to resolve the arguments, you will see how difficult it is to sort out competing claims and put all the arguments into perspective. Try it! Once you have listened to a round, think of what could have been done differently or try to guess how the decision will come out (and for what reasons). Such analysis will aid your efforts to be persuasive in future tournaments.

When you return from a tournament, you and your colleague and coach should conduct a debriefing. Go over the tournament round by round. You may wish to redeliver some speeches. In this exercise, drop out the weakest arguments and concentrate on what you think were the most important. Do this with arguments you lost and arguments you won. Both deserve strengthening.

After assessing your tournament performance, take a look at the affirmative case and most often used briefs. Try to reach an agreement with your colleague as to the likely direction that developments will take. For arguments that are strong, see if there are ways to make them even stronger. Your opponents are more likely to work on arguments they lost than on arguments they won. Perhaps updating the evidence will provide an edge the next time. Perhaps you will want to narrow a claim so that there is less ground to attack. In any event constant improvement is necessary to make sure that a strong argument remains competitive.

Weak arguments should be either strengthened or eliminated. Some arguments are so weak that they do not merit further research. It is difficult to give up on an argument once time has been spent researching it. However, if an argument is not successful and judges see either a consistent flaw or a different flaw every time, then there may be little value in putting in further time on the issue.

A final post-tournament activity should be looking for new ideas or arguments. Judges tire of hearing the same kind of argument, tournament after tournament. Moreover, the issue grows stale and too complicated for clear adjudication. Debaters should look for new sources of evidence, new variations on old arguments, or entirely new ideas on a topic. Not all of your time can be spent in this pursuit. Often, however, a new idea can make all the difference at a future tournament.

Hosting a Tournament

Your team may wish to host a forensic tournament. If so, examine a calendar of events in your area and see if there is an available weekend. Examine the tournament invitations for last year to determine what local customs govern participation rules and the appropriate kind and range of events. Contact programs in the area to see if they would be interested in attending the tournament at your school. The following is a checklist of activities necessary for putting together a tournament.

1. *Facilities.* The tournament planners should get a list of open rooms, including an auditorium or central meeting area, and reserve these facilities. The number of events and tournament entries and schedule will depend on what facilities the school can make available.

2. *Schedule.* Get the tournament on the local schedule of tournaments. Send out invitations that specify rules, regulations, dates, and times

of events. Set entry fees and judges' fees so that you will be able to cover the costs of hosting and to hire appropriate judges.

3. *Judges.* Require coaches to judge, one per two teams. Look to school service organizations for guest judges. Hire limited numbers of guest judges if coaches are not available.

4. *Pairing.* Preset tournament preliminary rounds and assign rooms and judges to individual events sections and debates. Type a schedule for distribution to tournament participants.

5. *Tabulation room.* Set up a tabulation room that will keep track of results during the tournament for purposes of power matching and selection of elimination round participants. The tabulation room should also keep track of ballots and distribute results at the end of the tournament.

6. *Special events.* A tournament may have one or more assemblies at appropriate times to announce changes in preset rounds or elimination round results. The tournament might also wish to sponsor special seminars for the participants.

Needless to say, hosting a good tournament takes time and patience. Excellent tournaments are run efficiently, fairly, and graciously.

Summary

Competition is the final stage of debate preparation. Debaters spend many hours researching a topic and formulating affirmative cases and negative positions. Strategic thought goes into the selection of arguments. The process is not complete until debate is taken beyond the classroom and practice rounds and put to the test in a tournament setting.

Participation in tournament competition is a unique opportunity for you to try out new ideas, refine arguments, polish critical listening skills, and speak. Beyond the performance aspects of debate, the tournament also affords you an opportunity to make friendships. The skills you cultivate will help you win in competition; the ability to test yourself under fire will last a lifetime.

Through competition you learn to persuade others, sometimes contrary to their initial prejudices. You will sometimes find yourself being required to argue positions not exactly in line with your own personal beliefs. This should help you learn the values and beliefs of others. Over time, debate competition will give you the opportunity to serve as both participant and judge. The first tournament is exciting, often scary. While the fear leaves after experience, the thrill of exciting competition continues.

Questions for Discussion

1. After learning the basics of debate, why should you consider participating in a debate tournament?

2. In the tournament setting there are several types of rounds. Explain the following: preliminary rounds (preset rounds and power-matched rounds), elimination rounds.

3. Typically there are four categories of judges at a tournament. What are the differences among judges and how should one adapt to those differences?

4. How do you decide what level of competition is appropriate to you and your colleague?

5. What is the best way to prepare for tournament competition?

6. Why should you observe debate rounds when you are not participating in competition?

Activities

1. Attend a local tournament. Take your flow and the judge's ballot from one of your preliminary rounds. Explain why you won or lost the round and what arguments could have been developed differently.

2. Using the flow and ballot from a round you lost, rework the arguments the judge outlined as the reason for his or her decision.

3. After you have been eliminated from a debate tournament, listen to debate rounds. Flow the rounds. Write out a ballot explaining your reason for your decision. See if the judges voted the same way.

4. Develop a schedule for a possible debate tournament. You should assume four preliminary rounds and 12 teams. Remember each team should have the same number of affirmative and negative rounds.

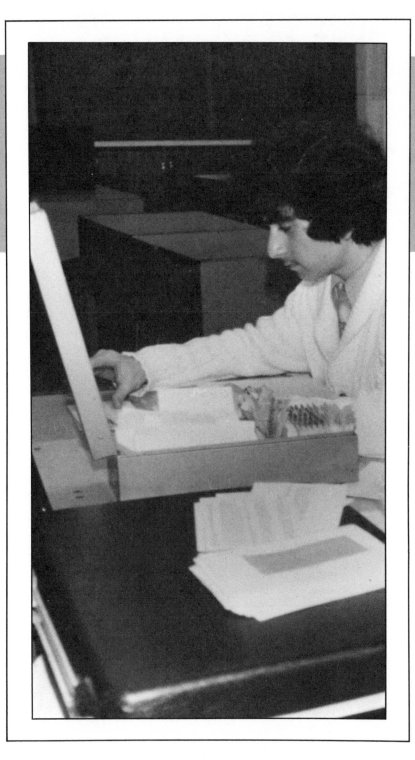

Chapter 9

Communicative Persuasion in Strategic Debate

Objectives and Key Terms

After studying Chapter 9, you should be able

1. To explain and demonstrate the difference between performance and communication.

2. To explain, with examples, the criteria different kinds of judges use in a round.

3. To develop an understanding of the nature of the debate speech— why it contains so much material and why it is delivered at such a rapid rate.

4. To explain how the debater can develop high source credibility.

5. To explain and demonstrate the tactics of effective communication.

To communicate persuasively, you will need to understand the following terms:

communication	source credibility
"balance of arguments" judge	highlighting
"better job of debating" judge	forecasting
"maverick" judge	signposting
rate of delivery	

I t should be clear by now that debate is a very complicated activity. It demands a great deal from students, who must be theoreticians thoroughly familiar with the fundamentals of debate and the logic of formal argument. They must also be researchers who are capable of doing exhaustive research on a broad policy question. They must know how to combine analysis and research to build sound constructive cases. They must be tacticians who study the best strategies and tactics of competitive presentation. Finally, they must be good public speakers.

No matter how effective the debater is at other tasks, success ultimately depends on the ability to communicate ideas and evidence to a neutral but critical party: the judge. In fact, this is one of the strongest educational justifications for academic debate. In this age, when everyone is deeply concerned about communication, a large number of scholars in speech and other fields are studying communication theory, trying to find out what goes wrong in human communication and what can be done about it. The student who studies debate is doing something about it.

Every weekend debaters are faced with tremendous communication problems as they try to communicate a host of very complicated ideas to their critics. While other students are at home reading books about how to improve communication, the debater is actively engaged in practicing communication skills. Thinking debaters constantly reevaluate and adjust their techniques to make themselves more effective communicators.

As students proceed through their debate careers, they should learn the techniques of communication on a very practical and personal level. They will find that there are specific things they can do to be effective public speakers. In fact, individuals must develop their own theories about how they can be effective. This is why it is so difficult to write about the ways to communicate—the answers are different for each person. Fortunately, the debater is one of the few persons who can practice before qualified judges who are there to provide feedback on the effectiveness of the communication. The only regret is that many debaters fail to take full advantage of this feedback.

The basic point of this chapter is that thinking debaters should make serious, careful studies of themselves as speakers. Through feedback from judges, coaches, opponents, and colleagues, debaters refine their skills to make themselves as effective as possible.

The best way *not* to learn to be a better persuasive communicator from the debate experience is to follow the nonthinking approach. The debater who merely follows the stereotype debaters learns nothing about public speaking. Debaters who blame judges for mistakes that the debaters themselves made learn nothing. Debaters who do not develop their own style and who never change the way they speak learn nothing.

The rest of this chapter, then, is not "the truth" about being a persuasive communicator (the truth is different for each debater). It is a compilation of the authors' observations on some generalizations that can be made about the debate setting and how you can communicate more effectively in it. The first topic for discussion is the debate setting. It is followed by the strategies and tactics of persuasive communication in debate.

Setting

Almost every communication setting can be broken down into four parts: audience, speech, occasion, and speaker. And this is certainly true of debate. The audience, for the purpose of this analysis, is really just one person: the judge. The speech is the set of arguments and ideas that the debater wishes to communicate to the judge. The occasion is the rather carefully defined competitive setting, which includes everything from the debate room itself to the speakers on the other team. The speaker is the debater, who must adjust to the other three elements in the most appropriate manner. These are the four topics for this section, but first a very important matter must be mentioned.

Communication, Not Performance

The basic strategic assumption that the student must make about the debate setting is that debate is **communication**, not a performance. There are times, however, as in oral interpretation contests, when students might be said to be performing. On these occasions they will be graded on the quality of the performance. Some debaters carry this attitude over to debate, but this is a great mistake. Debaters must think of themselves as people who are trying to communicate with other persons, not as students who perform before teachers. The decision in a debate most often rests on the debater's ability to communicate, rarely on the ability to perform as a debater.

Debaters who understand this basic idea have already gone a long way toward becoming effective as speakers in the debate setting. They understand, for example, that—as speakers—it is *their* responsibility to communicate. If the judge misses the analysis, the debater is at fault for not having communicated well.

Judges

It would be helpful if debate judges were like computers that take in all the ideas they hear, process them, and make decisions. It would be wonderful if judges were always objective, always attentive, and always correct in their decisions. This, however, is not the case.

The first thing the debater must learn about judges is that they are just human beings—trained human beings, to be sure, but not machines. Judges may not always be objective; in fact, they can be very subjective if a debater angers them. They may not always be attentive; even though every speaker's ideas are fascinating to the speaker, a judge can be bored, tired, or even uninterested. And, sad to say, the judge's decision will not always please the debater.

Those students who understand what this means have learned something important. They have learned that they must provide objective and subjective data that will help the judge understand the debater's case. They must keep the judge's interest and attention. Only the speaker can provide the data that make the judge give the "correct decision." If the debater feels that the judge has voted incorrectly, it is the debater's fault because the only thing that matters—as far as the decision goes—is who won the debate in the mind of the judge.

In other words, the debater must understand that there is just one correct decision in a debate: the judge's decision. The debate ballot does not say that "the _____ team did the better job of debating." It does not say, "If a computer were judging this debate it would say that the _____ team did the better job of debating." It *does* say, "In *my* opinion the _____ team did the better job of debating." Therefore, unless the judge knowingly votes for the weaker team, whatever decision the judge gives is the correct answer to the statement on the ballot.

Now the question becomes: How does the debater win the debate in the mind of the judge? This, of course, is really the subject of this chapter. The first step is to understand something about how most judges reach their decisions in the debate.

Although no one knows *exactly* how debate judges reach their decisions, debaters can make some fairly accurate predictions about the kinds of judges they will have. The starting point is the place on the ballot where the judge is asked to fill in the space in the sentence: "In my opinion the _____ team did the better job of debating." How does the judge decide whether to write "affirmative" or "negative"? What criteria are used?

Successful debaters understand how different judges reach their decisions.

"Balance of Arguments" Judge

The criterion that many judges use is which team established its arguments during the debate. The **"balance of arguments" judge** listens carefully to the debate and usually takes copious notes on the flow sheet. As the debate progresses, the judge analyzes its basic issues and the arguments and evidence that support them. The decision is based on the judge's determination as to which team did the better job of meeting its basic responsibilities.

For the affirmative this means that the judge weighs the affirmative's issues. If it used a traditional need case, the judge considers whether the affirmative established the need for a change, the affirmative's proposal was shown to be capable of solving the problems of the present system, and the advantages were maintained throughout the round. The "balance of arguments" judge may well award a loss to the affirmative team if any of the basic issues was significantly damaged.

If the affirmative has presented a comparative advantages case, the judge considers whether the affirmative has established that its advantages will truly be beneficial to the interested parties and whether these advantages could be expected to be gained from the affirmative's proposal. In addition, the judge carefully weighs the affirmative's response to the negative's plan objections to see if serious disadvantages still remain at the end of the debate.

Whether the affirmative has met its burden of proof is the major concern of the "balance of arguments" judge, who looks closely at the negative argument. Did the negative adequately defend the present system? Did its arguments and evidence penetrate the affirmative's case? Did the negative establish the disadvantages of the affirmative's proposal?

The decision, then, may well boil down to a single issue and to which side seemed to win it. The "balance of arguments" judge is likely to indicate on the ballot the points that decided the debate in his or her mind. These judges are likely to be much more content-analysis oriented than other judges. They may well award the decision to a less articulate team, even though its opponents were more persuasive debaters, if that team won a really significant issue.

"Better Job of Debating" Judge

Many debaters are disturbed if some of their judges do not take detailed notes during the debate. In truth, some judges just sit back and listen to the round, without seeming to care about the specific arguments and evidence the debaters use. Such judges are not incompetent; they are using different standards for judging the debate.

The **"better job of debating" judges** do not weigh the arguments to determine which team was more effective in the round; they base their decisions solely on which team did the better job of debating. Their decisions may be totally subjective or even impressionistic, but it is more likely that the judges have used specific criteria. Despite appearances, chances are that such a judge will gauge the debaters' effectiveness on the criteria that are listed on the debate ballot.

Typically, the ballot asks the judge to consider five criteria: analysis, reasoning, evidence, refutation, and delivery. The analysis judgment is based on how well a team analyzed the issues of the proposition and the debate. Reasoning is judged by examining the debaters' logic, whether their conclusions were reasonable on the basis of the evidence they provided and how good that evidence was. Delivery ratings are based on the students' overall effectiveness as speakers. Did their delivery facilitate the communication of their case, or did it detract from it?

"Better job of debating" judges generally follow the debate ballot in reaching their decisions. They interpret the criteria on the ballot as guides in deciding who won the debate. They take the statement on the ballot literally: Who did the better job of debating? On the other hand, "balance of arguments" judges view the ballot as a means of providing feedback to the student, not as a guide to decision making.

Clearly, these two styles of debate judging overlap considerably. The general skill of a debater significantly affects the balance of arguments, and the balance of arguments is a significant factor in deciding which team did the better job of debating. Chances are, if both a "balance of arguments" judge and a "better job of debating" judge are listening to the same debate, they would come up with identical decisions. Nevertheless, debaters should be aware of the different types of judges, both to help them develop their communication skills and to relieve their frustration over some decisions.

Debaters, who seem to prefer "balance of arguments" judging, frequently are upset if they feel they have won an important issue in a debate, but the judge hasn't given them the decision. The chances are that the judge based the decision on general effectiveness and felt that the other team had the better debaters, even though they may have lost one or two issues. The student who knows that there is more than one kind of judge knows that it is necessary to win the decision of both types.

"Maverick" Judge*

It is time to be even more frank about debate judging. Probably the most frustrating thing about debate is that debaters feel they occasionally get bad decisions. The old line, "I've never lost a debate, but I sure get a lot of bad decisions" is a common refrain among many debaters. The authors will say unequivocally that in the vast majority of cases, this is just a rationalization. Debate is an intellectual activity, and participants feel a strong urge to excuse their defeats because they feel their intelligence is somehow at stake. This is understandable because few persons can see anything wrong with their own logic. But, unless the judge is wrong, this

---

*This phrase was coined by Otto F. Bauer and C. William Colburn in their excellent article "The Maverick Judge," which appeared in *Journal of American Forensic Association*, 3 (January 1966), 22–25.

means the debaters are wrong or perhaps are not as bright as they thought they were.

If the old rationalization contributes something to the mental health of debaters, it nevertheless is one of the major barriers to improving as a speaker. As coaches, the authors have found that debaters do not become really good until they admit that most of the time the judge is correct. Until they learn this, they have no reason to improve—they're always right and the judge is always wrong. If these kinds of debaters could just get perfect judging every round, they would be the undefeated national champions!

Another bit of knowledge attaches to being mature enough to admit that the vast majority of losses are due to the weakness of a team: All judges are not perfect. Indeed, a few judges consistently deviate from the decisions of other judges, even in rounds that have several judges. This does not mean, however, that the former are wrong by the "in my opinion" standard; it means that debaters cannot predict how such judges will make their decisions—as can be the case with the two types of orthodox judges.

Bauer and Colburn have called these kinds of judges the **"maverick" judges**. Whether they are debate coaches, speech teachers, or newcomers to debate circles, there is really no way to tell how or why they vote the way they do. They simply disagree with the "balance of arguments" judge and the "better job of debating" judge.

What can debaters do about this? Nothing. They must simply get used to the fact that they will occasionally draw a maverick judge. The debater can take solace, however, from three things. First, maverick judges are a rare breed; in all likelihood more than 90 percent of all judges will be of the other two types. This means that instead of losing sleep over maverick judges, debaters should concentrate on the other kinds. Second, they should realize that they are not the only debaters who will occasionally be judged by a maverick. Indeed, the competition labors under the same problem. If a team wins many debates, this does not mean it was lucky in avoiding maverick judges; it means the team members are good debaters. Finally, and most important, debaters should understand that a maverick judge is just as likely to vote for them as against them. If debaters want to excuse their losses by blaming maverick judges, they would have to regret some of their victories. But of course such immature debaters never complain about bad decisions in their favor.

Occasion

The debater's communication behavior is conditioned by more than just the judge. The debater should realize that the speaking occasion itself is an important influence on both the speaker and the judge. It should, therefore, affect the debater's communicative approach.

One can say several things about the debate setting. A debate usually takes place in a school classroom, on a weekend, with only a few persons present to hear the round. Also, it takes place as part of a series of rounds that make up the debate tournament. How does this affect the communication situation?

The main effect is that the debate is not a unique experience for anyone. The judge has already heard many debates and is likely to hear many more. In fact, the debate probably is only one of four or five debates that the judge will hear in one day. The occasion, therefore, forces debaters to be more conscious of their communication than are most other kinds of public speakers. The judge is likely to be tired and not very interested in the debate. Indeed, one of the first and major surprises for the debater-turned-judge is how long a debate seems from the back of the room and how short it seems from the speaker's stand.

Naturally, the occasion is likely to change as debaters approach the final rounds of elimination tournaments. Suddenly, there is a large audience of debaters and a crowd of interested spectators; there are several judges instead of one. Tension is high and people are very interested in hearing exactly what the debaters say. Debaters must then be able to adjust to the new situation. They should speak to the large audience as well as to the panel of judges, spending less time keeping the audience interested and more time concentrating on defeating the opposition.

Material

Some speech teachers complain strongly about the **rate of delivery** that students use during a debate. They feel it is uncommunicative, too hurried, and not enjoyable to hear. What they forget is that the debater, like any other speaker, must adjust to the material and to the time allotted for presenting it.

Debate material has several distinctive characteristics. First of all, there is a lot of it. As you can see by looking at any debate book, debaters must provide tremendous amounts of material just to meet their basic obligations. The material in only the first affirmative rebuttal would take much longer to give if it were presented at an orator's rate of delivery, but the debater doesn't have that much time. No one wants to sit through an all-night debate just so each speaker can speak at the rate and with the distinctness appropriate to other speaking situations.

Second, most debate material is objective in nature, and the advocate does not use flowery phrases or emotional appeals. Almost everything said must be documented, down to the page numbers on important material, and the debater must present a great deal of statistical material that would not make good listening, say, on a popular television show.

Finally, a great deal of the debater's material is delivered extemporaneously, some of it thought of during the speech, or as the debate progresses, or during a discussion of other points. This is why many debaters feel awkward when they first experience the activity. The nature of the material is such that they are forced to standardize much of what they say so that they can think better while talking. Among poor debaters this means that many clichés are used to facilitate debating. With better debaters it means that students have to standardize their own language—with "personal clichés"—so that they do not have to think of each new word as they argue.

The speech teacher who is repulsed by the delivery in debate is criticizing the students for doing what all good speakers should do— adapting to the nature of the material they are trying to communicate. Debaters would be poor communicators if they did not adjust. They are, however, poor public speakers if they overadjust—if they talk so fast that the debate judge can't understand them. Also, debaters are poor communicators if they carry their debate style into other speaking situations, in which different styles of delivery are appropriate.

The Speaker

Just as debaters must know the strengths and weaknesses of their case, they must know their strong and weak points as speakers. Although debaters tend to have the same general style because of the situation and the material, each individual must develop a personal style of delivery. This style should be based on sound self-evaluation. Speakers should cultivate their favorable points and minimize the factors that detract from their persuasive communication.

Strategies of Communicative Persuasion

The strategies of communication in debate focus on the speaker's special audience, the judge. Knowing something of the nature of the judge, the debater must have communication strategies that will help persuade the judge. The strategies should not be designed for the perfect judge—always attentive, always objective—but for the average judge whom the speaker expects to have. The overriding principle here is that good debaters do not have to have the perfect judge to win debates. They know that they will speak in a realistic communication setting and that it is their responsibility to transmit their ideas to another person.

Basic Strategy

Debaters know that many factors influence a critic's decision in a debate. Many judges objectively weigh the arguments and issues in the round to arrive at their decisions. Other judges gauge the debate through a subjective impression of the debaters' effectiveness. But most judges use a combination of objective and subjective factors.

Some teams are the kind that a judge would like to see win—good, pleasant communicators who favorably impress the judge from a personal point of view. Other teams are the kind a judge would like to see lose; they are ineffective, sarcastic, and perhaps rude in their approach to the other team. The majority fall in the middle, and the judge is relatively neutral toward them. Subjective impressions, however, cannot be discounted for even the most objective "balance of arguments" judge because subjective factors are likely unconsciously to affect the judge's judgment of which team had the better arguments and evidence.

Thus, the basic strategy should be built on communicating arguments so effectively that the judge will know, objectively, why the team thinks its arguments are valid. At the same time, the team wants the judge to *feel* that it should win the debate. The strategy, then, in one sentence is: When the debate is over, the judge should *know* that the team has won and should feel that it *should* have won the debate.

The content of this book has thus far been designed to help the debater with the first part of the strategy, winning the debate from the objective standpoint. But now it is necessary to consider how to make sure that a judge understands the arguments and how to convince that judge that your team should have won.

Strategy of Communicating, Not Performing

This factor was mentioned earlier as an attitude that the speaker should have about the debate setting. It now becomes a definite strategy for the advocate of either side of the proposition. The debater must plan to communicate ideas, not show off skills—a distinction that is basic to persuasive speaking. If students assume that they are performers, the responsibility for understanding what they do is with the audience. If they know that they are communicators, they understand that the responsibility for effectively transmitting thoughts lies squarely on their own shoulders.

Form, Language, and Style

Arguments are the raw material of debate. One of their functions is to form constructive reasons for meeting the affirmative's burden of proof of the proposition or for maintaining the negative's presumption. Another role of argument is to attack the position of the opposition or to rebuild positions that have been attacked. Arguments are derived from research and are presented on the basis of competitive strategies and tactics, but the most perfect set of arguments, arranged in perfect form, is useless if it is not communicated to the judge. Thus, one of the strategies of the debater has to be to present arguments in the language and style that are most appropriate for the judge and in the form that will best help the judge receive the information.

Source Credibility

It is difficult to say anything with full certainty about the persuasive setting except that source credibility is a major factor in the effectiveness of persuasive communication. **Source credibility** is a social-psychological term that refers to the judgment the receiver makes of the believability of the source of a message. It is roughly equivalent to Aristotle's term *ethos*, which he applied to the character of the orator.

Experimental data tell students of persuasion that source credibility is a basic element in effectiveness, and experimenters have manipulated such things as introduction and dress to show the importance of source credibility. Using the same speaker, the same speech, and an experimentally equivalent audience, experimenters have introduced the same man as a "major authority" at one time and as an "interested layperson" at another time. Audiences believed the man when he was "an expert" but not when he was a "layperson." The same speaker appeared before an audience in army fatigues one time and in a business suit another time, and the audience found him more "believable" when he appeared in the suit.

Thus, the total impression or image that a speaker creates makes an important difference in the persuasive effect achieved. It can even influence a judge's decision on whether an argument is valid, which supposedly is limited to the evidence the speaker presents. Therefore one of the strategies of the speaker in debate is to have high source credibility. It becomes necessary to eliminate things that detract from the impression made and to do things that contribute to it.

Tactics of Communication

The strategies of communication are necessarily general because the communication process isn't as well-defined for debate as is, say, the research process. However, the tactics of communicative persuasion are specific enough to help the beginning debater. Advanced students will have to expand on the basic information that is provided here and form their own tactics as they best fit their personal idiosyncrasies.

Once debaters know what they are going to say, they must decide what formal devices, language devices, and style of delivery they will use to facilitate communication with the judge. The tactics used should be designed to advance the basic strategy of doing the best job of communicating with the judge so that at the end of the debate the judge will "know" the team won and will "feel" it should have won the debate.

Formal Tactics

Debaters work in a very difficult communication situation. What they have to say is not easy for anyone to understand because often the material they use is technical and the logic they use is subtle and complex. In addition, debaters have a great deal to say and very little time in which to say it. They must therefore use tactics that help the listener better understand the material. The most useful tactics are noted below.

Highlighting

The first step that speakers can take to facilitate communication is to arrange their materials in a form that makes the important points stand out from the material that is less important. In short, debaters use well-written statements of their major issues, highlighting them so that they will be easy to remember. These contentions should be short, clear, and worded in an interesting way. One debater, for example, described the entire analysis by saying, "Ladies and gentlemen, we are going to argue today that it is time to take the dollar sign out of medicine."

By highlighting in such a manner, the speaker can be fairly certain that at the end of the round the judge will remember the team's basic philosophy and major contentions. Although this is very important for the affirmative speaker, it should not be forgotten by the negative speaker. It also is helpful for the negative to develop a clear-cut statement of its philosophy and to highlight its contentions so that the important parts of its case stand out. Some teams have solved the problem of the negative by developing "points of clash" that they can state early in the debate to help the critic visualize the negative's attack. These might include: "The affirmative has misanalyzed the present system" and "There are several compelling reasons for rejecting the affirmative proposal."

Forecasting

This is an elementary tactic in debate. Speakers know that if the audience is made aware beforehand of what is going to be said, it will be easier for them to understand it. Nor do good debaters want to surprise the judge. They are willing to forego surprising the other team so that the judge will be ready for what is to come.

Each major argumentative development, then, should begin with a short statement of what is to come. First affirmative speakers, for instance, might begin with an overview of what they are about to do and might indicate the major divisions of their need-for-a-change argument before going into subpoints and evidence. The essence of forecasting is to clear away the trees to show the judge the forest—to forget about evidence and arguments for a moment and to let the judge see the highlights of the logical development.

Signposting

Just as the forecast tells the judge where the debate is going, the signposts tell the judge where the debater is at a particular time. After developing an argument, all the debater has to do is provide the judge with a brief perspective. What does the argument mean in terms of a particular segment of the case? What else has to be done to finish the analysis?

Summary

Thus far our speakers have told the judge where they are going and where they are in the case. After this it is time to tell the judge what has come before. Most logical units (such as major contentions), therefore, should be capped with a very short summary of the argument. Also, most experienced debaters know that a one- or two-sentence summary at the end of their speeches can help etch the major ideas in the mind of the judge.

The four tactics detailed above can do much to improve the speaker's persuasive communication during a debate speech. There is nothing new about the techniques, however. Debaters have been using them for innumerable years and have found them very useful. Unfortunately, because they have been used so long, these tactics also have become part of nonthinking debate. Again, the reader is warned to use the tactics thoughtfully. One should not, for example, begin every speech with a summary of the debate simply because everyone else does so. This would be a ritual, not communication. Debaters should employ the tactics only when they seem necessary for improving the communication of the material. Using them without thinking does not help communication, and it wastes much valuable time.

Language Tactics

Debaters should choose language that advances the strategy of effectively communicating with the judge. The cardinal principle here is to develop language habits that will help debaters explain what they mean and will hold the attention of the critic.

Choice of Words

Judging some debaters is like watching the fiftieth rerun of a very dull movie. The debaters seem to be saying what all the other speakers have said, and in just the way they said it. It is difficult for the judge merely to listen to the speakers, much less try to understand them. The basic prob-

lem is that many debaters "learn" the language of argument simply by listening to other debaters. As a result they sound like everyone else; everyone chooses the same words to describe the same things.

Thinking debaters know this and carefully choose the words they
will use in a debate. They look for descriptive phrases, use words that
will help keep the attention of the judge, and avoid the terminology
that everyone else seems to be using. If others invariably say "status
quo" and "plan," the thoughtful debater might say "present system"
and "proposal."

The good debater also avoids language fads. If a pair of good debaters
wins the national championship or gains the respect of many debaters,
other debaters want to emulate them and, perhaps unconsciously, imi-
tate them. If the pair frequently uses "that affirmative team," "that need
argument," and "that affirmative plan," the phrases soon become a fad.
But by the time the fad has filtered down to most debaters, the best
teams wouldn't even think of using the terms. The good team, instead,
avoids all debate clichés and chooses the words that are most appropriate
for the team.

Redundancy

Skillful repetition is another language tactic of good teams, who deliberately describe a difficult concept two or three times, perhaps using different words each time. They know that very few persons understand everything the first time they hear it, and therefore they are not afraid to
repeat themselves. Again, however, the difference between thinking and
nonthinking debaters is shown in *what* they repeat. Thinking debaters
repeat what needs repeating. Nonthinking debaters repeat because this
is what everyone else does. What point is there in repeating something
like "Therefore there is a need for a change"? Of course it is good to repeat the *reasons* why there is a need for a change—to say it several ways so
that the judge will fully appreciate the debater's logic.

Tactics of Style

It is partly through their style of delivery that debaters convey many ideas
and attitudes and develop source credibility. Obviously, individuals
should find the style that is best for them, but there are four techniques
most speakers can use to become more effective.

First, debaters should deliver their speeches as if they are talking to each individual. They should convey the impression that they are persons, not computers. Speakers should, therefore, be conversational and relatively casual, without losing the formality of the public speaking situation.

Second, debaters should develop in their speeches an extemporaneous quality that creates a corresponding reaction in the judge. The judge should feel that the speakers are tailoring their ideas to the debate and to the judge, not that they are simply delivering memorized speeches or reciting long sets of debate clichés.

Third, the student should use bodily actions to facilitate persuasive communication. Any gestures, facial expressions, and body movements used should help emphasize the arguments and help keep the interest of the judge. Debaters, likewise, should avoid any bodily actions that detract from their communication. This includes everything from the obviously distracting things, such as playing with one's pencil, to the subtly distracting habit of doing what everyone else is doing, which is apt to lull the judge into inattention.

Fourth, speakers should carefully analyze their general effectiveness. With the help of the coach and by scrutinizing ballots, debaters should seek to eliminate all factors that seem to detract from their speeches. They should eliminate vocal and physical mannerisms and everything else that seems adversely to affect the majority of their listeners. Debaters should, instead, cultivate habits that seem to contribute to their general effectiveness as speakers.

Tactics for Developing Source Credibility

Quintilian described the perfect orator as a "good man speaking well." He believed that an audience could be moved only by a truly good person and, therefore, he thought that only a really good person could be a great orator. This is also true in debate; the best way to have high source credibility is to be truly credible. If debaters are honest in the research and development of their ideas, critics are likely to believe them. If, on the other hand, they are not credible, critics are likely to see through the smoothest exterior.

There are few ways for school and college debaters to develop extrinsic prestige, unless it is derived from the school they attend. Debaters are not perceived as actual experts on the topic, no matter how much research they do. Instead, they are expected to use the prestige of their sources to lend credibility to their arguments. Beyond that, there is a lot debaters can do to use their own intrinsic expertise to win an argument. Extensive, careful research is, in itself, the key. The best debaters, then, use the evidence they have in a competent, fair way to show they know what they are doing.

The next element in credibility is character, and many decisions turn on this issue. Good character cannot be faked. Therefore, beyond morality, honesty and reliability are important for tactical reasons. Curiously, there are relatively superficial things that even the most honest person can do that will arouse suspicion in an audience. Good debaters are aware of that, and they study themselves to work toward a positive image. They know that dress and eye contact have a direct impact on how they are perceived. They know that they must treat their opponents fairly and honestly. Any ground debaters might gain by distorting their opponents' arguments or by distorting key evidence is surely more than lost in credibility.

Dynamism is a matter of delivery. As the authors have already noted, it can be a very potent factor in debate. Unfortunately, far too many debaters seem to throw this asset away. This is just what happens to speakers who sound like talking machines, using too much jargon and too many clichés. The best debaters develop styles that are their own. They let their own personality come through. They even smile!

It is one thing, though, to say, "Go forth and be credible," and quite another to do that. Relatively recent work by rhetoricians and social scientists sheds light on the strategies for high source credibility. It is now generally agreed that three components come together to determine whether speakers are judged credible by their audiences: expertise, character, and dynamism.

Audiences judge expertise in at least two ways. First, if they do not know the speaker well as a person, they look for *extrinsic* signs that would indicate high or low credibility. Does the speaker have an impressive title? Does he or she come from a school that is well known and respected? Second, as the speaker proceeds, audiences tend to look at factors that are *intrinsic* to the speaker as a person. Is the speaker well prepared? Has the speaker developed an interesting, coherent pattern of logic? In brief, is the speaker expert on the topic? If the answers are positive, listeners will be disposed to judge the speaker's message in a positive way.

Judgments about character are essentially questions of trust. In the world outside of debate, listeners want to know if the speaker's motives are honest and want to be assured that the speaker is not taking advantage of them. In debate, the judge does not worry about whether the speaker honestly believes in the side of the question she or he is arguing. Instead, the judge wants to know that the speaker is intellectually honest and accurate.

Dynamism is a word that is often used to describe a very powerful and elusive element in source credibility. For a long time, dynamism was a kind of X-factor in communication. That is, sometimes audiences might see the speaker as expert and of good character but would still assign a relatively low credibility rating. At other times, expertise and character might be perceived as average but credibility would be high. Recently, more refined studies shed light on that issue. Audiences respond to the human qualities of a speaker. If the person is warm, likable, and extemporaneous, credibility will tend to be high.

Knowing all this, effective debaters work to develop tactics that will yield positive credibility impressions. They work hard to be expert. They have strong values about honesty. And they develop speaking styles that are natural to them, extemporaneous, and dynamic.

Rate of Delivery

The authors have already discussed the unusual nature of the debate setting. Among other things debaters must speak very rapidly if they are to meet their obligations in the very limited time they have. The best debaters can do that and yet remain communicative and clear. However, the authors are concerned that too many debaters have surpassed the limit of rapid delivery.

Again, debaters should find the rate that is appropriate to them, the setting, and the judge. What good does it do to cover more if the judge understands less? The best debaters slow down when they cover the most important points, moving more rapidly over the less important. Good debaters analyze the judge in terms of how much he or she can handle. If it's early in the season or the judge is relatively inexperienced, a slower rate is definitely warranted. It is also often wise for a team to adjust to its opponents. To do and look their best, stronger teams often slow down when debating a weaker team.

Summary

It must have become apparent that the authors are sold on academic debate as a competitive-educational activity. If it is properly practiced, debate can be one of the most enjoyable and rewarding experiences students can have. The intellectual competition is exciting and enjoyable, and in their pursuit of competitive excellence the students learn many things that could be gained in no other way. They learn principles of debating that not only prepare them for academic debate, but also acquaint them with the fundamental concepts of Western law. Debaters learn to research an issue in great depth, something that most students fail to experience unless they enter graduate school. They develop organizational and presentation skills that are not unique to debate, but apply to all language activities.

Most important, students of debate learn the principles of oral communication in a way that no other students of communication theory can. Debaters are faced, again and again, with a tremendously difficult persuasive communication task. This experience is valuable in itself, but debaters also have the advantage of having a different judge almost every time they speak. The judges listen to the debaters and provide the speakers with feedback on their communication skills. No other educational setting provides this.

The authors, however, aren't sold on *all* academic debating. For too many debaters, it has become merely a ritual instead of a strategic, critical clash between the opposing sides of a proposition. It is much too easy for students to engage in debate but learn almost nothing at all—to fake it. All they have to do is automatically follow the patterns of research, organization, presentation, and delivery, and they need never strain a brain cell. In short, there are too many nonthinking debaters.

The answer to this problem should be self-evident. The only way that students—beginners or champions—can maximize their competitive-educational experience is by approaching debate as a *thinking* activity. They must realize that it is an activity in which critical thinking, careful research, strategies, tactics, and communication theory are thoughtfully employed.

Debaters can learn what they must do by studying the theory of strategic debate, and then they must learn enough about debating so that they can develop their own ideas about debating most effectively, considering the demands of the proposition, their research, and their personal liabilities and assets. There is no *easy* way to do all this. Debaters, if they are to be successful, must think and must work hard. They must follow the path of most resistance.

Questions for Discussion

1. The authors state that a debate takes place in the mind of the judge. What does this mean?

2. Tape record a debate and listen to the tape just for the debaters' use of formal tactics. How did they do? How might they improve their use of highlighting, forecasting, signposting, and summaries?

3. If you were debating before a "balance of arguments" judge, what criteria could you assume the judge would be using? A "better job of debating" judge? A "maverick" judge?

4. Describe the distinctive characteristics of debate material.

5. What role does source credibility play in the persuasive setting?

6. What role does the choice of language play in a debate?

7. Many judges complain about the rate of delivery in debate. Is it appropriate for the debater to always try to speak as fast as possible in order to deliver as many arguments as possible?

Activities

1. After listening to several debates, make a list of the debate clichés you noticed. What mannerisms, gestures, or other elements of stereo-typed delivery did the debaters seem to use? How could they have been changed?

2. Using the tape of a debate, choose one of the constructive speeches. Reconstruct the speech using better highlighting, forecasting, signposting, and summaries.

3. Using the same tape from Activity 2, rework the first affirmative rebuttal with better highlighting, forecasting, signposting, and summaries.

4. After each of your debate rounds in class, outline several ways you could improve your rebuttal speech.

5. Tape one of your debate rounds. Go back through the rebuttal speech, outline the arguments again, and examine your choices of ar-guments and evidence. Prepare a new rebuttal speech.

6. Using your first affirmative or one of the speeches you have pre-pared for a previous chapter activity, work on your rate of delivery. Begin by delivering the speech very slowly, and then increase your speech speed until you find a speed that is both comfortable for you and understandable.

Appendix A
Duties of the Speakers in Standard or Cross-Examination Debate

First Affirmative Constructive Speech

Strategy:
To present the strongest possible case for the proposition and to leave the affirmative in a strong offensive position.

Tactics:
1. Give a brief, pleasant introduction that capsulizes the affirmative's approach.

2. State the resolution.

3. Define the important terms of the resolution if not incorporated in the plan.

4. Forecast the affirmative's rationale for a change.

5. Present the affirmative's rationale for a change.

6. Present the affirmative's proposal, derived from the rationale for a change.

7. Present the inherent advantages of the affirmative's proposal.

8. Give a brief summary-conclusion of the affirmative's case.

The order in which 4, 5, 6, and 7 are presented depends on the type of affirmative case, as discussed earlier. For example, in a comparative advantages case, the plan would be presented first, followed by the advantages and rationale for change.

First Negative Constructive Speech

Strategy:

To maintain the negative's presumption, to take away the offensive, and to expand the debate beyond the arguments presented in the first affirmative speech.

Tactics:

1. Give a brief introduction and forecast that stress the nature of the negative's philosophy in the debate.

2. Defend the presumption by summarizing the aims of the present system and its effectiveness in meeting its goals.

3. Provide the negative's organization for analyzing the affirmative's argument.

4. Argue that the affirmative team has not presented an adequate rationale for changing the present system.

5. Give a brief summary-conclusion of the negative's stand, stressing the negative's organization.

Second Affirmative Constructive Speech

Strategy:
To uphold the affirmative's burden of proof, to remain on the offensive, and to narrow the range of arguments.

Tactics:
(This speaker may present additional advantages.)

1. Give a very brief introduction and highlight the affirmative's strongest rationale for change.

2. Stay on the offensive by returning to the affirmative's organization to answer the attacks of the negative team.

3. Try to incorporate the negative's defense of the present system into the affirmative's case. If this is impossible, use refutation.

4. Review the affirmative's advantages, which may not have been attacked at this point.

5. Provide a brief summary, lamenting the fact that the negative failed to discuss the proposal and advantages when given the chance to reply.

Second Negative Constructive Speech

Strategy:
To use the negative block to carry out the basic negative strategies: maintaining the presumption, taking the offensive, and expanding the debate. The emphasis of this speech, though, is the outlining of disadvantages to adopting the affirmative proposal.

Tactics:
1. Forecast the negative block, including the first negative rebuttal. (Some would argue that it is not necessary to forecast the first negative rebuttal.)

2. Show why the affirmative's proposal will not correct problems of the present system.

3. Show why the affirmative's proposal is unworkable or impractical. This might involve three or four separate and numbered arguments.

4. Detail the disadvantages of the affirmative's proposal. This might involve five or six specific harmful side effects of the proposal.

5. Give a very brief conclusion.

First Negative Rebuttal Speech

Strategy:
To further the negative's strategies. Keep in mind that time may not allow the first negative to return to every point. Carefully choose what is important, develop these, and explain why they are the most important case arguments in the debate.

Tactics:
1. Return to the argumentation in the first negative speech, refuting the affirmative's objections.

2. Look again at the affirmative's rationale to show why the proposition should not be accepted, even if the proposal were effective.

3. Give a summary-conclusion of the negative block.

First Affirmative Rebuttal Speech

Strategy:
To further the affirmative's strategies of fulfilling the burden of proof, maintaining the offensive, and narrowing the debate.

Tactics:
1. Refute the negative's plan objections. Try to consolidate as many arguments as possible. Point out fallacies in reasoning, as well as miss-

ing links in arguments. Where possible try to show how negative disadvantages are really affirmative advantages.

2. Return to the affirmative's case to rebuild it at major points of attack.

3. Attempt to narrow the debate by focusing the affirmative's argument on a few issues.

4. Maintain the offensive by giving a brief summary that emphasizes the strength of the affirmative's case.

Second Negative Rebuttal Speech

Strategy:
To continue the negative's strategies by overcoming the affirmative's attempt to center the debate around a few of its arguments.

Tactics:
1. Give a brief introduction and forecast.

2. Briefly reestablish the negative's defense of the present system.

3. Reattack the affirmative's rationale.

4. Review the plan objections and disadvantages, refuting the affirmative's replies and pointing to the issues the affirmative neglected to discuss. Here again time may not allow reviewing all of the second negative arguments. Carefully choose the disadvantages that are most important to the negative position. If necessary drop the rest and proceed to case.

5. Summarize and conclude, calling for the rejection of the proposition.

Second Affirmative Rebuttal Speech

Strategy:
To conclude the affirmative's attempt to advance its basic strategies in the debate.

Tactics:

1. Give a brief introduction and forecast.

2. Review plan objections. Take special care to refute major disadvantages (particularly those covered by the second negative rebuttalist).

3. Try to center the speech on three or four major arguments on which the affirmative's case depends.

4. Review the basic affirmative analysis and call for the acceptance of that analysis.

Appendix B
Duties of the Speakers in Lincoln-Douglas Debate

Affirmative Constructive Speech

Strategy:
To present the strongest possible case for the value proposition and leave the affirmative in a strong offensive position.

Tactics:
1. Give a brief, pleasant introduction.

2. State the proposition.

3. Define the important terms of the proposition.

4. Forecast the affirmative's rationale for a change.

5. Present the affirmative's rationale for a change.

6. Give a brief summary-conclusion of the affirmative's case.

Negative Constructive Speech

Strategy:

The negative has a responsibility to clash with the affirmative, either with the affirmative interpretation of the topic or with the topic itself. The negative's best position is to use both straight refutation and the negative case. When doing so the negative offers straight refutation first and ends with the negative case.

Tactics:

1. Give a brief introduction and forecast the negative position in the debate.

2. Directly refute the affirmative case.

3. Build a negative case—direct attack on the topic itself. The negative must refute the assumptions inherent within the topic. This involves developing a case with definitions and contentions. The negative usually spends three to four minutes on the negative case.

First Affirmative Rebuttal

Strategy:

To cover as many negative arguments as possible while still rebuilding the affirmative position.

Tactics:

1. Pay careful attention to the value term. Repair any damage to affirmative arguments made by the negative.

2. Have new evidence ready to rebuild arguments on the affirmative case.

3. Restate or reaffirm contentions if they have not been attacked by the negative.

4. Give a brief summary that emphasizes the strength of the affirmative case.

Negative Rebuttal

Strategy:
Respond to the affirmative attacks while stressing what the negative believes to be the key issues of the debate.

Tactics:
1. Give a brief introduction and forecast.

2. State where you are in the debate.

3. State the affirmative's response.

4. Provide the negative's response.

5. Outline the impact of the argument. If there are a lot of arguments, the negative will need to do one of two things: 1) if developed in-depth, focus on basic analysis behind each contention; 2) if developed shallowly, the negative may be able to respond to each point directly. This should take three to four minutes.

6. Focus on the negative case.

7. Summarize and conclude, calling for the rejection of the proposition.

Second Affirmative Rebuttal

Strategy:
Focus on the case issues the affirmative is winning while pointing out the issues you believe you have beaten that were presented by the negative. The affirmative should try to center the speech on a few major arguments to develop these clearly and explain why they turn the debate for the affirmative.

Tactics:
1. Give a brief introduction and forecast.

2. State where you are in the debate.

3. Outline the negative's responses.

4. Outline the affirmative's response.

5. Outline the impact of the arguments.

6. Review the basic affirmative analysis and call for the acceptance of that analysis.

Appendix C
Forms of Debate

Three forms of debate are listed here, although there are many more. The traditional debate format, cross-examination debate (which varies between high school and college debate), and Lincoln-Douglas debate are the typical forms of debate in forensic tournaments.

Traditional Debate Format

	Form A	Form B
First affirmative speech	10 minutes	8 minutes
First negative speech	10 minutes	8 minutes
Second affirmative speech	10 minutes	8 minutes
Second negative speech	10 minutes	8 minutes
First negative rebuttal	5 minutes	4 minutes
First affirmative rebuttal	5 minutes	4 minutes
Second negative rebuttal	5 minutes	4 minutes
Second affirmative rebuttal	5 minutes	4 minutes

Cross-Examination Debate

	High School	College
First affirmative speech	8 minutes	10 minutes
Negative cross-examination of first affirmative speaker	3 minutes	3 minutes
First negative speech	8 minutes	10 minutes
Affirmative cross-examination of first negative speaker	3 minutes	3 minutes
Second affirmative speech	8 minutes	10 minutes

Negative cross-examination of second affirmative speaker	3 minutes	3 minutes
Second negative speech	8 minutes	10 minutes
Affirmative cross-examination of second negative speaker	3 minutes	3 minutes
First negative rebuttal	4 minutes	5 minutes
First affirmative rebuttal	4 minutes	5 minutes
Second negative rebuttal	4 minutes	5 minutes
Second affirmative rebuttal	4 minutes	5 minutes

The time limits vary from contest to contest. Also, there is considerable variety concerning which speaker cross-questions which speaker. Each speaker must take at least one turn, however, as examiner.

Lincoln-Douglas Debate

Affirmative constructive	6 minutes
Negative cross-examination of affirmative	3 minutes
Negative constructive	7 minutes
Affirmative cross-examination of negative	3 minutes
First affirmative rebuttal	4 minutes
Negative rebuttal	6 minutes
Second affirmative rebuttal	3 minutes

Preparation Time

Most tournaments, both in high school and in college, have placed restrictions on an individual's or team's preparation time. While there are some standard formats, time limits may vary from tournament to tournament at the director's discretion. Three commonly used prep-time restrictions are explained below.

Two-Minute Rule

This rule applies to the individual speaker. Each speaker is given two minutes to prepare his or her speech. This time is calculated from the ending of the previous speaker's speech. Should the speaker need more than the allotted two minutes, the time is subtracted from the actual speaking time.

Eight-Minute Rule

This rule applies to the affirmative and negative as a team. Each team is given eight minutes of preparation time to use as they wish. Preparation time is calculated from the moment one speaker stops speaking until the next speaker begins. For example, if three minutes elapse from the end of the first affirmative speech until the first negative speech begins, then the negative has used three minutes of preparation time. Once a team has used all eight minutes they must be ready to speak immediately in their remaining speeches or have the preparation time taken off their actual speaking time. With a little practice, teams should seldom run out of preparation time under the eight-minute rule.

Ten-Minute Rule

This rule also applies to the affirmative and negative as a team. The procedure is the same as for the eight-minute rule, except that each team has ten minutes instead of eight. This form is most commonly used in college debate.

Appendix D

Suggestions for Successful Debating

Analysis

1. The debater should seek the most thorough knowledge of the topic and the most complete evidence to support her or his arguments.

2. The debater should choose arguments that are important enough to have adequate evidence available to support them.

3. The debater should not be afraid to use the "standard" case idea that many other teams are using. Often it can be refined or intensely developed during the season to become the best case. Nonthinking teams frequently are lulled into a false sense of security by what they think is a standard case but what is really a case that is capable of important refinements.

Organization

1. Choose the pattern of organization that best fits the analysis.

2. Carefully check the feedback of judges to see how effective the organization is. This should be done both during the debate as well as by carefully reading ballots.

Presentation of Arguments

1. Affirmative

   a. The affirmative should actively support its burden of proof.
   b. The affirmative should remain on the offensive.
   c. With few exceptions, the affirmative should narrow the range of arguments in the debate.

2. Negative

   a. The negative should actively support the presumption that goes with the present system.
   b. The negative should try to become the offensive team and put the affirmative team on the defensive.
   c. With a few exceptions, the negative should try to expand the range of arguments in the debate.

Refutation and Rebuttal

1. The debater should listen carefully to the opposition's arguments. It does little good to argue against an argument that has been misinterpreted.

2. The debater should state the arguments being attacked and indicate to the judge why they are being attacked.

3. The debater should state his or her counterargument.

4. The debater should present the evidence for the counterargument.

5. The debater should lend perspective to the development of the counterargument by showing how it affects the debate.

6. The debater should realize that it is possible for the opposition to tell the truth and not contest obviously valid arguments. Instead, the debater should analyze the relationship of the argument to the larger case or should move on to arguments that are contestable.

Delivery in Debate

1. The debater should realize that the debate takes place in the mind of the critic.

2. The debater should highlight important arguments by wording them in an interesting and memorable way. One should avoid long drawn out sentences.

3. The debater should forecast her or his attack.

4. The debater should erect signposts to help the judge know where he or she is in reference to case arguments.

5. The debater should provide a brief summary and perspective at the end of the speech.

6. The debater should avoid all speaking mannerisms that detract from delivery.

7. The debater should avoid debate chichés. Language should be appropriate to the material and an expression of one's own personality. Listening to tapes of your debates will help you to recognize the use of clichés and inappropriate language.

8. The debater should avoid sarcasm or other personal attacks on the opposition. Little is gained from hostile debating.

9. The debater should maintain poise throughout the debate and should not talk or be otherwise rude during the opposition's turn at the speaker's stand.

Bibliography

Baron, Joan Boykoff and Sternberg, Robert J. *Teaching Thinking Skills: Theory and Practice.* New York: W. H. Freeman and Company, 1987.

Branham, Robert J., ed. *The New Debate: Readings in Contemporary Debate Theory.* Washington, D.C.: Information Research Associates, 1975.

Brock, Bernard L., et al. *Public Policy Decision Making: Systems Analysis and Comparative Advantages Debate.* New York: Harper and Row, 1973.

_____. "The Comparative Advantages Case." *The Speech Teacher* 16 (March 1967): 118–23.

Brydon, Steven R. "Presumption in Non-Policy Debate: In Search of a Paradigm." *Journal of the American Forensic Association* 23 (Summer 1986): 15–22.

Burgoon, Judee and Montgomery, Charles. "Dimensions of Credibility for the Ideal Debater." *Journal of the American Forensic Association* 12 (Spring 1976): 171–77.

Cheseboro, James W. "Beyond the Orthodox: The Criteria Case." *Journal of the American Forensic Association* 7 (Winter 1971): 298–315.

Church, Russell T. and Wilbanks, Charles. *Values and Policies in Controversy: An Introduction to Argumentation and Debate.* Scottsdale, AZ: Gorsuch Scarisbrick, 1986.

Copeland, James M. *Cross-Examination in Debate.* Lincolnwood, IL: National Textbook Co., 1981.

Cox, J. Robert. "Attitudinal Inherency: Implications for Policy Debate." *Southern Speech Communication Journal* 40 (1975): 158–68.

Cross, John D. and Matlon, Ronald J. "An Analysis of Judging Philosophies in Academic Debate." *Journal of the American Forensic Association* 15 (Fall 1978): 110–23.

Dempsey, Richard H. and Hartman, David T. "Mirror State Counterplans: Illegitimate, Topical, or Magical?" *Journal of the American Forensic Association* (Winter 1985): 161–66.

Dick, Robert C. *Argumentation and Rational Debating.* Dubuque, IA: Wm. C. Brown Co., 1972.

Dowling, Ralph E. "Debate as Game, Educational Tool, and Argument: An Evaluation of Theory and Rules." *Journal of the American Forensic Association* 17 (Spring 1981): 235–36.

Dudczak, Craig A. "Direct Refutation in Propositions of Policy: A Viable Alternative." *Journal of the American Forensic Association* 16 (Spring 1980): 232–35.

Ehninger, Douglas and Brockriede, Wayne. *Decision by Debate.* 2nd ed. New York: Harper and Row, 1978.

Eman, Virginia and Lukehart, Jeffery. "Information Use in Academic Debate: An Information Theory Perspective." *Journal of the American Forensic Association* 12 (Spring 1976): 178–83.

Flaningam, Carl D. "Value-Centered Argument and the Development of Decision Rules." *Journal of the American Forensic Association* 19 (Fall 1982): 107–14.

Fogelin, Robert J. *Understanding Arguments: An Introduction to Informal Logic.* 3rd ed. New York: Harcourt Brace Jovanovich, 1987.

Freeley, Austin J. *Argumentation and Debate: Reasoned Decision Making.* 6th ed. Belmont, CA: Wadsworth Publishing Company, Inc., 1986.

Fryar, Maridell, Thomas, David A. and Goodnight, Lynn. *Basic Debate.* 3rd ed. Lincolnwood, IL: National Textbook Co., 1988.

Goodnight, G. Thomas and Zarefsky, David. *Forensic Tournaments: Planning and Administration*. Lincolnwood, IL: National Textbook Co., 1980.

Goodnight, Lynn. *Getting Started in Debate*. Lincolnwood, IL: National Textbook Co., 1987.

Goodnight, Tom, Balthrop, Bill and Parson, Donn W. "The Problem of Inherency: Strategy and Substance." *Journal of the American Forensic Association* 10 (Spring 1974): 229–40.

Hample, Dale. "Testing a Model of Value Argument and Evidence." *Communication Monographs* 44 (June 1977): 106–20.

Hemmer, Joseph J., Jr. "The Comparative Advantage Negative: An Integrated Approach." *Speaker and Gavel* 13 (Winter 1976): 27–30.

Hensley, Dana and Prentice, Diana. *Mastering Competitive Debate*. 2nd ed. Caldwell, ID: Clarke Publishing Co., 1982.

Hoaglund, John. *Critical Thinking*. Newport News, VA: Vale Press, 1984.

Hollihan, Thomas A. "An Analysis of Value Argumentation in Contemporary Debate." *Debate Issues* 14 (November 1980): 7–10.

Kahane, Howard. *Logic and Contemporary Rhetoric: The Use of Reason in Everyday Life*. 4th ed. Belmont, CA: Wadsworth Publishing Co., 1984.

Kaplow, Louis. "Rethinking Counterplans: A Reconciliation with Debate Theory." *Journal of the American Forensic Association* 17 (Spring 1981): 215–26.

Kemp, Robert L. *Assignment: Directing the School's Forensic Program*. Clayton, MO: Alan Company, 1985.

————. *Lincoln-Douglas Debating*. Clayton, MO: Alan Company, 1984.

Klopf, Donald W. and Cambra, Ronald E. *Academic Debate Practicing Argumentative Theory*. 2nd ed. Denver: Morton Press, 1979.

Klopf, Donald W. *Coaching and Directing Forensics*. Lincolnwood, IL: National Textbook Co., 1982.

Lewinski, John D., Metzler, Bruce R. and Settle, Peter L. "The Goal Case Affirmative." *Journal of the American Forensic Association* 9 (Spring 1973): 458–63.

Lichtman, Allan J. and Rohrer, Daniel M. "A General Theory of the Counterplan." *Journal of the American Forensic Association* 12 (Fall 1975): 70–79.

————. "The Logic of Policy Dispute." *Journal of the American Forensic Association* 16 (Spring 1980): 236–47.

Ling, David A. and Seltzer, Robert V. "The Role of Attitudinal Inherency in Contemporary Debate." *Journal of the American Forensic Association* 7 (1971): 278–83.

McAdoo, Joe, ed. *Judging Debate*. Springfield, MO: Mid-America Research, 1975.

Matlon, Ronald J. "Analyzing and Debating Propositions of Value in Academic Forensics." *Journal of Communication Association of the Pacific* 6 (July 1977): 52–67.

————. "Debating Propositions of Value." *Journal of the American Forensic Association* 14 (Spring 1978): 194–204.

Mayer, Michael. "Epistemological Considerations of the Studies Counterplan." *Journal of the American Forensic Association* 19 (Spring 1983): 261–66.

Meyers, Chet. *Teaching Students to Think Critically*. San Francisco: Jossey-Bass Publishers, 1986.

Newman, Robert P. "The Inherent and Compelling Need." *Journal of the American Forensic Association* 2 (May 1965): 66–71.

Patterson, J. W. and Zarefsky, David. *Contemporary Debate*. Boston: Houghton Mifflin Company, 1983.

Paulsen, James W. and Rhodes, Jack. "The Counter-Warrent as a Negative Strategy." *Journal of the American Forensic Association* 15 (Spring 1979): 205–10.

Perella, Jack. *The Debate Method of Critical Thinking: An Introduction to Argumentation.* Dubuque, IA: Kendall/Hunt, 1986.

Pfau, Michael W., Thomas, David A. and Ulrich, Walter. *Debate and Argument: A Systems Approach to Advocacy:* Glenview, IL: Scott, Foresman and Company, 1987.

Prentice, Diana and Kay, Jack. *The Role of Values in Policy Debate.* Kansas City, MO: National Federation of State High School Associations, 1986.

Rowland, Robert C. "The Debate Judge as Debate Judge: A Functional Paradigm." *Journal of the American Forensic Association* 20 (Summer 1984): 183–93.

Sanders, Gerald H. *Introduction to Contemporary Academic Debate.* 2nd ed. Prospect Heights, IL: Waveland Press, Inc., 1983.

Sayer, J. E. *Argumentation and Debate.* Sherman Oaks, CA: Alfred Publishing, 1980.

Shelton, Michael W. "In Defense of the Studies Counterplan." *Journal of the American Forensic Association* (Winter 1985): 150–55.

Terry, Donald R., ed. *Modern Debate Case Techniques.* Lincolnwood, IL: National Textbook Co., 1970.

Thomas, David A. and Hart, Jack. *Advanced Debate: Readings in Theory, Practice and Teaching.* 3rd ed. Lincolnwood, IL: National Textbook Co., 1987.

Ulrich, Walter. *Guidelines for the Debate Judge.* Kansas City, MO: National Federation of State High School Associations, 1986.

————. *An Introduction to Debate.* Kansas City, MO: National Federation of State High School Associations, 1986.

————. *Judging Academic Debate.* Lincolnwood, IL: National Textbook Co., 1986.

————. "The Strategic Limitations of the Spread." *Debate Issues* (January 1984): 3–11.

————. *Understanding the Counterplan.* Kansas City, MO: National Federation of State High School Associations, 1986.

Warnick, Barbara. "Arguing Value Propositions." *Journal of the American Forensic Association* 18 (Fall 1981): 109–19.

Wenzel, Joseph W. and Hample, Dale J. "Categories and Dimensions of Value Propositions: Exploratory Studies." *Journal of the American Forensic Association* 11 (Winter 1975): 121–30.

Wenzel, Joseph W. "Toward a Rationale for Value-Centered Argument." *Journal of the American Forensic Association* 13 (Winter 1977): 150–58.

Wood, Stephen and Midgley, John. *Prima Facie: A Guide to Value Debate.* Dubuque, IA: Kendall/Hunt, 1987.

Young, Marilyn J. *Coaching Debate.* Clayton, MO: Alan Company, 1975.

Zarefsky, David. "The Role of Causal Argument in Policy Controversies." *Journal of the American Forensic Association* 13 (Spring 1977): 179–92.

————. "The Traditional Case— Comparative Advantage Dichotomy: Another Look." *Journal of the American Forensic Association* 6 (Winter 1969).

Ziegelmueller, George W. and Dause, Charles A. *Argumentation: Inquiry and Advocacy.* Englewood Cliffs, N.J.: Prentice-Hall, Inc., 1976.

Glossary

The language of debate is specialized. It is filled with terms that are meaningful to persons who understand the concept and theory of debate. The same terms are necessary in the explanation of debate. The following list of terms, which have been used in this text and in many others, makes up the body of literature relating to debate. Each term is concisely defined. Although the definitions provided here were written by the authors, an effort was made to be consistent with the meanings and interpretations that are found in standard argumentation textbooks.

AD HOMINEM ATTACK. An attack on the person rather than the person's arguments.

ADDITIVE ADVANTAGE. An advantage developed by the affirmative for the first time in the second affirmative constructive speech. It is generally an advantage that flows from adopting the affirmative plan.

ADVANTAGE. A significant improvement over the status quo that can best be gained by the affirmative plan.

ADVOCATE. (v.) To support a position. (n.) One who advocates; a debater.

AFFIRMATIVE. The side that favors (affirms) changing the status quo to conform to the debate resolution.

AGENT OF CHANGE. A person or persons responsible for carrying out the work of the plan. Sometimes this kind of plan plank need only indicate what agency, bureau, or level of government will be responsible for seeing to it that the plan mandates are carried out. The affirmative may also create a new board or agency.

ALTERNATIVE CAUSALITY. Causes for the problem other than those dealt with by the affirmative. This term also can be used in negative plan-meets-need arguments and disadvantages.

ANALOGY. A comparison used to draw a general conclusion. The conclusion drawn is strong in relation to the number of likenesses between the things compared. Classical reasoning indicates that analogies are for clarification rather than proof; however, contemporary argumentation accepts generalizations based on strong analogies.

ANALYSIS. The process of breaking down an idea or a proposition into its elements. In debate, analysis traditionally follows a fairly standard procedure of seeking pro and con positions on the stock issues.

ARGUMENT. Two senses of this term are important to debaters. In the first sense, an argument is a message consisting of a conclusion supported by a reason documented by evidence. The emphasis is on credible proof and logical structure. In the second sense, an argument is a confrontation between two parties in disagreement over a claim. The emphasis is on refutation. Thus, a debater can make an argument that is tested against the standards of evidence and logic; two debaters can have an argument with each other that one or the other wins on the basis of his or her refutation of an opponent.

ARGUMENTATION. The study or use of argument, consisting of the dual process of (1) discovering the probable truth of an issue through analysis and research and (2) advocating it to an audience through appropriate logical, ethical, and persuasive techniques.

ASSERTION. An unsupported statement; a conclusion that lacks evidence for support.

ATTITUDINAL INHERENCY. A claim that the attitudes of the bureaucracy— i.e., government or industry— prevent the present system from solving the affirmative problem.

AUDIENCE. The person or persons to whom a message is directed. In academic debate, the audience consists of a judge who listens to the debaters, weighs the arguments presented by each side, and then makes a decision about which team's position is the most acceptable.

AUTHORITY. A person whose experience, training, position, or special study makes her or his testimony or opinion acceptable as evidence; an expert.

"BALANCE OF ARGUMENTS" JUDGE. A kind of debate judge who bases his or her decision on which team established its arguments during the debate. The decision is based on the judge's determination as to which team did the better job of meeting

its basic responsibilities. This kind of judge is likely to be much more content-analysis oriented than other judges.

BENEFIT. In a need-plan case, a positive effect of the plan in addition to the solution of the major need areas.

"BETTER JOB OF DEBATING" JUDGE. A kind of debate judge who does not weigh the arguments to determine which team was more effective in the round, but bases his or her decisions solely on which team did the better job of debating. Decisions may be totally subjective or even impressionistic, but it is more likely that this kind of judge will use specific criteria (usually those listed on the ballot).

BIAS. A prejudiced attitude on the part of the source of evidence quoted in a debate. If quoted sources are biased, their opinions are therefore questionable as credible proof. Bias exists in sources when it is shown they have some vested interest in the policy being debated. There can be political or economic bias by a lobby group or political party. As a rule, academic and scholarly research reports, or nonpartisan analytical "think tanks," are accepted as relatively unbiased sources in debate. Debaters should seek unbiased sources when possible.

BIBLIOGRAPHICAL INDEX. A bibliography of bibliographies.

BLACK'S LAW DICTIONARY. The standard work for legal terms and court precedents for concepts of law.

BOOKS IN PRINT. An annual listing of published works by subject, author, and title.

BRIEF. An outline of all the arguments on both sides of the debate resolution. An affirmative or negative brief consists of all the arguments on the respective sides of the resolution.

BROOKINGS INSTITUTE PUBLICATIONS. A series of in-depth analyses of important issues.

BURDEN OF PROOF. The burden of proof rests on the side that desires a change from the status quo. If the proposition was correctly stated, the burden of proof should rest with the affirmative. The affirmative must show that some serious fault is inherent in present conditions and that the proposed solution will remedy the fault in a way that is practical and desirable.

Affirmative

1. Either must prove that the status quo includes at least one important deficiency or harm or demonstrate that the affirmative plan would be superior to the status quo in one or more significant respects.
2. Must prove that deficiency is inherent to the status quo—i.e., that causal factors make the shortcoming inevitable and that a solution is impossible unless the cause or causes are removed or counteracted.
3. Presents the plan.
4. Shows that the proposal will solve alleged needs or result in the advantage.

Admitted matter

Weak points that do not matter. The negative can admit that the status quo is imperfect but that the imperfections are slight and minor changes would solve the imperfections. This would shift the focus of the debate from whether the

point is true to how significant the point is and whether the status quo has the capabilities to solve it.

Waived matter

Issues that are granted for purposes of debate. For example, constitutionality is granted. Most plans would require a constitutional amendment; thus the need for amendment is granted so the debate can concentrate on more important issues.

BURDEN OF PROVING. The obligation of debaters on either side to prove any argument they initiate.

BURDEN OF REBUTTAL. The obligation of the negative in any debate to meet and clash with the affirmative case.

BURDEN OF REFUTING. The obligation of either side to respond to relevant constructive arguments presented by its opponent and to advance its own arguments.

CARD FILE. An organized collection of evidence recorded on index cards. A card should contain only one idea or bit of information, preferably verbatim from the source, together with complete labeling of the contents of the card and information about the source, such as the authority's name and qualifications and publication data, including the date of the source.

CASE. A debate team's basic position on the resolution, made up of all the arguments that the team presents in support of that position.

CASE-RELATED DISADVANTAGES. Potentially bad consequences implied by the specific affirmative case. What is being argued is that to gain an advantage in one area of the topic will only make things worse overall. This is a powerful argument in most rounds. If it is won by the negative, the affirmative cannot win.

CAUSATION. A relationship between two phenomena in which one is believed to cause the other.

CIRCUMVENTION. Countermeasures will arise that circumvent the objectives of the affirmative plan. This area of analysis becomes particularly fertile when the case depends on the attitudes of interest groups or social agencies (attitudinal inherency). Unless the attitudes that perpetuate the problem are changed, the old problem will simply reappear in a new form. A circumvention argument always has two parts: the motive and the means. The motive for circumvention is generally isolatable from the inherency presented by the affirmative. The means for circumvention are various.

CLASH. The process of meeting and dealing directly with an argument of the opposition. Dealing with an argument implies denial or minimization, but not agreement with it.

COACH JUDGE. A coach from one of the schools participating in a tournament who judges other participants. Coach-judges are trained in debate and know the issues.

COMPARATIVE ADVANTAGES CASE. A case in which the affirmative shows that although existing programs could possibly be modified in the present system to achieve a solution to the problem area, the affirmative proposal could do a better job. The argument focuses on the comparison between the affirmative plan and the present system. The entire case is presented in the first affirmative constructive speech.

COMPUTER INDEXES. One type of computer system contains items you would find in a card catalog (primarily books). Most are indexed by author, title, and subject. Another type of system carries periodical listings.

CONDITIONAL COUNTERPLAN. A negative strategy of arguing the superiority of the present system over the affirmative plan. But, on the condition that the judge agrees with the affirmative that the present system should be changed, the negative also suggests a counterplan it is willing to defend in preference to the affirmative plan. This strategy is risky because it potentially places the negative in a self-contradictory position of claiming no need for a change and then advocating a counterplan to change the present system.

CONGRESSIONAL QUARTERLY. A weekly résumé of activities in Congress.

CONSTRUCTIVE. (adj.) A constructive argument is one offered in support of, or in opposition to, the resolution. A constructive speech is a time period in which it is permissible to present constructive arguments.

CONTENTION. A subdivision of an issue; the statement of a claim; an argument essential to support a position on an issue. Contentions may consist of either observations or indictments. In debate, a number of contentions make up the affirmative case.

CONTRADICTION. Statements or arguments within a given position that are in direct opposition to each other.

CORPUS JURIS SECUNDUM. A text that clarifies the implications of legal rulings or the current state of the law. Available at law libraries, major courthouses, and many general libraries.

CORRELATION. A statement of a logical relationship between two phenomena showing that the two appear together and that they also vary together, either directly or inversely. In other words, correlation would establish a relationship less strong than causality.

COST-BENEFIT RATIO. An on balance comparison of the advantages and disadvantages of alternative proposals for change. The emphasis is on quantified measures of both costs and benefits, with the greatest value assigned to the most favorable ratio between costs incurred for benefits received.

COUNTERARGUMENT. An argument designed to contradict a specific affirmative argument. The debater puts the argument in perspective by showing how the defeat of the particular argument affects the affirmative's case.

COUNTERPLAN. Generally, the negative will agree that there is a problem in the status quo and will present a plan that it believes is better than that of the affirmative. First negative presents the plan and begins supporting. The negative must show that the counterplan is inconsistent with the affirmative plan. In other words, the negative should be ready to show that the counterplan and the affirmative cannot be adopted at the same time. The negative must assume the burden of proof for the counterplan. The counterplan cannot be resolutional; the plan must be adopted on a state, local, or voluntary, level. If it requires federal action, then it has met the terms of the resolution.

CRITERIA-GOALS CASE. An elaboration on the comparative advantages case, with greater emphasis on the policy goals of the present system. The affirmative incorporates the identification of the goal of the present system as an integral part of its analysis. Affirmative sets up the criteria to judge the fulfillment of those particular goals. The affirmative shows its proposed plan meets the criteria better than the present system does.

CROSS-EXAMINATION. A form of debate in which debaters are permitted to ask direct questions of an opponent during specified time periods, usually immediately following the opponent's constructive speeches.

DEBATE. A contest of argumentation. An affirmative team presents arguments in favor of a resolution, and a negative team presents arguments against it. The contest is won by the team that presents the best arguments in the opinion of the judge.

DEDUCTION. A reasoning process that takes general statements or premises and draws a conclusion about particular or specific elements. In formal logic, deduction is contained in a chain called a syllogism. This form of reasoning is formal, and the validity of such an argument is based on the logical relationship between premises and conclusion, not necessarily on the truth content of any premise.

Example:

Major Premise: All elementary schools are entitled to public tax support.
Minor Premise: Parochial schools are elementary schools.

Conclusion: Therefore, parochial schools are entitled to public tax support.

DEFENSE OF THE PRESENT SYSTEM. A refutation of affirmative claims that involves two arguments: first, that life under the present system will be worse in the future; and, second, that the future looks promising in respect to the harm area isolated by the affirmative.

DEFINITION. A formality of a debate wherein the affirmative team declares the meaning of the terms of the debate resolution. The definition of terms serves the useful function of limiting the areas encompassed by the resolution. While the affirmative team has the privilege of defining the terms, the negative team has the privilege of challenging any definition considered unacceptable. The most frequently used methods of defining terms are references to authorities, examples, or the dictionary.

DEFINITION BY AUTHORITY. A definition of terms based on such sources as *Dictionary of Economics and Business, The Oxford English Dictionary, Black's Law Dictionary,* and *Random House College Dictionary,* to name a few. It may also include authorities in the field being debated.

DEFINITION OF TERMS. The affirmative identifies each important term in the proposition and discerns its various meanings from a number of sources.

DESIRABILITY. A condition or state of favorability; a value judgment attached to a particular outcome of a plan, especially a benefit or an advantage. Desirability is a state lower in degree than necessity.

DILEMMA. A situation in which choice is between only two alternatives, both of which are undesirable.

DISADVANTAGE. A harmful effect, or series of effects, brought about by the affirmative plan. Any disadvantage is composed of two parts: the links and the impacts. The link is the "why" part of the disadvantage. It is the proof that explains why the affirmative plan will cause an undesirable effect and why it is unique to the affirmative plan. A link may be either direct or indirect. The impact is the end result or outcome of the disadvantage.

DISTORTION. A misrepresentation of a piece of evidence.

DROP. To neglect to carry on an argument after the opponent's response.

EDITORIAL RESEARCH REPORTS. Available only to newspapers and libraries, this publication presents in-depth analyses of currently important topics.

ELABORATE ALPHABETICAL FILING SYSTEM. A note-card filing system that involves an affirmative file and a negative file. The cards are filed behind the major affirmative and negative headings.

ELIMINATION ROUNDS. Debate rounds in which teams with the best records are matched. Depending on tournament size, the rounds could begin with double octofinals, octofinals, quarterfinals, or even semifinals. A single loss in a tournament elimination round eliminates a team from the tournament, while the winner goes on to the next higher level of competition. Usually, there are multiple judges.

EMPIRICAL EVIDENCE. The results of controlled observation to obtain factual and inferential data.

ENCYCLOPEDIA OF ASSOCIATIONS. A

comprehensive list of American associations.

ENFORCEMENT. That plank of a plan that provides for seeing that the performance or prohibition planks of the plan are carried out.

EVIDENCE. Data that form the basis for conclusions.

EXAMPLE. Single objects or events used to show the possibility of generalized categories of similar groups of examples; a type of factual evidence. Negative examples are those used to disprove generalities.

EXPERIMENTAL DATA. The evidence reporting the results of a scientific experiment that has been conducted to explore some causal relationship. It is often considered the best debate evidence because it represents the best way to establish causation. In evaluating experimental data, the debater should ask three questions:

1. How well were the variables controlled?
2. Has the experiment been replicated with the same results?
3. Can the results of the experiment be generalized to more than just the cases that were used in the experiment?

EXPERT JUDGE. A kind of judge who is familiar with the latest forensic theory and practices. He or she generally requires less explanation in apprehending the nature and weight of the argument and is less responsive to general persuasive rhetoric, as he or she understands and is concerned with the technical issues involved in debate.

EXTEND. To carry an argument another step forward in rebuttal; to answer the opponent's challenge and advance beyond it.

EXTERNAL CRITICISM. Criticism directed at the source of evidence. This kind of criticism pertains to the excellence of the publication from which the evidence is drawn and the competence of the author of the evidence.

EXTRATOPICALITY. An advantage or solvency that is gained from means other than the resolution. An advantage is extratopical when it comes about because of a plank in the plan that is not resolutional. For example, if the plan causes unemployment by banning hazardous products, it cannot claim an advantage of employment by a plank in the plan for employment of these people or an advantage from the work these people might do in public works programs.

FABRICATION. To make up evidence.

FACT. An actual, observable object or event in the real world. Useful as evidence in debate, facts usually fall into these categories: (a) examples, (b) statistics, (c) empirical studies.

FALLACY. A mistaken inference; an erroneous conclusion based on faulty reasoning.

FIAT. An assumed power to put a proposal into effect; a legal mandate binding on the parties involved, overriding their personal attitudes. Fiat power is limited to matters subject to law; it is not a "magic wand" to avoid substantive argument. For example, an energy bill could be adopted by fiat, but a new oil supply cannot be discovered by fiat.

FLOW SHEET. A diagram of the arguments in a debate and of their relationships. Arguments are charted in parallel columns, with the affirmative case written in the left-hand column, the negative arguments in the next column, the affirmative responses in the next column, and so forth. Thus, a "flow" of the arguments can be seen at a glance by tracing each argument and its responses across the flow sheet.

FORTHCOMING BOOKS. A bimonthly listing of all books scheduled for publication within the next five months.

GENERALIZATION. Conclusions drawn from evidence or data.

GENERIC DISADVANTAGE (Policy Disadvantage). A negative effect of the affirmative case deriving from its impact on society as a whole. The disadvantage derives from the policy in general and not from a specific action of the affirmative plan. The concept of generic disadvantages is based on the idea that there is no such thing as a discrete action or a delimited area; all policies are interrelated to some extent. When looking for possible disadvantage areas, the debater should first examine possible higher-order impacts—e.g., earth-ending threats.

GOAL. A general objective; an aim. Systems of policy are thought to exist in order to achieve goals. Affirmative cases may be developed on the premise that a laudable goal can best be met through the affirmative proposal.

HARM. An undesirable impact resulting from the operation of a policy system. The impact may be stated in terms of deprivation of or injury to parties affected by the policy. Harm exists where needs are denied or suffering or loss of life is caused.

INDEX SHEET FILING SYSTEM. A notecard filing system in which the evidence cards are lettered and numbered. A master notebook is kept for the entire filing system. All the material in each file box is noted on a single index sheet to which the debater can quickly refer for the code numbers that apply to specific subjects.

INDEXES (Guides). Alphabetical listings by author, title, and general subject of magazine articles that have appeared in a particular group of periodicals.

INDICTMENT. An accusatory conclusion; a charge. A contention in a debate will usually state an indictment.

INFERENCES. Conclusions based on possible relationships between known facts.

INHERENCY. Presumption holds that the present system should be continued unless someone can prove otherwise.

INTERNAL CRITICISM. A kind of criticism that questions the truth of the evidence. What does the evidence say? How consistent is the evidence?

ISSUE. A question concerning which the affirmative and negative teams take opposite sides; a major point of disagreement.

JUDGE. The person who stands in for a larger audience and renders a decision in accordance with tournament custom and good educational practices.

JUSTIFICATION. A fulfillment of the standards of judgment. A justification argument is one in which it is charged that an affirmative case fails to "justify the resolution." As a negative strategy, the argument shows how the advantages of the affirmative case do not stem from the resolution itself but rather from other extratopical features of the plan.

KEY WORDS. A list of words put together by a researcher when investigating a subject area. Looking up the words in various indexes and the card catalog will provide a tremendous supply of possible sources.

LAY JUDGE. A kind of judge who comes from the community. Although this kind of judge is interested in current affairs and may have a high level of intellectual accomplishment, he or she is not a specialist in debate theory and might not be an expert in the topic under discussion.

LINCOLN-DOUGLAS DEBATE. A kind of debate that utilizes a two-person format centered around a value proposition.

LOGIC. The system of analysis that shows the nature of relationships between statements, facts and conclusions, causes and effects, and deductions and premises. Logic is reasoning based on rules concerning the form in which an argument is put rather than on the nature and quality of the evidence.

"MAVERICK" JUDGE. A kind of judge whose basis for decision making is unpredictable.

MEANS OF CHANGE. The affirmative may specify an exact means of enacting the resolution, or it can create a number of choices from which the board (agent of change) might choose. When the affirmative wants to defend specific alternatives, those alternatives should be listed in the plan.

METHODOLOGY. The procedure by which an empirical study is conducted. An empirical study's methodology may be challenged along such lines as the size of the sample, the amount of time, or the presence of a control group. To challenge the methodology is to test the validity of the conclusions drawn from such a study. Debaters who quote from empirical studies should be familiar with the methodology of the studies.

MINOR REPAIRS. Alterations that can be made in the present system not requiring federal action or the adoption of the affirmative plan or the resolution. The aim is to show how the present system can solve the problem with mechanisms that currently exist. For example, if the affirmative is arguing the harms of unemployment, the negative could minor repair by adding money to the current programs that are designed to take care of the unemployed. This would not change the structure of the present system but could solve the harm of unemployment.

NFL (National Forensic League). Sponsor of high school speech and debate activities. Located in Ripon, Wisconsin.

NEED. An evil or harmful situation inherent in the status quo, which the affirmative plan will remedy. The need is a necessary element of a traditional need-plan case.

NEED-PLAN CASE. A kind of case that develops the argument that a need for change exists. The case develops the plan and shows how the plan meets the need. The case develops the argument that the plan would be beneficial.

NEGATIVE. In a debate the side that opposes (negates) the affirmative position and therefore the resolution.

NEGATIVE BLOCK. The section of a debate that consists of the second negative constructive speech and the first negative rebuttal.

NET BENEFITS CASE. A kind of case

based on systems analysis. The case incorporates four steps: (1) Apply systems analysis to the problem area; (2) determine the components that make up the system and the rules that govern how the components are interrelated; (3) analyze and project the differences that can be predicted following a change in policy governing the interrelationships; and (4) determine the most favorable ratio between the costs and the benefits of the proposed change in the system.

NON SEQUITUR. A Latin phrase that means "does not follow." It is used by logicians to describe any fallacious argument in which the conclusion does not follow from the evidence.

NONTOPICALITY. The condition of failure to encompass the scope or intent of the resolution. A case is nontopical if it fails to justify all the terms included in the resolution.

NOVICE DIVISION. A division for beginners who enter a tournament for the first time or are just beginning in a forensic career.

OBSERVATION. A descriptive conclusion or assumption.

OBSERVATIONAL DATA. Information that reflects controlled observation of events. Types of observational data include statistics and carefully developed examples. The main criteria for judging the quality of observational data are validity and reliability.

OPEN DIVISION. A tournament division that mixes beginners and advanced students.

OPERATIONAL DEFINITION. The terms of the resolution are defined by way of the affirmative plan. The plan serves as an example of the resolution. When using an operational definition, the affirmative merely states this fact after stating the resolution.

OPINION EVIDENCE. A kind of evidence that is divisible into two categories: expert testimony and testimony from a lay person. Expert testimony is the only variety that can be used for proof. Testimony from lay people should be reserved for the persuasive effect of illustration.

PMN OR PMA (Plan-Meets-Needs or Plan-Meets-Advantages). Does the plan meet the need or advantage of the affirmative case? While general research can be done ahead of time, specific application will generally need to be done after hearing the affirmative plan. For example, if the affirmative argues that people are unemployed because of U.S. trade policies, the negative would want to demonstrate that the number of unemployed is a fairly constant number and that to change the trade policies would not change the overall unemployment figures. At best, the plan may only shift unemployment from one sector of the work force to another.

PO (Plan Objection). An objection that is generally the responsibility of the second negative. These arguments include a combination of workability, plan-meets-need arguments, plan-meets-advantage arguments or disadvantages.

PARALLEL ORGANIZATION. A method of organization based on contingency. The team argues that if any one of several contingencies is true, the proposition should be accepted.

PARAMETERS OF THE RESOLUTION. The collegiate topic committee provides a statement of what the committee had in mind when framing the resolution. Although this statement is not binding on the debater, it does help the negative to build a framework for a topicality argument against any off-the-wall affirmative definitions.

PLAN. The specific program proposed by the affirmative team to implement the debate resolution. The plan is a necessary part of every affirmative case.

PLAN PLANK. A specific provision within the affirmative plan; a set of particulars about the plan. Individual planks might specify (1) goal or intent, (2) agency of change, (3) duties or powers, (4) enforcement, or (5) financing.

PLAN SPIKES. A provision in the plan designed to eliminate a potential disadvantage or a plan-meets-need argument.

POLICY. A means of achieving a goal; an action. In a narrow sense, a policy is a governmental program, such as the financing of public schools through property tax revenues. In debate, a policy proposition is the proposal of some new governmental program that the affirmative team claims should be adopted.

POST HOC ERGO PROPTER HOC. A Latin phrase meaning "After this, therefore because of this." A logical fallacy based on the assumption that, because one event is closely followed by another event, the first is the cause of the second.

POWER-MATCH ROUNDS. Matches based on the accumulated record of teams at the tournament.

PREEMPT. A plank in the plan to prevent the development of a negative disadvantage. For example, if a plan causes unemployment, some sort of subsidy might be provided to prevent the disadvantages of harms to unemployment.

PRELIMINARY ROUNDS. Debate rounds usually consisting of four, six, or eight debate matches per team, with each team alternating sides between affirmative and negative. The teams with the best record advance to the elimination rounds. Usually, there is one judge.

PREMISE. A general statement of a goal or value from which arguments and conclusions may be drawn.

PREPARATION TIME. In a debate, the time that elapses before the beginning of each debater's speech. After the first affirmative speech, each team has a strictly regulated amount of cumulative preparation time allocated to it for the entire debate, which the team members may utilize as they wish. The amount of time and the rules governing its use are determined by the tournament director.

PRESET MATCH. A round set by the tournament host before the tournament begins.

PRESUMPTION. Traditionally, the assumption that conditions and policies should remain as they are. The affirmative side has the burden to prove that the status quo should be changed. The present system is presumed to be adequate until the affirmative team meets its burden to prove that a change in the status quo is needed or would be advantageous. Presumption is analogous to the legal principle that the accused person is presumed to be innocent until proven guilty.

PRIMA FACIE. The Latin phrase may be translated as "at first look." A prima facie case is one that a reasonable and prudent person would accept "at first look." In debate, a *prima facie* case must include a specific plan to implement the resolution

and a justification for the plan—
either an inherent need in the status quo, a comparative advantage of
the plan over the status quo, or
some other accepted justification.

PROBABILITY. (1) The relative degree of
certainty with which an inference
may be drawn. (2) In statistical language, the level of confidence that
may be placed in a conclusion expressed as a percentage.

PROBLEM AREA. The domain of issues
that pertain to a topic. A problem
area includes issues of long-
standing social concern.

PROCESS DISADVANTAGE. A flaw in the
affirmative method of producing results. It relates neither to the particular content area of the topic nor to
extrinsic considerations of policy
effect. The judge is asked to reject
the case because the plan is an inappropriate method of achieving any
advantage.

PROOF. That which reduces uncertainty
and increases the probable truth of
a claim. Evidence is transformed
into proof through the use of reasoning, which demonstrates how
and to what extent the claim is believable. Proof is a relative concept,
ranging from possibility through
probability to certainty. The
amount of proof needed to establish a claim depends on a number of
variables, such as the importance of
the claim, the strength of opposing
claims, and the credibility of the
person making the argument.

PROPOSAL. The specific affirmative
plan.

PROPOSITION. A debatable statement;
a statement open to interpretation; a statement about which reasonable people may accept arguments on either side. Debate
theory incorporates three types of

propositions: fact, value, and
policy.

PROPOSITION OF FACT. A statement
about a person, thing, or event, the
truth or falsity of which is determin-
able by direct investigation.

PROPOSITION OF POLICY. A statement
calling for a specific action. A proposition of policy requires that the
debater (1) find the facts that afford a sound basis for making predictions, (2) reason cogently from
these facts to the probable results,
and (3) show that these consequences would be desirable.

PROPOSITION OF VALUE. A statement offering a value judgment about a person, thing, or event. Two sides could
agree on all the facts of a case but
disagree about whether the facts
constitute justice or whether the actions were prudent.

QUOTE CARDS. Material (evidence) recorded on index cards for use in debate rounds.

RATIONALE. (1) The philosophical
framework within which a case is
constructed. (2) The criteria for accepting a premise or conclusion.

REBUTTAL. A short speech devoted to
(1) rebuilding arguments that have
been attacked, (2) refuting opposing arguments, and (3) summarizing the debate from the perspective
of the speaker.

REBUTTAL SHEETS. Sheets on which the
arguments most likely to arise in a debate are listed, along with the replies
and the best evidence. Rebuttal
sheets can also be made without specific reference to pieces of evidence.

REFUTATION. An attack on the arguments of the opponent.

RELIABILITY. A criterion for evidence
that asks if the same results would
be obtained if the observations were
repeated or if they had been gath-

ered at the same time by a different observer.

RESEARCH. To search again; to gather information and evidence and to classify it so that it is easily retrievable for use.

SANDBAGGING. The practice of presenting an argument initially in skeletal form, with little or no evidence, so that it appears weak, and saving a bulk of evidence for second-line presentation only if the argument is attacked. The strategy is to make your strongest point look like the weakest so that the opposition will focus the debate there.

SENIOR (VARSITY) DIVISION. A division for more experienced debaters.

SERIAL ORGANIZATION. A method of organization in which each argument depends on the preceding argument for its support. If one argument can be destroyed, the whole case or series of arguments fails.

SHIFT. To abandon an original position and take up a different one.

SHOTGUN. (1) A strategy of presenting a profusion of unrelated, scattered attacks against an opponent's case; (2) a loud, bombastic style of delivery.

SHOULD. A term generally defined by the affirmative as meaning "ought to but not necessarily will." The word means that the proposal of the affirmative would be the most desirable policy at the present time.

SIGNIFICANCE. (1) The degree of importance of a conclusion. Significance may be qualitative or quantitative. Qualitative significance rests on an established value; quantitative significance rests on concrete units of measurement. (2) In statistical language, the level of confidence at which a predicted conclusion may not be rejected, usually ".05 level of significance," or "95 percent probability."

SIMPLE ALPHABETICAL FILING SYSTEM. A note-card filing system that involves dividing the evidence cards into subject areas and filing them accordingly.

SINE QUA NON. A Latin phrase meaning "without which not." It signifies something that is indispensable or essential. As a test for the post hoc fallacy, the sine qua non question is "Would the second event have occurred if the first had not occurred?"

SOURCE CREDIBILITY. A social-psychological term that refers to the judgment the receiver makes of the believability of the source of a message.

SPEAKER AWARDS. Recognition given to contestants who have accumulated the greatest number of quality points during the preliminary rounds. Many tournaments drop the highest and lowest points awarded each speaker. Ties for awards are often broken by comparing ranks.

SQUIRREL CASE. A case idea that the affirmative tries to work into the topic. It usually involves an unusual definition that will incorporate the case idea. To challenge a squirrel case, the negative challenges the definitions by placing them back into the resolution. Most of the time, when this is done the resolution will make no sense.

STATISTICAL ABSTRACT OF THE UNITED STATES. An exhaustive summary of current statistics.

STATISTICAL NON SEQUITUR. A claim in which the statistics are valid, but the evidence and the conclusion pertain to two different things. Therefore, the evidence does not follow from the conclusion, even if the evidence and the conclusion separately are valid.

STATUS QUO. The present system; the existing order; that which would be changed by adopting the affirmative plan.

STOCK ISSUES. A series of broad questions encompassing the major debatable issues of any proposition of policy. Some stock issues are (1) Is there a need for a change? (2) Will the plan meet the need? (3) Is the plan the most desirable way to meet the need?

STRAIGHT REFUTATION. For every claim that the affirmative asserts is true, the negative offers a counterclaim asserting that what the affirmative says is false.

STRUCTURAL INHERENCY. The affirmative argues that the problem cannot be corrected until basic changes have been made in the structure of the present system. The problem cannot be solved simply by doing more of what is presently being done, nor can it be corrected simply by spending more money on present methods. Generally, the affirmative will identify some law(s) or set of regulations that stand in the way of the affirmative solution.

STUDENT JUDGE. A kind of debate judge who is a peer of the participants in a tournament.

SWEEPSTAKES AWARDS. Recognition given to the schools who have had the best performance at a tournament.

TABULATION ROOM. The place at the tournament in which results are tracked for purposes of power matching and selection of elimination round participants. Tabulators also keep track of the ballots and distribute the results at the end of the tournament.

THRESHOLD. The significance of the causal relationship between the link and the harm of the disadvantage.

TOPICALITY. A jurisdictional question. For a case to be topical, it must come under the jurisdiction of the resolution. For it to be nontopical, it must be beyond the jurisdiction of the resolution. For example, if a judge has the power to decide whether a person is guilty or innocent of a felony and someone brings to court a question of drunk driving, the judge does not have the power to say whether the person is guilty or innocent, because drunk driving is not a felony.

TREATIES IN FORCE. The Department of State's annual list of all the treaties to which the United States is bound.

TRENDS OF THE PRESENT SYSTEM. A defense of the status quo based on the assumption that new programs or measures have been designed to combat the problem to the extent possible, and additional efforts (by the affirmative) would be premature—perhaps even making the situation worse. The logic behind this position is that the multifaceted present system is better than the single approach suggested by the affirmative.

TURNAROUND. An argument that the meaning of an opponent's contention is the opposite of its apparent intent so that it counts against the opponent. For example, if the negative team makes a disadvantage argument, and the affirmative rebuttalist points out that the result of that disadvantage is more positive than negative, then the argument becomes a turnaround for the affirmative team.

UNIQUENESS. In comparative advantage

analysis, the condition of inherency or inseparability of the proposal and the effects that are claimed to result from it, either advantages or disadvantages.

UNITED STATES GOVERNMENT PRINTING OFFICE: CONGRESSIONAL INFORMATION SERVICE INDEX. Contains annotated listings of all publications from the legislative branch since 1970.

UNITED STATES GOVERNMENT PRINTING OFFICE: MONTHLY PUBLICATIONS CATALOG. A reference catalog listing all government publications by subject headings.

VALIDITY. A criterion for evidence that asks whether the observer actually observed what he or she claimed to be measuring.

WHO'S WHO IN AMERICA. A standard source for substantiating the qualifications of authors.

WORKABILITY. A criterion for judging the affirmative's plan. The negative bases its attack on an "even if" analysis. Even if a need for a change exists and even if the affirmative's proposal could meet the need, even in theory, the affirmative's plan would be unworkable. The attack focuses on the mechanisms of the affirmative's proposal.

Index

NTC DEBATE AND SPEECH BOOKS

Debate
Advanced Debate, *ed. Thomas and Hart*
Basic Debate, *Fryar, Thomas, & Goodnight*
Coaching and Directing Forensics, *Klopf*
Cross-Examination in Debate, *Copeland*
Forensic Tournaments: Planning and Administration, *Goodnight & Zarefsky*
Getting Started in Debate, *Goodnight*
Judging Academic Debate, *Ulrich*
Modern Debate Case Techniques, *Terry, et al.*
Strategic Debate, *Wood & Goodnight*
Student Congress & Lincoln-Douglas Debate, *Giertz & Mezzera*

Speech Communication
The Basics of Speech, *Galvin, Cooper & Gordon*
  The Basics of Speech Workbook, *Galvin & Cooper*
Contemporary Speech, *HopKins & Whitaker*
Creative Speaking, *Buys, et al.*
Creative Speaking Series
Dynamics of Speech, *Myers & Herndon*
Getting Started in Public Speaking, *Prentice & Payne*
Listening by Doing, *Galvin*
Literature Alive!, *Gamble and Gamble*
Person to Person, *Galvin & Book*
  Person to Person Workbook, *Galvin & Book*
Public Speaking Today!, *Prentice & Payne*
Self-Awareness, *Ratliffe & Herman*
Speaking by Doing, *Buys, Sills and Beck*

For a current catalog and information about our complete line of language arts books, write:
National Textbook Company,
a division of NTC Publishing Group
4255 West Touhy Avenue
Lincolnwood (Chicago), Illinois 60646-1975 U.S.A.